They gave us a
TELEVISION STATION
to
PLAY WITH

Tom, I hope you find something of interest in here and thanks to Steph for her support.

Richard

17 Mile N.T.
4.12.21

When ABC TV came to Darwin
Richard Creswick

Richard Creswick: Author.
They gave us a television station to play with: when ABC TV came to Darwin.
Text © Richard Creswick 2021.
Original photographs © Richard Creswick 2021, unless otherwise attributed.

ISBN: 978-0-646-83999-8

Design and layout by Michael Pugh: michael.pugh@bigpond.com.

Subjects:
Darwin.
Northern Territory: arrival of televison.
Australian Broadcasting Commision: ABC—ABD 6.
Australian Aborigines: Larrakia—Land Rights.
Cyclone Tracy.
Northern Territory: self government.
Australian Prime Ministers: William McMahon—Gough Whitlam—Malcolm Fraser.
East Timor (Timor L'Este).

Front Cover: The 'Hairy Newsroom', 1972, ABC Darwin.

Contact: richard.creswick6@gmail.com

A catalogue record for this book is available from the National Library of Australia

Dedication

This book is dedicated to the memory of my father Alexander Harold Creswick whose life was never so exciting after service in World War 2 when he would have had his family believe it was almost all fun and games. The fact that three of the ships on which he served were subsequently sunk by enemy action; the fact that he became one of the Rats of Tobruk for being part of the naval breach of the siege of that North African irritant to Rommel and the fact that, many years afterwards, he became one of a handful of Australians awarded a medal by the Russian government for their part in the deadly Murmansk convoy escorts which helped keep Russia re-supplied in its war against Germany hinted that there were more serious stories to tell. We didn't press him hard enough.

And to my beloved granddaughter, Robin Park Creswick, so that one day she will know, if not understand, what her Poppa did all those years ago.

This book was written on and
about the land of the Larrakia people.
Their claim to traditional ownership is acknowledged.
Their elders past and present are recognised.

Foreword

And it seems like yesterday … 50 years ago this year ABC Television finally came to Darwin—the last capital city to join the network—a momentous occasion for the locals who until then could only rely on radio for the latest ABC Australian and local news. In this sympathetic, painstakingly researched and insightful book, retired ABC journalist Richard Creswick brings to life the struggles, obstacles and eventual triumphs of those who were involved from the beginning and those who followed soon after in a tale of human ingenuity and a determination to succeed.

The book has many delightful anecdotes of some of the Darwin characters around at the time (some of us are still here!) providing a human backdrop of humour and detail which should be remembered and celebrated in a story as rich in colour as modern day television.

Cyclone Tracy devastated Darwin in 1974, and in the midst of the ensuing chaos the ABC crew was eventually able to bring the stark reality of that time to the rest of Australia—and the world.

The persistence and dedication of the entire local ABC team over the past 50 years (notwithstanding the difficulties of cyclones and southern 'advisors') is a tale of triumph over adversity and a demonstration that 'Our ABC' has the will and the expertise to excel and service the people of the Northern Territory with professional skill and dedication.

Thank you Richard—this book is a great contribution to the history of Television and the Northern Territory in its triumphs and tragedies and will be enjoyed by many.

Dawn Lawrie, AM
Former MLC, MLA and Administrator of the Cocos (Keeling) Islands.

Contents

The author, his wife Patsy and their cats in 1972.

Introduction

This book has been a long time in the writing. It comes about, finally, because this year, 2021, is the 50th anniversary of the start of television in Darwin and as one of only three surviving journalists involved in the first production of what are known as full length television news bulletins and because I have always been a writer, it has fallen to me to chronicle this subject.

I have been a writer professionally for about 45 years in various guises, but privately for much longer, or even, still. I don't keep a daily diary, a bit of a disadvantage when trying to write something like this, but I do keep a rain diary which for nearly 40 years has included activities of interest and when something really notable happens I tend to record it in some form for either the enjoyment of family and friends, or, occasionally, a wider potentially interested audience.

I have had items published in a number of publications ranging from the *Melbourne Age* to the, now-defunct Ansett Airlines in-flight magazine, *Panorama*, as well as both government and private publications in the Northern Territory.

Looking back, I realise that nearly all of my longer form pieces have something to do with seafaring. Only one is mentioned in this book, a bamboo raft adventure, but I have written of a risky venture delivering a traditionally built Indonesian perahu (or prau) from Bali to Darwin via occupied East Timor; an account of being a cook/deckhand on a mackerel fishing boat, the MV *Rachel*, chartered by a group of scientists to travel from Darwin to Broome in search of the elusive Irrawaddy Dolphin, or at least the Australian genus of it; a hilarious sail aboard a large catamaran on a delivery voyage from Darwin to Dili, East Timor and a sail around the Indonesian Archipelago after participating, as crew, aboard the yacht, *Malaika*, with our friends Lex and Jo and their daughter Ally, in the 2008 Darwin to Ambon race and rally.

A three-month visit to Japan in 2005 was recorded in a series of letters from Japan written with my wife Patsy when she provided English language lessons to an eclectic collection of children and adults in the city of Nakatsu on the southern island of Kyushu.

Increasingly, as the events described in this book faded further and further into the past, when the subject of the early days of television cropped up and anecdotes were told, I would be urged to write it down.

In 2005, having just retired from working in the media unit of the first Labor Chief Minister for the Northern Territory, and first woman Chief Minister, Clare Martin, also a former ABC journalist, colleague and presenter of the local *7.30 Report*, I decided it was time to finally tackle this subject. Fate, in the form of the Japanese sojourn mentioned above, intervened and a first attempt went onto the back-burner. Several times, in the intervening years, I have pulled up the document, desultorily added another few thousand words to it, corrected a few mistakes, then hit the save button and put it aside.

Other events also intervened; a couple of the nautical adventures referred to above and some extensive Australian travel using the fancy camping trailer bought with my severance payment, including at least three circumnavigations of the western third of Australia because we both had ageing mothers, among other relatives and friends, in Perth.

Then there were the interesting overseas travels to Mexico, Vietnam, India, Myanmar, Japan again, Hong Kong, South Korea, Timor L'Este, and Java as well as regular visits to Bali where we have friends and a surrogate daughter, a young Balinese woman and more recently her daughter.

Seriously enjoying our retirement further delayed the book and then, suddenly, it was going to be the 50th anniversary and surely that must be impetus enough? The question then became, had I left myself enough time? Hopefully yes but it certainly provided the necessary kick in the pants to get the project going again, and time will tell.

A project such as this is not a one person job and despite the time interval many of those who were part of this story are still alive, a tribute to the fact that we were, mostly, very young when they gave us a television station to play with. ABC management at that time was predominantly in the hands of older white men because there were certainly very few women in management at any level.

To come to Darwin as a 26 year old and be part of a service provided by people around the same age or only a few years older, was exciting. We, particularly those of us in the newsroom, might sometimes have been more frivolous, and certainly less hidebound, than was the case elsewhere but when it came to our professional responsibilities, the respect for Accuracy, Brevity and Clarity that was drummed into us, we all took our jobs seriously.

In those days there was a clear delineation between news and comment. News was about reporting the facts, or at least reporting what were claimed to be facts and woe betide us if we ventured an opinion in a story—not that we did. But now I am writing a book and because it is neither an academic treatise nor an ABC news story, but is largely based on my personal memories, occasionally I will offer an opinion in addition to what I hope will be addressing the facts around an historic time in Darwin's, and the Territory's, history.

As always in a venture like this, many people have provided me with information and confirmed or corrected my imperfect memory. I have also relied on a variety of publications which are acknowledged at the end of this book. And as is usual, I apologise for any mistakes and sins of commission or omission. They are entirely my own.

Richard Creswick
17 Mile, NT, May 2021

In the beginning

The colony of New South Wales was not yet forty years old when, in 1825, it incorporated the area which would eventually become known as the Northern Territory by expanding its western boundary to the 129th degree of longitude thus taking in what would become both South Australia and the Northern Territory. That ownership would be relatively short lived because in 1856 South Australia established its own two-house parliament and seven years later, annexed the lands which would become the Northern Territory, incorporating them into one of its own electoral divisions.

Thus began a connection with Adelaide and South Australia which continues to this day even though, by 1906, the increasing cost and difficulties in maintaining this large, sparsely populated part of Australia had forced South Australia to approach the newly formed Commonwealth with a proposal to surrender the Northern Territory, a surrender finally accomplished in 1911.

But this story is about a much more recent period in the history of the Northern Territory, its subject matter being the coming of television to Darwin in 1971.

In 1971 Adelaide was still the administrative capital for many of the state type functions carried out in Darwin, even though it had by then been sixty years since South Australia had returned control of the northern outpost to the Commonwealth.

The Commonwealth, through its Department of the Interior, might have run the Northern Territory bureaucracy, called the NT Administration (NTA), from Canberra and appointed the heads of the federal departments who effectively ran the Territory, but on the ground many of the links and allegiances were still to South Australia.

It was why, among other things, the education system in the Northern Territory was still tied to the South Australian Curriculum and largely

Darwin aerial, iron ore wharf foreground. Shows Administration buildings, Government House and Hotel Darwin. Photo, Old Darwin; maybe NT Government photographer.

staffed by South Australian teachers, even though the Commonwealth Teaching Service was by now the employer of teachers; it was why most of the bank branches, with their two-year terms for staff, were linked to Adelaide and was why the ABC in Darwin had, since the war, also been administered from Adelaide.

That was why it seemed logical that the ABC in Adelaide should play a major role in establishing a new Darwin television service.

In August 1971, the senior officers of the Australian Broadcasting Commission, as it was then, were in Darwin for the launching of ABD Channel 6, the last of Australia's capital city television services, and the forty-ninth in the Commission's network extending from Geraldton in the west to Brisbane in the east and now, from Hobart in the south to Darwin in the far north.

It had been a long time coming. After all, television had been launched in Sydney fifteen years before, in 1956, in time for the broadcast of one of Australia's most memorable and exciting events, the 1956 Olympics, even though they were being held in Melbourne. Melbourne got television in November that year.

2

Darwin at that time was Australia's fastest growing capital, with an annual population growth rate of about ten per cent but still had a population of only 36 828, according to a June 1971 census conducted by the Australian Bureau of Statistics (ABS).

The census showed the town's population had increased by 71 per cent compared with the figure from the previous census in 1966. The only comparable period for such an increase was in the years between 1947 and 1954 when the population increased by a huge 218 per cent, largely reflecting the return of the civilian population to Darwin after the war. The Japanese bombing of Darwin, beginning in February 1942, had led to mass evacuations of the town's civilian population when it was placed under military control.

In a short history of *Recognising indigenous populations in the Census*, Glenn, a self-styled census expert, wrote in his blog: 'the 1971 census, which was the first after the famous 1967 Referendum on Aboriginal recognition, was the first to officially include Aboriginal people as part of the total population'.

It is possible that the 71 per cent population increase in five years could also have reflected the inclusion of Aboriginal people in the count, but I was unable to find a specific census reference to Aboriginal people.

Despite its small population, Darwin was the capital of the Northern Territory which, perhaps, was justification enough for establishing a state type television service.

In 1971, the majority of Darwinites were comparatively well-paid Commonwealth public servants, defence personnel, police, fire, ambulance staff, teachers, doctors, nurses and other health practitioners and the private employees of service industries like the airlines, banks, insurance and real estate companies. Others in well-paid positions included those servicing the expanding mining and pastoral industries. Many came from states where television was an accepted service and perhaps felt they deserved the same in Darwin.

No less deserving of the benefits of television were the unionists, tradespeople, council day labourers, shop staff, café workers, hotel bar staff and the myriad others who kept the economic and social wheels of the city turning.

3

Within the ABC there was at the time, and it might continue even to this day, a belief that Sydney, birthplace of the Commission with the start of radio broadcasts back in the '30s, the spiritual home of the ABC, host to its major physical presence and its administration, was disproportionately more well off in every aspect of its operations than the other parts of the ABC empire.

Melbourne, to a slightly lesser extent, demanded and was given resources, but the further one went from Sydney, the poorer the resources. There was a nomenclature within the ABC which illustrates this hierarchy. It is the way in which all of the state services outside New South Wales were lumped into the groups known as the BAMPH states, for the letters of their state capitals. If Melbourne was to be excluded, they became the BAPH states, or BADPH when TV came to Darwin, and within these states (and Territories) other than Sydney, there was a significant antipathy to headquarters for what was seen as its hoarding of resources and reluctance to distribute them.

This even extended to the system of allocating journalists gradings across the News division which is still the biggest division within the ABC, even with recent slashing of journalist numbers due to funding cuts from an unsympathetic federal government. At the time of which I am writing journalists were graded, and thus paid, according to their experience with the top grading being A2, followed by A1, A, B, C, and D Grades; then came the trainees, known as cadets, who were supposed to do a four-year cadetship, unless they had a university degree.

If they did, it elevated them to the position of a fourth-year cadet, thus requiring them to do only one year of their cadetship, before reaching the lowest grading. In practice few cadets actually completed four years of training often being graded earlier if they showed ability.

As a result most of the A2 gradings were awarded to journalists in Sydney, with a few trickling out to the other states. Likewise the bulk of the A1s were in Sydney with slightly larger numbers filtering out to the states and so it went on.

As to facilities, should a new piece of equipment be found to be essential it would first be acquired for Sydney, with the superseded model being passed on to another state, and this practice continued down the hierarchical line.

This system meant that when television was to be introduced to Darwin, there was no suggestion the new station would be given new and modern equipment. Instead, the task of building up the facilities which would be required, the videotape machines, the telecine (film) chains, the racks of wires, relays, switches and other essentials, was delegated to the ABC in Adelaide.

The man who would become the first Senior Broadcast Officer (SBO) in Darwin, Rodger Andrews (now living in Queensland with his wife Maxina) some years later wrote his memories of the process of establishing that television station and has generously allowed me to quote extensively from those memories. He has also supplied a number of the photographs which are in these pages.

> Because it would prove far too expensive to send a large team to Darwin to support the construction of a complete television station, the decision was made to prefabricate the entire electronics in Adelaide.
>
> An area known as Studio 52 in ABC Adelaide was set aside to allow the building up and testing of racks, consoles, telecine chains, videotape and studio facilities. All the racks and consoles were built with connecting plugs which would allow wiring to be completed and then, after testing, be disconnected for shipping with the interconnecting cables cut to the length required for reconnection on arrival in Darwin. As the hardware arrived in Darwin it was then a simple matter of placing it within the control rooms and running the new connecting cables out. It sounds easy but of course there were always unforeseen problems to be overcome by the technicians on the ground.

Rodger had been recruited to Adelaide after nine years of working on outside broadcasts (OBs) for the ABC in Tasmania. He spent two months in Adelaide getting to know the technical staff who would be working in Darwin and finalising some of the administration required before relocating to Darwin.

Like so many newcomers, Rodger didn't really know what to expect on his arrival but found the climate something of a shock, particularly arriving towards the end of the wet. Rodger arrived at the end of March and the station was due on air in August. He wasn't confident the deadline could be met.

> I was met by the well known Regional Manager, Don Sanders. After a quick tour of Darwin and an inspection of the new ABC homes we looked at the new home for television on the corner of Cavenagh and Bennett Streets. An empty shell, it was still under construction. Dirty, dark with builders' tools and supplies all over the place, it had no electricity or water and certainly no airconditioning.

Rodger described the building as being like a small fortress:

> Constructed of a double thickness of concrete blocks it had a ground floor with a second inner shell in the centre which would accommodate the future studio, and then a second floor and above that a higher roof. The cavity between the two courses of concrete blocks was sealed with a metal mesh to act as screening from outside electromagnetic forces. This shielding proved to be a nuisance during installation and later, as nothing could enter or leave the building (cables, conduits, antennas etc,) which would interfere with the integrity of the shielding.
>
> The main reason for this extreme shielding was the thinking that Darwin port, airport and naval radio and radar installations were quite close and could cause interference to our service.
>
> Towards the end of May 1971 the installation crew began arriving in Darwin. Some of the equipment had arrived earlier but as would be expected <u>not</u> the things required to begin the job.
>
> In the meantime there was still no electricity, the builders were still trying to finish the building, the place was dirty and full of dust no matter how many times an attempt was made to clean it up. The temperature in Darwin was always around 32 degrees so without power the temperature inside the building was the same as outside and often higher.

According to Rodger, the working conditions were simply appalling and the fact that the facilities were completed on time was due only to the dedication and hard work of those involved.

I have already commented on the penny-pinching propensities of the ABC with regard to facilities outside Sydney and this is confirmed by Rodger who says:

> It would be fair to say that 80 per cent of the station facilities consisted of second-hand equipment gathered (some would say scrounged) from other ABC stations and ABC Training departments. These facilities comprised two Pye Telecine Chains capable of playing not only the common film formats known as Composite Magnetic (Commag) and Composite Optical (Comopt) but also the more cumbersome Separate Magnetic (Sepmag) system of which more later; one Turret Caption Scanner, containing 'the clock' and a card magazine; one Ampex 1100 series 2 inch videotape machine; two AWA Vidicon studio cameras; one Astor Audio Desk with eight input channels and four outputs and two Evershed remote control pan & tilt heads for the studio cameras, unaffectionately known as Nodding Neddys, again more of which later.

Time was racing by and there was still no power.

The Electricity Supply Undertaking (ESU) would not connect power while the building was still under construction. The air conditioning contractor had not finished his installation and there were delays in the arrival of equipment.

At that time when rail extended only to Alice Springs from the south, the equipment had to be railed from Adelaide to Alice Springs and then transshipped onto road trains for the remaining 1000 miles (1600 kilometres) to Darwin. 'There were times', Rodger says, 'when we thought it was coming by camel train'.

Finally both power and air conditioning were operational but there were only a few weeks until 'On Air' day and the production staff were arriving and very eager to get their hands on their new empire.

Meanwhile the installation crew was working not only to hook up the equipment but attending to the myriad faults which had occurred as a result of the vibration caused by transportation and the lack of use over the previous months.

> The videotape machine would prove to be the greatest headache for some time even after the station went to air.

The ABC's New TV studios. Photo, Rodger Andrews.

The normal time for head wear (the heads are the particular item which convert the electrical signal recorded on the tape into the sound and picture) in those days was at least 100 hours of use but we couldn't get more than 20 hours before we had noise and excessive head switching and banding. (This translates to distortions in the picture and bands of instability at the bottom of the picture, not something that technicians like to see or put to air).

The re-supply of refurbished heads became critical and we were borrowing heads from all states.

As we had only one machine it was a dire situation. The program staff had decided to alternate vision sources by using film then videotape and then back to film. The videotape machine *had* to be kept in service. The problem of identifying faults was exacerbated by the fact that the techs had no other machine with which to compare results or swap boards.

We could not work out why we had such excessive head wear. There were all kinds of theories such as pollution from the iron ore dust from the nearby wharf area or the high humidity of the climate. Technically we could not find an electronic problem with the machine, everything was within the specifications laid down by Ampex.

With just a couple of weeks to go we were able to allow the presentation staff to begin training the future on-air and production staff.

Dummy news runs were most important in this training as initially news would be the first locally produced program to air. Not all the production staff had television backgrounds, in the main being drawn from radio.

Finally the day arrived: Friday August 13 1971. Senior ABC officers were arriving. Telegrams and telexes were being received. Well wishers from all over the country were sending their good luck wishes.

The first transmission went without a hitch, glitch or serious problem and, as Rodger wrote:

Time to relax. All the nervous tension of the previous months goes. Yes, time for a drink or two, let the hair down, pats on the back all round. Well done.

But then the reality sinks in:

OK that's the first night over but now we are committed to a service seven days a week. There is no back up. We are totally on our own. Reliant on 99 per cent of film and recorded programs arriving from south in time. Certainly no PMG coaxial cables from the south. We must provide a service that much of the Darwin population has been accustomed to in the southern states.

The small screen era begins

The coming of television had been a fairly widely anticipated event with the ABC taking out advertisements in the local paper, The *Northern Territory News*, for weeks beforehand advising readers of the programs they could expect to see in 'The look to look forward to', the ABC's promotional jingle.

These included light entertainment programs such as that of the Greek songstress, Nana Mouskouri or Johnny Cash; the dark comedy, *Steptoe and Son*; comedy series, *The Ghost and Mrs Muir*, billed as the hilarious love affair between a 19th century ghost and a 20th century woman, and *Dad's Army*, the popular comedy series following the exploits of a Home Guard detachment in England during the Second World War; *Softly Softly*, a fast moving BBC crime series with Stratford Johns; *Dynasty*, a contemporary drama about people, issues and events in the news as influenced by the family owners of a powerful Australian newspaper and

Alf and Annette Jervis.
Photographer unknown.

television empire; films such as *Portrait of a Lady* and *Mr Deeds goes to Town*; *Monday Conference* promoted as Australia's first national weekly television interview program with Robert Moore and current affairs programs *This Day Tonight* and *Chequerboard*.

The local paper was also flooded with advertisements from electrical appliance stores offering a huge variety of quite expensive television sets for sale or rental. There were stories of the difficulties faced by these television sellers in adjusting and tuning sets which had been jostled and jolted in their long journey to Darwin. Tuning had to be done using the test pattern with which most people would be familiar but as this was only shown for two hours between 12 midday and one o'clock and from 5 to 6 p.m., the ABC came under pressure to extend the test pattern broadcast, eventually to five hours a day. A lot of people were entranced by that.

And there was an almost gleeful item in the newspaper's *True North* column which, three days after transmission started, noted people waiting for television sets would have to wait a bit longer as 200 were written off when a transport overturned 60 miles (100 km) south of Darwin the previous day. The driver, from Queensland was not hurt.

The newspaper also carried articles profiling those who would be involved in putting the programs to air. These people included announcer Glenn Taylor, who would be given the task of presenting the programs on the opening night.

Glenn, readers were told, was the most recent newcomer to the announcing staff having previously appeared in ABC radio plays and schools broadcasts before being appointed a full-time announcer in Adelaide. Glenn was also expected to soon be contributing items to the proposed new TV current affairs program, *This Week in Darwin*.

There was an introduction to another announcer, Alfred Jervis, an Anglo-Indian whose mellifluous tones made him a natural as a newsreader and led to his becoming the main reader when longer television news bulletins finally began some time later.

Alfred, born and educated in Bangalore (now Bengaluru) India, worked as a tank farm foreman on the oilfields of Kuwait before becoming a field instructor for the Ferguson Tractor Company.

He and wife Annette and two daughters decided to migrate to Australia to continue his work with agricultural machinery. He told his interviewer that, one day, out of the blue he had walked into the offices of the ABC in Adelaide and asked for an audition to become an announcer. He was engaged for a one-month trial and, after three months, applied for a permanent job as an announcer in Darwin coming north in March 1965.

According to Alfred, his first few months in Darwin were pretty rough, living in a hostel away from Annette and two children but six years later he considered himself settled in Darwin and 'now that TV's arrived, Darwin's got everything'.

Another announcer profiled was Richard Peach described as a much travelled young man with a wide and diverse experience. Before arriving in Darwin two years earlier, he had been an announcer on Australia's first 'pirate' radio station, a short lived venture conceived by Adelaide University students but declared a flop. He had gone on to work as an office boy at the ABC, then briefly at Adelaide's commercial television station Channel 7, but as a result of giving an interview about his pirate radio experience, he was subsequently given a trial run as an ABC announcer with work in a variety of positions following until his move to Darwin.

Glenn Taylor informs me, and Wikipedia confirms it, that Richard was the long running voice of the PMG's talking clock, known as George, a free telephone service which the public could ring on 1194 to check the absolutely correct time: 'At the third stroke it will be ...'. This service was only discontinued on October 1, 2019

Senior presentation officer, Adrian Payne and ABC Board Chairman, Sir Robert Madgwick in Master Control on launch day. Photo courtesy of ABC Archives.

Also introduced, though they were already well known to ABC Radio listeners, were the rural reporter and country hour presenter, Peter Knudsen, sports reporter (part time) Peter Turnbull and talks officer, Tom Wilkinson.

On the day television broadcasts began, the *Northern Territory News* gave extensive coverage to the event.

This included reports of the opening being attended by the Chairman of the ABC, Sir Robert Madgwick, the other eight members of the Commission (though they went unnamed) and the General Manager, Mr TS (Talbot) Duckmanton. The Commission was said to have also taken the opportunity to hold its regular board meeting while in Darwin.

In a separate article reporting on festivities surrounding the station's launch, the *NT News* noted Sir Robert hosted a party poolside at the Darwin Hotel, then the town's premier hotel, where 200 invited guests, who according to a staff member of the time did not include staff, were able to watch the launch program on twelve TV sets arrayed around the pool. This particular news item included a photograph of Sir Robert watching his own pre-recorded message go to air.

The launch party, for which I have not been able to find a guest list, must have been one of the social events of Darwin's year and surely brought together the cream of Darwin's society. Guests we do know of included the Administrator, Fred Chaney and, as the Legislative Council, the territory's hybrid form of a parliament, was sitting at the time, all seventeen of its members, both official and elected, would have been invited. Certainly the guest list would have included the then Senior Judge, Bill Forster, Magistrates Don Miles and David McCann and the well known senior public servant and assistant administrator, Martyn Finger and his wife Audrey, described by lawyer and later Lord Mayor, Cecil Black, as the 'King and Queen of Darwin Society'.

Don Sanders, as a member of a group of men of similar status would have ensured members of his coterie of Darwin Club Friday drinking mates, known as the Thirsty Club, would have been included, among them being the Port Authority Chairman, Captain Tom Milner, and heads of the three domestic airlines then serving Darwin, TAA, Ansett and MMA, as well as the heads of the major banks then represented, the ANZ, the English Scottish and Australian, the bank of New South Wales and the Commonwealth and Commercial Banks.

The guest list would certainly have included the Mayor, Ken Waters, and Darwin Town Council aldermen (the town would not be granted city status, and thus a Lord Mayoralty until eight years later) among them Ted D'Ambrosio, Royce Fitzgerald, Ken Slide and Grant Tambling, who would later be able to state that he had served at every level of government, going on to be a member of the first Legislative Assembly, a Member of the House of Representatives and a Senator in the Australian Parliament and then as Administrator of Norfolk Island.

Despite the pre-publicity, Glenn Taylor did not provide the voice for introductions to the evening's program. That task was carried out by the senior announcer, Alfred Jervis who, according to Glenn, pulled rank. The night's entertainment began at 7.00 p.m. with a news bulletin followed by a special Darwin newsreel which featured, among other things a dance routine featuring the wife of presentation officer Adrian Payne, Yuleen (who was also regional assistant), Pat Harris, wife of the film clerk, Arthur Harris and film assistant, Amanda Taylor, to the ABC promotional theme of the time, 'The look to look forward to'.

This was followed by Sir Robert Madgwick's official speech of welcome for the new service and the official opening by the Federal member, Stephen Edward (Sam) Calder both with mercifully short speeches.

Good evening I am delighted to be able to take part in the official opening of ABD Channel 6 Darwin. The opening of a new station is the end result of a lot of work, particularly by the Australian Broadcasting Control Board, the Australian Post Office and the Australian Broadcasting Commission. Tonight I speak to you as Chairman of the ABC. The ABC's responsibility is to provide programs through stations approved by the government on the recommendation of the Control Board and through transmitters provided by the Australian Post Office. The provision of programs always poses a host of problems. The ABC by the Act of Parliament under which it operates must provide an adequate and comprehensive program. This means that it must provide a program for all types of people with all sorts of tastes. It is rarely possible to provide a program that will please everybody or satisfy everybody's needs and so the spread of programs provided covers everything from news and current affairs to music of all kinds, sport, religious broadcasts, educational broadcasts and drama of all types from serious drama to light entertainment. You will find in this feast of programming much that you will like although as I suggested a moment ago, everybody will have a different set of priorities and probably nobody will like everything. Most people experiencing television for the first time do tend to watch everything but after a while they become more selective, more critical. And while I am certain that you will find through your national television channel a very satisfactory selection of programs from which to choose, I hope that you will not hesitate to let us know what you think, to let us have your views and comments about what you see. We try to meet as many of your needs as we can and we always respond to suggestions and constructive criticism. It now gives me very great pleasure to ask Mr Calder to speak to you and to declare ABD Channel 6 Darwin officially open.

Sam Calder's official opening speech, perhaps reflecting an unfamiliarity with television, was halting and somewhat patronising with its warning to viewers not to let the new medium control their lives.

Thank you Sir Robert and welcome to you and members of Commission on your first executive of meeting in Darwin. I would like to thank Postmaster General, Sir Alan Hulme for asking me to open the first ABC television station in the Northern Territory and also to recognise the efforts of Sir John McEwen and my parliamentary colleagues in supporting me when I first raised the call 'TV for the North'. I'd like to thank the members of the ABC staff for the excellent programming they have produced for us down through the years. The coming of television to Darwin will bring some exciting new views on international sport and also keep us abreast of world and Australian affairs and later will bring some first class programs to our schools and our homes. But I hope that it will all be not one way for there are some local items of tremendous interest which can be shown to Australia such as the world class catamaran championship, the Darwin Eisteddfod and all that goes to back it up, the first class horsemanship, cattle, horses and riding at the shows and rodeos up and down the Northern Territory and the unique features such as the Henley-on-Todd and the Tennant Creek Gold Rush. I am glad to see that the excellent rural program is to be continued with, also that there is to be a mobile videotape recording van which can give us a first hand and factual news coverage of our everyday events. We will get great advantage from this station, and also from the commercial station shortly to be opened but remember, television like radio is controlled with one switch so remember to control television, do not let it take over the best of life in Darwin which I think is the equal of any in Australia.

> So now with pleasure and humble thanks to the Postmaster
> General and to the ABC I declare ABD Channel 6 Darwin
> to be open. You can all look forward to pleasant viewing.

There followed a program line-up which consisted of the *Rolf Harris Show*, a *Big Country* episode titled *Six Days with Killen*, the *Magic of Music, Marty, a Montreux Special; Tommy Steele and Things* and ending with an episode of *FBI*.

Readers of the *NT News* had been advised that when regular programming began it would run from 5 p.m. to 10 or 10.15 p.m., and 10.45 p.m. on Saturdays. Consistent with the station's stated aim of promoting as much local content as possible, initially there would be a nightly five minute bulletin of regional news and three minutes of weather, two weekly presentations of local sport, a 15 minute rural program and a 10 minute magazine program.

Darwin's national news coverage would initially consist of the 6.30 p.m. national radio news bulletin replayed on air behind a caption (a picture of a territory scene or feature).

It was reported that this was to be an interim measure until a national and regional TV bulletin could be introduced from 1972. It was envisaged that from the beginning the national news would be followed by a 10 minute newsreel Monday to Friday, prepared in Sydney and flown to Darwin each week. Darwin viewers would, for the time being, see delayed coverage of national or international events such as cricket, football and other sporting fixtures on either film or videotape air freighted to Darwin.

In a profile accompanying the preview, the ABC's Regional Manager, Don Sanders, noted that with the coming of television, staff numbers had grown from five to more than 35, and the number of ABC staff houses from four to 31. As will be shown, Sanders slightly underestimated the number of people employed by the ABC prior to the coming of television.

Sanders had been Regional Manager for 11 years, having joined the ABC in Adelaide in 1941. During a three-and-a-half-year stint with the RAAF he was based at the 32 Mile (south of Darwin) with No. 2 Squadron.

Back at the ABC after the war he was transferred to Perth in 1947 and later relieved in Port Moresby, PNG. He was appointed Northern Territory Regional Manager in 1960.

One of Don's claims to fame, although presented modestly, was for long-distance running; he held the South Australian state junior record for the mile for a number of years as well as winning the Perth to Busselton Air Race. Events, he said, which occurred when his then portly figure was more suited to such pursuits.

Perhaps presciently, Don Sanders said that while it [TV] would undoubtedly change the pattern of living in Darwin it was still his hope that the people 'will not lose the art of conversation and making their own entertainment'.

Entertainment, before television

And what was that entertainment? Within the public service, Darwin was still considered a hardship post. It had a reputation as a town supported by and dedicated to, the consumption of alcohol, principally beer. Some were proud of the claim that Darwin's per capita beer consumption was the highest in the world, or perhaps that was discounting Germany.

The Sea Breeze Hotel, Nightcliff, was a favourite drinking spot at weekends.
Government Photographer collection, NT Library.

It was said that Darwin's biggest imports were beer and public servants, and its biggest exports, empty beer bottles and full public servants.

Despite a comparatively small population, the town sustained two breweries, Carlton, which produced the world-famous Darwin Stubby holding half a gallon of beer, and Swan and each week tons of packaged beer, cans, stubbies and the less popular 26-ounce long-necks, were imported from every state ranging from Castlemaine XXXX from Queensland, to Resches and Tooheys from New South Wales, Foster's Lager, Victoria and Melbourne Bitters from Victoria (with their cans being ordered according to their colour, blue, green and red); Boags and Cascade from Tasmania; Southwark and West End from South Australia and Swan Lager, Emu Export and Emu Bitter from Perth. Some bottle shops also carried a variety of imported beers.

Most hotels were tied to one or other of the breweries so for serious drinkers the beer you preferred determined which hotel you supported, though not exclusively. After all, any beer in any pub is welcome on a hot day, and Darwin's days were hot.

The hotels generally closed at 10 p.m., but there was a later closing time of 11.30 which by agreement rotated between the town's hotels: The Darwin, with its Green Room lounge, Regency Room or Red Restaurant and Hot and Cold Bar; The Victoria (or Vic), the oldest hotel in Darwin on Smith Street which had several bars as well as a popular Chinese Restaurant operated by soon to be Lord Mayor, Alec Fong Lim; the new Don Hotel with its Schooner Bar, Gallery Bar and soon-to-open Post Bar, the newly opened, and quite luxurious Koala Motel at the end of Mitchell street and, moving out of town, the Fannie Bay Hotel, overlooking the bay of the same name; the Parap Hotel, the Dolphin at Millner which billed itself as a family venue but attracted a less salubrious clientele, the Seabreeze overlooking the sea at Nightcliff and the new Marrara on McMillan's Road, Jingili. Along the Stuart Highway heading south from the Bagot Road intersection there was the Maranga at Winnellie, a working man's hotel notorious for its lunchtime strip shows and topless barmaids, then the Berrimah hotel, another workers' pub and the last licensed drinking place until either the Humpty Doo Hotel on the Arnhem Highway or the Noonamah Pub.

Two other irregular drinking establishments deserve mention: The upstairs bar or Qantas Lounge at Darwin Airport, open for a few hours either side of an arrival or departure, was a regular late night/early morning drinking spot as visitors or workmates were welcomed or farewelled on the unsociably timed early morning 'red eye' specials of the domestic or international airlines. At that time the Darwin airport terminal was a converted wartime aircraft hangar in the walls of which could still be seen bullet holes from the Japanese bombing thirty years before. It was also unusual for sharing the airport with the Royal Australian Air Force which had a strong presence in the town. The bar was noisy and departure announcements were often not heard so airline staff would appear at the door and shout: 'if you're planning to fly, your aircraft is about to leave'.

The other unusual drinking place was Kaissis Store on Berrimah Road just south of the Stuart Highway intersection. This was a service station and licensed store which, after work on weekdays, became a gathering point where workers from the expanding industrial area nearby rubbed shoulders with public servants from the Berrimah Farm, home to the Department of Primary Industries and various agricultural enterprises. Though drinkers were supposed to remain within the confines of the service station, numbers grew so large that they invariably spilled into the surrounding area which was certainly illegal but officials, including police, turned a blind eye to it.

There were a number of nightclubs including the Penthouse overlooking the Sailing Club on Vestey's Beach, Steve Pastrikos's Aspa and later the provocatively named Dix and Fannies run by notoriously gay entrepreneurs Ben Tumminello, Peter Morgan and John Spellman, who had a wine bar in Smith Street called Pianola Palace, and would go on to operate several fine dining establishments. Eating places included the Hong Kong in Cavenagh Street, the Latin Tavern in Dashwood place, the DR, or Darwin Restaurant, in Stuart Park and Martina's at Nightcliff, not to mention a couple of more upmarket places like the Regency or Red Room at the Hotel Darwin and the Carlton Chinese restaurant in the Vic Hotel. Fast food outlets in those pre-KFC and Maccas days included Uncle Sam's, Rocky's Place and Eva's bar and grill.

There was a plethora of social clubs established to support sporting or other pursuits but often, though not always, dedicated once again to drinking. These included the exclusive Darwin Club, a gentleman's club located in a tin shed in an older part of Mitchell street; the RSL and Worker's Clubs in Cavenagh street, the Waratahs Club, claimed to be the biggest, and linked to the football club of the same name, the PINT (or Postal Institute) club established at the radio and now television transmitters at Blake Street, also a handy venue for a free viewing of whatever entertainment was on at the Amphitheatre, which it overlooked, the Royal and Ancient Order of Buffaloes (RAOB) or Buffs Club in Stuart Park.

Along the inner suburban foreshore there were the Water Ski Club, the Darwin Sailing Club and the Trailer Boat Club while inland there was the Darwin Aviation (or DAC) Club which occupied a new building adjoining a former QANTAS aircraft hangar, a relic of the days when Darwin's airport was what is now Ross Smith Avenue.

Not to be forgotten were a number of cultural clubs such as those run by the Greek, Italian, German and Portuguese and Timorese communities as well as the Chinese Chung Wah Society, though the latter was not known for drinking. It was also rumoured that a number of gambling clubs operated above certain shops.

The easy availability of alcohol was aided by the fact that most community supermarkets, and there was usually one in each suburb, had what were then called gallon licences, meaning they were allowed to sell liquor from 10 a.m. to 9 p.m., six days a week but it had to be a minimum of a gallon, a dozen 26 ounce beers or the equivalent in wine. On Sundays, takeaway alcohol could only be bought from a hotel bottle shop.

Of course there were entertainment options that did not necessarily involve the consumption of alcohol. Darwinites had the option of three film venues: The Star Theatre in Smith Street, opposite the Vic where one could slip across for a beer during interval in the usually two-film program; the Parap Theatre and the Paspalis Nightcliff Drive In. The Star and Parap picture theatres were both partially covered and partly open air with the Star being famous not only for its Wednesday and Saturday cowboy nights particularly popular with Aboriginal patrons but other regular social or red-carpet events.

Tomaris Sweep commemorative plaque. Author, photo.

YEAR	NAME	HORSE	1st PRIZE	YEAR	NAME	HORSE	1st PRIZE
1934	W. BYERS	PETER PAN		1971	A. ANDERSON	SILVER KNIGHT	$9000
1935	K. McDONALD	MARABOU	£40	1972	LYN & INGE	PIPING LANE	$9900
1936	E. ROGERS	WOTAN		1973	F.A.VAUGHAN	GALA SUPREME	$9500
1936	D. McMILLAN	THE TRUMP		1974	FRED ARMSTRONG	THINK BIG	$9300
1937	H.CALLANAN	CATALOGUE		1975	Mrs VIOLET LEE	THINK BIG	$8000
1938	Mrs G. CANUTO	RIVETTE		1976	L. HAY	VAN DER HUM	$17000
1939	A. COLLINS	OLD ROWLEY		1977	Mrs E. DUFTON	GOLD & BLACK	$17000
1940	A. GILGE	SKIPTON		1978	G. FOMIN	ARWON	$17000
1945	A. GILGE	RUSSIA		1979	G. MONCK	HYPERNO	$10000
1946	G. LIM	HIRAJI	£505	1980	G. McSKIMMING	BELLDALE BALL	$10000
1947	W. ARMBRUST	RIMFIRE	£707	1981	E.M. YEARBY	JUST A DASH	$12000
1948	NIP & SNIFF	FOXZAMI	£1200	1982	ROBERTS & FORMIN	GURNERS LANE	$14000
1949	H.GOOD	COMIC COURT	£1500	1983	J. TILLEY	KIWI	$15000
1950	D.& B. CHIN	DELTA	£1750	1984	D. KARP	BLACK KNIGHT	$20000
1951	D. LOFTHOUSE	DALRAY	£2000	1985	M. MAXWELL	WHAT A NUISANCE	$20000
1952	Mrs G. FOMIN	WODALLA	£2240	1986	J. SCOURFIELD	AT TALAQ	$20000
1953	Mrs L GREEN	RISING FAST	£2750	1987	L.OAK	KENSEI	$20000
1954	H.E. KNIGHT	TOPAROA	£2880	1988	J. COBB	EMPIRE ROSE	$20000
1955	A. LIM	EVENING PEAL	£2880	1989	K. O'BRYAN	TAWRIFIC	$20000
1956	H.M. CHIU & J. CHIN	STRAIGHT DRAW	£3250	1990	A. RUGGIERO	KINGSTON RULE	$20000
1957	R. CANT	BAYSTONE	£3250	1991	STEINERT FAMILY	LETS ELOPE	$25000
1958	LIBRA	Mac DOUGAL	£2880	1992	R. EDDY	SUB ZERO	$25000
1959	B. KAY	HIGH JINX	£3340	1993	W. HOHN	VINTAGE CROP	$25000
1960	K. SEABROOK	LORD FURY	£3116	1994	SONIA RAMSAY	JUENE	$25000
1961	K. KERSTING / D. COLE	EVEN STEVENS	£3056	1995	S. MILES	DORIEMUS	$25000
1962	R. KEMP / R. YEPP			1996	J. WYATT	SAINTLY	$25000
1963	G. GRAHAM	GATUM GATUM	£3060	1997	M.V. ALIFF	MIGHT & POWER	$25000
1964	B.M. PAINE	POLO PRINCE	£3030	1998	P. McINNES	JEZEBEEL	$30000
1965	L WARBURTON	LIGHT FINGERS	£3025	1999	NAT. BANK NIGHTCLIFF STAFF	KOGAN JOSH	$30000
1966	Mrs D. de FRAINE	GALILEE	$7200	2000	MARY JANE GODLOVE	BREW	$35000
1967	F. SEBASTIAN	RED HANDED	$7200	2001	J. ROLI	ETHEREAL	$25000
1968	H. CON FOO	RAIN LOVER	$7200	2002	A. POULOS	MEDIA PUZZLE	$25000
1969	G. HOISSER	RAIN LOVER	$7200	2003	P. BLACKBURN	MAKYBE DIVA	$25000
1970	P. IMHOFF	BAGHDAD NOTE	$8000				

For many years the Star had another claim to fame as the venue of the annual Tomaris sweep, a charity event operated from 1934 until 2003 and named for the theatre's owner, Tom Harris, which gave patrons the opportunity to bid for one of the horses to run in that day's famous nation stopping Melbourne Cup. Along with a substantial prize the lucky person who drew the winning horse would have their name added to a commemorative plaque (still) displayed in the foyer of the theatre.

Meanwhile, on the night television came to Darwin, according to the program guide in the *NT News*, patrons of the Star Theatre could see *The Appointment* starring Omar Sharif and Anouk Aimee plus Dan Rowan, Dean Martin and Carol Lynley in *The Maltese Bippy*; the Parap Theatre was showing *Count Yorga Vampire* starring Robert Quarry and Roger Perry plus Boris Karloff, Peter Lorre and Vincent Price in *Comedy of Terrors*.

At the Paspalis Drive in the bill included *Two Mules for Sister Sara* starring Clint Eastwood and Shirley MacLaine while Jeff Chandler and Ty Hardin starred in *Merrill's Marauders*. With television only being offered in black and white, it's perhaps not surprising all three cinemas highlighted the fact that their programs were in colour.

Cyclone-damaged Brown's Mart, formerly known as Solomon's Emporium, then the police station before becoming Brown's Mart. Photo, NT Library, NT Government photographer.

Live entertainment was also on offer, with the world famous pianist Winifred Atwell at the Gardens Amphitheatre supported by Australian crooner, Lionel Long.

In an accompanying news article, it was noted the vivacious Atwell had brought 19 pieces of luggage which did not include her fabulous, upright honky tonk piano which the artist explained had been honourably retired having become too old, and too valuable to travel. It was also noted that Atwell was showing off a new look having shed six stone (almost 40 kg) in weight saying she now weighed between ten and a half and eleven stone (66 to 70 kg).Ms Atwell told the *NT News* she really meant it when she said that by coming to Darwin she had achieved an ambition of ten years prior when she had missed Darwin and Alice Springs during an Australian tour.

Thespian board treaders

Darwin did not want for theatrical events, supporting three performing groups, the Darwin Amateur Musical Comedy Society housed in the Cavenagh Theatre in Cavenagh Street West; the Darwin Theatre Group (DTG) which would later operate out of Brown's Mart, one

Brown's Mart today. Author photo.

of the few surviving buildings constructed from the local porcellanite rock which underpins most of Darwin and the Adult Education Theatre Group.

A group from DTG was in the midst of successfully fighting off a proposal by the NT Administration to hand control of the property to the Town Council which, it was feared, would demolish the building. It had been built in 1885 as a shop, Solomon's Emporium, for Vabien Louis Solomon, a businessman who went on to become an elected member of the South Australian parliament when that colony took over administration of the Territory.

In 1971, the small group of actors and theatre activists driving the bid for Brown's Mart's independence were also making their mark in street theatre. In that year they entered a politically themed decorated double decker bus in the Darwin Festival street parade.

A tribute to Harold 'Tiger' Brennan who was about to end his term as a member of the Legislative Council but with designs on becoming Mayor the following year, its theme echoed his election promise to cut red tape.

The Darwin Festival to be held in June of that year was one of the highlights of the town's cultural activities and was, according to Bill Richardson, the Mayor at the time, to include the Jaycees Rodeo,

23

concerts, musical performances, art exhibitions, tennis championships and an all-nations ball.

DTG and the separately administered Brown's Mart, would go on to be mainstays of local entertainment, both theatrical and musical, until the present day.

My friend Ken Conway who was one of the proponents of the preservation of Brown's Mart had come to Darwin from Adelaide to join a local law firm.

When Brown's Mart later became an independent entity with a Board of Trustees, Ken gave up a potentially lucrative legal career to become its long serving Executive Officer. To an outsider and friend most of his time seemed to be taken up writing grant applications to keep the various enterprises functioning. These included spin-offs such as TIE DIE (Theatre in Education, Drama in Education) a touring theatrical troupe; the highly successful Corrugated Iron Youth Theatre, now in its 37th year; Tracks Dance; the NT Writers Centre and Darwin Fringe.

In 2010 Ken was appointed a Member of the Order of Australia (AM) in recognition of his contribution to the Arts. His investiture, performed coincidentally by his long time friend, fellow thespian and then NT Administrator, Tom Pauling, was celebrated at a private function at Government House where Patsy and I were among the small group of diners.

He, Brown's Mart and DTG would provide many stories for ABC television in future years.

There were occasional entertainments at the Darwin Town Hall on Mitchell Street, also a popular venue for weddings, birthdays, dances and other celebrations. Darwin's Trade Unions, the North Australian Workers Union, led by the irascible Paddy Carroll; the Waterside Workers Federation under the control of Brian Manning and 'Curly' Nixon, the Transport Workers Union, the Electrical Trades Union and others organised the annual May Day March; and there were annual commemorations of aspects of the World Wars including Anzac Day, Armistice Day, and the WW2 Bombing of Darwin each February.

One of the biggest cultural celebrations was the annual Eisteddfod which drew recital, musical and dance contributions from across the Territory, including from schools and a number of the Aboriginal Missions.

Street parade, c. 1973, Old Darwin, photographer unknown.

And, of course, there was sport. For a town of its relatively small size, Darwin boasted a wide array of opportunities for both players and spectators.

There was Aussie Rules football, played on two ovals at Gardens Park or other ovals in the suburbs during the wet; two codes of rugby, League and Union, with League headquartered at Richardson Park in Ludmilla named after the town's first post-war Mayor, Lucius (Bill) Richardson and both played in the dry. Soccer was fiercely contested by teams reflecting some of the ethnic groups which had colonised and helped develop the town.

Netball was believed to be the strongest sport numerically bringing together teams in a wide range of age groups from young girls to mature women.

Greyhound racing took place at Winnellie Park on Friday nights and there were regular horse races at Fannie Bay on Saturdays with a highlight being the annual Cup Carnival in August. Cricket was another dry season sport, played either at Gardens Ovals or grounds across the suburbs. Both the Army and Air Force had teams and games were often played at Batchelor, the town south of Darwin built to support the Rum Jungle uranium mine.

Darwin Ski Club regatta, boats lined up on Vestey's beach. No fear of crocodiles then. Old Darwin, photographer unknown.

Other sports included tennis, squash, cycling, both circuit at the velodrome on Bagot Road, and road; softball and baseball, hockey, water skiing, a sport less hazardous then because there were fewer crocodiles; and there were gun and archery clubs.

The petrol heads of the town could watch or participate in dirt track circuit racing at the Bagot Park Speedway or take part in organised drag races conducted from 1969 by The King Cobra Rod and Custom Club on one of the many abandoned wartime airstrips which were located down the 'track', as the Stuart Highway was known.

From time to time illegal street racing occurred with Berrimah Road a favoured location for its long straight stretch of bitumen leading to the East Arm Leprosarium being virtually abandoned after work hours.

Golf had been played from the 1930s, initially on a course close to the Fannie Bay Gaol and around the runways of the former airport, but the course was forced to move to East Point as suburban development took place.

It remained there until another move was necessitated by the planned, but not yet built, Palmerston Freeway and a new course was eventually opened in 1974. By 1971 there was also a golf course situated on the RAAF Base alongside Bagot Road intended for Australian Defence Force personnel but also open to social players.

A particularly popular dry season sport was boating, reflected in the fact that there were three clubs aimed at those with sea craft, either sail or powered: the Trailer Boat Club, which was the earliest of the boating venues dating from 1958, the Darwin Sailing Club which—apart from dry season yacht races—looked to the future with classes for beginners as well as the experienced, and the Ski Club. There was also a nascent sports fishing scene.

At that time Darwin was starting to build a reputation as a jumping-off point for sailors seeking to sail further afield to explore the thousands of islands making up the Indonesian Archipelago or the Portuguese Colony of East Timor which, with Bali, was a popular holiday destination for both sailors and air travellers.

Also around that time Darwin was becoming known as a destination for both arriving and departing travellers on the so called 'hippy trail', an overland route between Australia and England taking in many exotic countries as yet not totally impacted by wars, including India, Afghanistan, Iran, Iraq, Turkey, Greece, Italy and Europe.

Some of those arrivals or departees whiled away the time at informal encampments known colloquially as the Royal Beach Hotel on Lameroo Beach and its cliffs close to the centre of town and the necessary public amenities.

Periodically there would be purges by the town council or police, particularly if there had been a spate of thefts of materials from building sites along the esplanade for the construction of humpies.

One such crackdown led later to a protest and occupation for several days of what was then the Mitchell Street Town Hall, long since subsumed into the Performing Arts Centre.

As mentioned, Darwin's population was predominantly male, with the number of men, at 19 096, outnumbering 16 185 women, for a total of 35 281. The whole of the NT at that time had a population of 85 519. Perhaps interesting to note was that 323 of those people were described as migratory. It's unclear whether this is a reference to the Indigenous population but some might have been the itinerants of Lameroo Beach.

*Nurses Quarters, old hospital. NT Government
Photographer collection, NT Library.*

*Front entrance to Wells building. Collection of NT Government
photographer, NT Library.*

Aerial, Darwin—old hospital in the foreground. Photo, Old Darwin.

Darwin from the south, circa 1968 showing (from the right). Naval Headquarters, Government Administration Blocks 4 and 5 (Ward and Brennan); and front from right to left, Block 1, Stuart; Block 2, Wells Building; Legislative Council, Block 3, Nelson. Blocks 6 (Gregory), 7 (Leichardt) and 8 (Chan) were still a twinkle in the Public Works Committee's eye. Work on them started in 1970 with Block 8 completed in 1974 and to become home to the Darwin Reconstruction Commission after Tracy. Also visible, the Supreme Court and Hotel Darwin. Photo by Don Donaldson, courtesy of his son, Bruce Donaldson.

Although a proportion of the populace was married, the town hosted large numbers of single men and women. Some of them shared rental houses or units with friends but by far the majority were accommodated in single men's or single women's hostels run by the Commonwealth, among them Marenah House on the Esplanade, a women's hostel until it became a barracks for the Police, the Commonwealth Hostel in Mitchell Street, with the Department of Civil Aviation, Ross Smith and Arafura Hostels accommodating other workers.

There was a women's section at the Mitchell street hostel, but the biggest hostels for single women were in Bennett Street, on the site later to become the ABC's television studio, or the Esplanade Hostel. The nurses' quarters at the hospital at the end of Mitchell Street, somewhat disparagingly nicknamed the 'bulk warehouse', was a popular place for young Lotharios to seek female companionship.

There were also hostels operated by employers like the banks which not only provided accommodation for their staff, but in some cases had canteens providing meals for the workers. One was above the Commonwealth Bank's offices on the corner of Bennett and Smith Streets.

An ABC newsreel of the time, eulogising the rapid expansion of development in Darwin, noted that a new multi-million dollar residential hostel was under construction for the YMCA and looking at the land and housing shortages and long rental housing waiting lists being created by this development found that many people were not only forced to live in caravan parks but were choosing to remain there because it was cheaper than the very high rents being asked for flats or houses.

That same newsreel talked of the 4.21 p.m. workday end with pictures of public servants exiting the three storey office blocks like ants, piling into cars and taking off to create the peak hour later referred to by Dawn Lawrie.

The Historical Society of the Northern Territory, in a May 2020 paper about the naming and numbering of the government office blocks, described them as being constructed in 'the Brutalist style of a monolithic blocky appearance, rigid geometric style and use of concrete'.

The first seven buildings, and the Legislative Council, were progressively demolished to make way for Liberty Square, the Supreme Court and new Parliament House.

Despite a reputation for godlessness at times, particularly in its very early days, the town was well supplied with opportunities for religious observance with the principal outlets being the Catholic 'Star of the Sea' Cathedral in Smith Street, and one of the oldest buildings, the Anglican Christ Church Cathedral, a grand name for a rather modest structure built of the same locally quarried porcellanite rock as Brown's Mart just down the road. Protestants had the Uniting Church, also in Smith Street while the Greek Orthodox Church on Cavenagh Street served the extensive Greek community. The large Chinese population could worship their ancestors at the Chung Wah

Colin Jack-Hinton. NT Government Photographer, NT Library.

*Top: The former 'Old Town Hall' was Darwin's museum when damaged
by Cyclone tracy.
Bottom: The ruins remain a permanent memorial. Author photos.*

Hall, or what was known as the Joss House, in Litchfield Street and local communities of churchgoers had a variety of suburban options available to them.

Finally, in terms of culture, there was the relatively new Museum of Arts and Sciences which occupied the building which was formerly the Town Hall. It had been presided over since 1969 by its founding director, the lushly bearded and colourfully eccentric, Colin Jack-Hinton who had been lured from the Museum of Western Australia. He inherited yet another of the town's old stone buildings, this one opposite Brown's Mart and comparatively small.

There he began building what would become an impressive collection of Aboriginal Art, a small but significant collection of paintings by early Australian artists and a comprehensive collection dedicated to the Oceania region with Darwin as its focal point. This process was severely hampered when Cyclone Tracy destroyed the building and much of the collection in 1974

One of Jack-Hinton's legacies was the exploration of the extensive rock art of Arnhem Land largely through the research conducted by George Chaloupka which resulted in several authoritative books on that art. He was instrumental in the inauguration and development of the National Aboriginal and Torres Strait Islander Arts (NATSIA) Awards, held annually at the new museum he had later commissioned on the shores of Fannie Bay.

Not such a dead hand

Despite the general negativity towards Canberra control of the Territory, there were some economic compensations. Public servants, and private employers able to match their conditions, were entitled to an additional two weeks Tropical Leave per year and those who chose to drive out of the Territory for their holidays could score a few extra days of travel time.

Many employees received either annual or two-yearly airfares to their home city and these could even be converted to overseas travel with the return airfare to Adelaide being the basic contribution. Electricity was subsidised, as were motor vehicle registrations and drivers' licences, and all

Territorians were eligible for the Federal government's Zone Tax Allowances, A (Darwin and the Top End) and B (Alice Springs and Central Australia). Those employed by the ABC fared even better also enjoying subsidised rent.

At that time journalists were regarded as temporary employees, only becoming permanent after a qualifying period of three years. One of the benefits of permanency was eligibility to join the ABC's very generous Superannuation Scheme linked to the Commonwealth Superannuation Scheme (CSS).

In those days journalists throughout Australia were covered by awards negotiated by the Australian Journalists' Association (AJA), an organisation just coming out of a long period of relative powerlessness held back by dinosaur leadership. Journalists at that time had no access to penalties for overtime, shift work, or working on week-ends or public holidays, but they were compensated with an extra week's leave above the then industry standard four weeks. Moving to the NT, I discovered that in addition to those five weeks, I was entitled to a sixth week of leave, plus the two weeks tropical leave.

This gave me almost as much leave as my teacher wife and meant that by judicious planning we could have extended holidays. For example it meant that in 1974 we were able to take the entire middle term of the school year, a total of twelve weeks, for an extended overseas tour.

These generous leave provisions were to have a significant effect on newsroom operations later because the South Australian News Editor, to whom we answered, declined to replace journalists on leave.

A quick calculation would show that six journalists each entitled to eight weeks annual leave meant we were essentially operating with one journalist down throughout any given year. Of course, in practice it wasn't that bad but when a journalist took leave the workload increased.

One other benefit of Darwin living for those with children, was the education system. As mentioned earlier it followed a South Australian curriculum and was largely populated by teachers from South Australia but this was changing as teachers from other parts of Australia were moving up, either as partners, or in their own right.

With the astonishing population growth came an explosion of new housing development with a new suburb of 600 to 1000 house blocks, plus school and shops, being developed each year.

In 1971 Wagaman was already under construction and the suburbs of Nakara and Wanguri were being carved out of the bush. Older Primary Schools had been operating for years in the settled inner suburbs including Darwin, Larrakeyah, Stuart Park, Parap, Ludmilla, Millner, Rapid Creek and Nightcliff. New schools had been built at Alawa, Jingili, Moil and Berrimah and there were three High Schools, Darwin High on Bullocky Point, site of the former Vestey's meatworks, of which the huge derelict water tank was the only remnant; Nightcliff High and the newly built Casuarina High.

There were also several Catholic primary and secondary schools, part of the Catholic Education system which also controlled schools on Catholic-run Aboriginal Missions across the Territory. Education in government schools for Aboriginal children was run by Welfare Education, led by Jim Gallacher but within the (Aboriginal) Welfare Department of Harry Giese.

Kormilda College in Berrimah, Dhupuma College outside Nhulunbuy and Yirara in Alice Springs had been, or were being, established as residential colleges designed to provide a secondary education for Aboriginal students from remote communities, a scheme which had mixed success until a decade later when they were either privatised or closed.

The combination of a dynamic, experienced and enlightened educationalist in Dr Hedley Beare as Director of Education and the increasing role of the Commonwealth in providing teachers, meant that government schools in Darwin enjoyed a level of facilities, staff and amenities which outshone schools in the older states.

For many young women and men, one of the highlights of working as teachers in the Territory was the knowledge that they were part of a small but dynamic and progressive education system where those at the coal face had ready access to the Education leadership: 'if you were doing something good, they knew about it and supported it,' plus you were quite likely to bump into them in the street, shop or café on Saturday morning.

Coincidentally it was in August 1971 that a new body representing the parents of students and pupils in the Territory's Public schools, the NT Council of Government School Organisations (NTCOGSO) was formed. The driving force behind its formation, Geoff Helyer, had been elected its first president.

A couple of years later I interviewed Geoff when he returned from Canberra having been elected president of the national government schools parents' organisation, the Australian Council of State School Organisations (ACSSO). Many years later I would also occupy both positions.

Access to tertiary education would not come until 1973 with the establishment of the Darwin Community College a combined College of Advanced Education (CAE) and Technical and Further Education (TAFE) temporarily located in premises in the city until the following year when a new campus at Casuarina was officially opened by the Duke of Edinburgh, but adult education classes were already being conducted below what was then the former Darwin High School building in Cavenagh street, before the Community College opened.

A friend notes that she was among a group of women who staged a polite protest at the DCC opening seeking the inclusion of childcare facilities at the Community College. She says the Duke showed interest in their protest and asked what it was about.

It would be 1989 before Darwin got its own university.

A small collection of stone buildings still standing in Darwin had survived a cyclone in 1897 which destroyed much of the town's ramshackle infrastructure, then the 1942 bombings of Darwin. This collection of

This building and adjoining offices have been erected on the site and from the ruins of the first Darwin Post Office and the Office of the British Australasian Telegraph Company which were badly damaged by bombs aimed from Japanese Aircraft 19th February, 1942. In the bombing, nine officers of the Postmaster-General's Department lost their lives on duty

The buildings are dedicated to the use of the Legislative Council for the Northern Territory and as Offices of the Government in the faith that work of lasting good will here be done in service to the people and form an enduring Memorial of past devotion and a continuing witness through the Ages that Patriotism shall ever rise more brightly from the ashes.

March 25th 1955

BAT Office and Post Office were virtually destroyed in the first wave of Japanese bombing in WW2. Jessie Litchfield collection, NT Library.

stone buildings included Government House, known as The House of Seven Gables; the former courthouse and police station but then known as Naval Headquarters just across the road from Government House and later to provide offices for the Administrator; the previously mentioned Brown's Mart and Christ Church Cathedral: the Museum also referred to above, the Victoria Hotel and a series of shops operated by Chinese merchants in Cavenagh street, still standing today and known as the Sue Wah Chin building.

One of the most historically significant of the stone buildings, also still standing is the former British Australian Telegraph house on the

Left and below: Commemorative plaques. Author photos.

THIS PORTION OF THE WALL, LEFT IN ITS ORIGINAL STATE, IS ALL THAT REMAINS OF THE DARWIN TELEGRAPH STATION BUILT IN 1872 WHEN THE OVERLAND TELEGRAPH STATION WAS OPENED. THE BUILDING WAS DESTROYED IN AN ENEMY AIR RAID ON THE 19TH FEBRUARY, 1942, WHEN TEN OFFICERS OF THE AUSTRALIAN POST OFFICE LOST THEIR LIVES VERY CLOSE TO THIS SPOT

Esplanade which was built to house engineer employees of the BAT. It is now known as Lyons Cottage in honour of a former mayor, John 'Tiger' Lyons who held office in 1958 and '59.

One of the stone buildings destroyed in the first wartime bombing was another BAT office which, with the Post Office, was then located at the top or eastern end of Mitchell Street. Ten employees, including the Postmaster, Hurtle Bald, died in that bombing raid.

A portion of a wall from the destroyed building was subsequently incorporated into the structure of the rather unpretentious building which was home to the Legislative Council until it too was demolished to make way for the new Parliament House.

Part of that section of original wall is again built into the entry foyer to the Library and Archives in the new Parliament House, together with two commemorative plaques: the one salvaged from the Legislative Council building and a new one which explains the provenance of the small wall segment remaining.

Communications in Darwin

The ABC had already been an important element in the town's communications system with a wartime Army operated radio service being transferred to ABC control soon after wartime controls were replaced by civilian administration. With the call sign 5DR (but later renamed 8DR) it provided what would become a state-service equivalent with News, Talks, Rural, Sports, Religious and other normal programming including serials such as *Blue Hills* and children's programs like *The Argonauts*.

There was also a Commercial Radio Station, 8DN, which by 1971 had a rudimentary News Service, a popular talkback program, various serials and lots of commercials.

There was just one newspaper, the previously mentioned *Northern Territory News*, a publication first started as a counter to the *Northern Standard*, a newspaper run by the North Australian Workers Union. The *Standard* had a long history of opposition to the government and was also perceived to be pro Communist.

In 1949 the Federal Government approached a Canberra journalist, Don Whitington to establish an alternative paper. With the support of

Eric White, founder of what was to become one of Australia's biggest public relations companies, Eric White Associates, and the local printer, John Coleman, the first edition of the weekly *Northern Territory News* was published in 1952 from what was known as the tin bank, the former English, Scottish and Australia (ES&A) Bank situated between Brown's Mart and the Anglican Cathedral.

Bought by News Limited in 1960, and becoming a daily in 1964, it had developed a reputation for supporting greater Territory self-government and many other local issues.

In 1971 its editor was the popular and renowned James Frederick (Jim) Bowditch. English-born Bowditch had a colourful past, having been a member of the elite Z-Force unit which operated behind enemy lines against the Japanese in Papua New Guinea and other occupied parts of the region.

Bowditch had come to journalism by a circuitous route. He had arrived in Australia from England in 1937, aged 18 and soon became involved in union activities in Melbourne, then Adelaide, activities which inevitably brought him into contact with communists. Although he was often called a communist, or alleged to be one, he never joined the movement. He became and remained a supporter of the Australian Labor Party and in later life would stand, unsuccessfully, as a Labor candidate for election.

Jim Bowditch always chafed under discipline and this difficulty accepting orders caused him to quit several jobs. It was a trait which also dominated his army career which ended with his discharge in 1946. By now married to his first wife Iris, daughter of a well connected military family, they moved to Alice Springs in 1947 where thanks to his father-in-law he got a position as a paymaster for the Department of Housing and Construction.

According to an (as yet) unpublished biography of Bowditch, written by a friend and colleague, Peter Simon, Bowditch threw himself into community life in Alice Springs becoming involved in politics, debating, amateur theatrics, cricket and union work. For some time he had been writing reports on union and other activities for various journals and expanded this to include colourful stories about the characters and happenings of the Centre which southern newspapers apparently couldn't get enough of.

39

Journalist and author Doug Lockwood at work.
Doug Lockwood collection, NT Library.

One of his friends was another writer, Alan Wauchope, a magistrate's clerk who had worked for both the *Melbourne Herald* and *Adelaide News*. Wauchope would become editor of the *Centralian Advocate*, a position Bowditch eventually inherited.

When his marriage to Iris broke down, due largely to his many outside interests and which included a growing interest in the plight of what were then known as 'half-caste' Aborigines, it was not unsurprising that Jim took up with a clever young 'half-caste' girl, Betty Hodgson, the well-educated daughter of an Aboriginal woman and an Englishman. It was a liaison that scandalised many in the conservative Alice Springs community.

The couple moved to Darwin in 1955 with Jim becoming editor of the *NT News*. In that capacity he rapidly earned the sobriquet 'crusading' because of his involvement with many notable causes usually arising from resistance to the heavy-handed actions of governments or police. These included hiding people who were about to be deported, or star-crossed lovers. He was, it was said, always a soft-touch for those in trouble or in need of some form of help.

As Simons' manuscript shows, Bowditch was often in conflict with authorities, and because of its obsession with communism was the subject of almost unrelenting and frequently bumbling surveillance by the Australian Security and Intelligence Organisation (ASIO). In later life he developed an increasingly severe drinking problem which led to many confrontations with police, friends and enemies. On several occasions he arrived home drunk to find what he thought was another man in bed with his wife, only to be told he was in the wrong house. Eventually his drinking caused problems at home and in his workplace. In 1972 he resigned over the principle of an unpublished editorial.

One of Darwin's better known media practitioners had been Douglas Lockwood who had been posted to Darwin by Melbourne's *Herald and Weekly Times* in 1941.

Doug was a mate of the writer Bill Harney, a notable and loquacious yarn spinner and author of more than a dozen books, many detailing his connections with Indigenous people. He had retired from a position as ranger at Ayers Rock (now Uluru) in 1962, and against the advice of Aboriginal friends who told him he would die if he left the Territory, moved to Mooloolaba, Queensland, where he died just six months later.

So close was their friendship that Doug Lockwood would go on to complete Harney's last, unfinished book. Lockwood also had a close friendship and working relationship with Jim Bowditch and, according to Peter Simon, Bowditch and Lockwood would exchange 'blacks' or copies of stories they had written.

This was partly to prevent demands by Lockwood's Melbourne editors to cover a story they had seen elsewhere. Many of these stories were written by fly-by-night writers who would drop into Darwin, write an often outrageous and sometimes completely fabricated yarn about some character or event, then disappear leaving Lockwood to have to explain the stories were bullshit. Mind you, Bowditch was not above concocting the odd outrageous story to boost newspaper sales including subjects such as UFOs, haunted houses, and the Mandorah Monster.

Douglas Lockwood wrote 13 significant books about the Northern Territory. He left Darwin in 1968 to take up the editorship of the *South Pacific Post* in Port Moresby, PNG with his place in Darwin being taken by Alan 'Bluey' Dearn, another colourful writer. Meanwhile another Lockwood, Doug's son Kim, had arrived in Darwin. As Kim explained, he had finished four years at university in Adelaide when he heard the

West Australian newspaper would waive a cadetship in journalism for those who had been to university.

In 1966 he applied and was accepted as a 'D' Grade final year cadet. 'The name probably helped', he told me recently.

Naturally he had known Jim Bowditch as a friend of his father, so when he wrote a story for the *West Australian* with a Darwin link, he sent a copy to Bowditch at the *NT News*. 'This immediately led to the offer of an A grading on the *News*, so I left', said Kim. Then, in 1972, when 'Bluey' Dearn left, Kim Lockwood succeeded to his father's old position as *Herald and Weekly Times* reporter in Darwin.

It was in this capacity that I first met Kim in the reporters' gallery in the old Legislative Council building tucked between two public service office blocks on Mitchell Street. Naturally our paths crossed frequently over the following few years until Kim left in 1975 just after Cyclone Tracy and Australian Associated Press (AAP) took over.

Slow but inexorable change

So, Darwin was a town not totally dedicated to the consumption of beer and not without its cultural, religious and sporting elements. But as ABC Television arrived in Darwin with much fanfare it proceeded to usher in a slow but inexorable and fundamental change to what had up until then, been a rather rough and ready, and sometimes primitive frontier town.

On Saturday, August 14, 1971, the day after the launch of ABD 6, the *NT News* noted that:

> TV's effects were 'not so harsh' saying the first television programs hit theatres, clubs and hotels but not as hard as expected. Dolphin Hotel manager, Noel Wilcock, said the family entertainment sections of his hotel were a little down but the rest was normal. Star Theatre Manager, Tom Harris said attendances were down for sure but not too bad, noting there appeared to be fewer people on the streets. However he said the Vic Hotel across the road was full. The Darwin Aviation Club patronage was said to be 'about average' though it was noted the club had installed a television set, and the Manager of the Darwin

RSL Club, Dave Dunstan, said the crowd there was 'amazing, just about normal'.

The *True North* column noted that:

> Last night saw the first round of the battle between live entertainment and television in Darwin and, surprisingly, it went 'on points' to the live entertainment.

The column quoted Mrs Nan Giese, publicity officer for the (Darwin) Eisteddfod, as reporting a packed house at the Greek Hall for the song section:

> She said it was rather amazing with more than 400 people and 'we were delighted to get such a good audience'.

Of course we don't know how many people were at home watching this historic first broadcast.

On Monday, August 16, three days after the opening, the *True North* column revisited its Darwin Aviation Club story, noting:

> It had adopted the modern adage 'if you can't beat 'em, join 'em' by installing a television, with its manager saying week-end attendance was well up to normal if not a bit bigger, showing that television was not going to make much difference to the Darwin way of life.

A subsequent article in the *NT News* headlined TV had little effect, reported that:

> Television kept people at home, but not as many as expected according to most theatre and restaurant people. The Manager of The Penthouse, Peter O'Shea said there were fewer diners out at the restaurant on Saturday night than normal but it was too early to say whether the lull would last. The Manager of the Martina Restaurant, Tom Harris junior, said while Friday's crowd was less than usual, no customers were lost on Saturday. He attributed this to the fact that a lot of people hadn't got television sets yet. The Aspa City Motel's Steve Pastrikos said there was no drop in business.

Star Theatre owner, Tom Harris senior reported lower than usual attendance but the Parap Theatre suffered no loss according to the manageress, Mrs Little.

Sadly, the picture was not so rosy just a short few months later. An item on the ABC TV News reported a big impact from television's arrival.

Overlaid with pictures of Darwin, including exteriors and interiors of the ABC TV studio, the script read thus:

> Australia's Top End capital took a big step forward this year. Television came to Darwin in August and in six months has had a noticeable influence on the life of The Territorian. A city [sic] reputed to have one of the highest rates of beer consumption is cutting down on going to the pub. The opening of ABD Channel 6 completes the ABC's television coverage of Australia's capitals and major cities ... More than 2000 television sets have already been formally licensed and several thousand more are on rental. Audiences at Darwin's three picture theatres are down 60 per cent while some hotels report a drop of 50 per cent in bar trade.

As noted earlier, the consumption of alcohol was a major preoccupation for many of the mainly male populace but that was less the case for the considerably fewer females. For many (mainly male) public servants, and some in the private sector, a two-year appointment to Darwin, where jobs were plentiful due to the constant turnover of staff, could mean a one or more level promotion which might have taken a decade to achieve had they stayed in their original departments down south.

As well, Darwin, and other parts of the Territory, offered a life of adventure they might never otherwise have experienced with the widespread availability of hunting, fishing for the famous barramundi, camping and off-road exploration of some of the Territory's spectacular scenery.

One of the first things many newly promoted arrivals bought was a four wheel drive and 'tinny', a fishing boat with outboard motor. The belief was that even the dumbest angler could catch a 'barra', and preferably many of these fish, renowned for their fight as well as their size.

The downside for many families was the isolation experienced by many of the wives, especially those with young children. Public transport was practically non existent and unless the family had a second car, wives had few options for entertainment during the days when husbands were at work, and later drinking with their new mates. Two radio stations, the ABC's 8DR and a commercial radio station 8DN, offered the only daytime entertainment with programs of news, current affairs, talk-back, music and a variety of serials of varying provenance and quality.

Women who were childless and/or had jobs fared better but it was recognised that the new much freer lifestyle, while a boon for most males, was less attractive for women and this was reflected in anecdotal evidence indicating Darwin had the lowest marriage and birth rates but the highest divorce rate compared with other jurisdictions.

Dawn Lawrie wrote that the town had the highest birth rate and highest illegitimate birth rate, the lowest death rate and, as far as could be ascertained, the highest percentage of common law marriages in Australia. It was, she said, 'a safe, happy conglomeration of diverse people'.

Not actually 'no place for women'

Although Darwin was seen as a hardship post and a difficult place for many women, particularly those housebound by personal circumstances, for many young women freed from the constraints of conventional expectations of their futures, Darwin in those days offered an interesting and often liberating lifestyle. Being an almost classless society where informality generally was the watchword, there was the opportunity to socialise with people from all walks of life.

In Darwin they lived in one or other of the many hostels but then joined with friends in shared houses where they led active social lives of dancing, barbecues, gathering with friends for communal meals at some of the popular meeting places like Alec Fong Lim's Carlton Restaurant in the Vic Hotel, Charlie Cagnetti's Olympic Café or The Regency Room at the Hotel Darwin.

There were social events like the Folk Club and other musical offerings, theatrical events and always the chance of meeting one or other of the town's better known characters among them Carl Atkinson, the diver and salvager and his partner Wendy who lived in a unique house at Doctor's Gully, the crocodile expert, Dr Harry Messell or the Museum's Dr Colin Jack-Hinton and George Chaloupka.

Resorts at Mandorah or Mica Beach, across the harbour from Darwin, were among other places where people enjoyed entertainment such as Aboriginal dancing. The Mica Beach resort, operated by Axel Sidholz had such a steep beach approach that revellers were transferred from a ferry onto a tracked amphibious ex-Army duck known as the 'Buffalo'.

Some speak of almost-weekly dances and balls, the annual Red Cross ball and The Waratahs Sports Club ball being highlights.

Some had access to films both on the RAAF base and at one or other of the town's public theatres or the drive-in while lots of basketball was played at courts on Daly Street near the old fire station, or at Batchelor. For others the Saturday night requests program on Commercial Radio station 8DN was compulsory listening as they tried to guess which of their friends had requested which song.

Young women who had jobs, mobility and money of their own found ample opportunity to explore beyond Darwin, discovering new and unusual places of natural beauty or in some cases deep spiritual inspiration. Some spoke of intangibles: a spiritual awakening, an awareness and expansion of self through the quality of light, the colour of light and when out of town, or out bush, the feeling of ancient presences the silent transmission of knowledge from Aboriginal people, sensations imbued in country but difficult to express in words. And for many, life was so unlike what they had left, they could not contemplate going back. Many would meet partners, marry and become life-long Territorians.

Light aircraft were an integral part of communications within the Territory both for business and recreation. Station owners, many of whom had their own light aircraft might fly into Darwin on a Friday afternoon with a load of prime meat and beef ribs for a week-end barbecue with friends.

Some years later, Independent MLA Dawn Lawrie was to write of her arrival in 1960 as the beginning of a time of change for Darwin with forced population growth bringing in large numbers of new settlers who very quickly adapted to a drinking, partying, easy going way of life and who also absorbed what she called 'a fair degree of the independent, anti authoritarian spirit of earlier Darwin people'.

But then there was another cohort of women who had a harder time of it: single mothers of young children, divorced, widowed, deserted or alone by choice, sometimes finding it hard to live on welfare or casual work who were able to find comfort and companionship in social activities such as bush-walking, picnicking with those in similar circumstances who understood and could appreciate their issues or perhaps by joining social groups like Parents Without Partners, a national organisation begun in Melbourne in 1967 and which held monthly gatherings where participants took turns to host the meetings and food was provided from within the group.

Much of what I have written is from the perspective of incomers, or those Dawn Lawrie referred to as new settlers but there were, as well as Indigenous people, already well-established communities of migrants from outside Australia including the Chinese, Greek, Italian, German, Filipino and other smaller groups, not to mention the many mixed-race people who had helped enrich the polyglot community of the time.

A group I haven't mentioned is those who returned to Darwin after the war with their parents or who were born here soon after civilians were able to return following the wartime evacuations.

Some of those in this category remembered almost idyllic childhoods of freedom to roam safe neighbourhoods finding places to play within a natural community environment where the only requirement was to be home before dark.

Young men became athletes, played sport, went bush to fish, or shoot feral pigs, crocodiles or buffalo or took part in the various car related sports, speedway racing at Bagot Park or drag races at the 33 mile airstrip.

Some talk of night time excursions with Indigenous friends, fishing, crabbing or getting 'long bums' in the mangroves bordering the harbour.

It has become accepted wisdom that, in those days of a more relaxed lifestyle, doors of houses were never locked and keys could be left in a car's ignition without fear that it might be stolen.

A brief history

To understand Darwin as it was when television arrived, it is helpful to have some knowledge of the Territory's history both distant and recent, and its development both physically and constitutionally. My brief history is compiled from a variety of sources and is designed only to give the broadest overview, a sort of taste teaser for those who might want to dig further. Anybody seeking a broader or deeper history of the Northern Territory can find much to inform them elsewhere including what many believe to be the definitive early social history, Ernestine Hill's *The Territory* first published in 1951 by Angus and Robertson.

Or perhaps you could read Glenville Pike's *Frontier Territory*, Douglas Lockwood's *Darwin's Front Door* or *I the Aboriginal*, the books of Tom Ronan, Tom Cole and Bill Harney or more recent historians such as Dr Allan Powell, Tom Lewis or Derek Pugh, and of course, in this day and age a quick search of the internet will turn up much of interest.

Any story which purports to be about a place, has to start with a potted history, but history, as we all know, has many authors and, generally, is told from the perspective of those who are successful, the winners of wars, not the losers.

Also, as recent controversies within Australia known as the history wars have shown, there can be considerable divergence in interpretations of even quite recent history, for example the real impact of white colonisation, settlement, invasion or whatever term you choose for the arrival in Australia of the colonists and their interactions with the original inhabitants, the first peoples or Indigenous Australians.

There is also the history of earlier contacts, difficult but not impossible to examine because of oral traditions of story telling, rock art of indeterminate age and the art and writing of the other cultures involved. I am talking here of the first people to interact closely and apparently regularly with the original inhabitants, the Macassan traders of what is now known as South Sulawesi in the Indonesian Archipelago, who brought plants, tools, customs, and their language to the north coast of the Northern Territory and took away trepang, also known as beche-de-mer or sea slug, a delicacy for the Chinese, and sometimes women, though this last might be disputed.

Although there were some conflicts, there appears to have been a relatively peaceful relationship between the Indigenous Australians and the Macassans. There is much evidence of ongoing contacts between the two groups, the many Malay words to be found in indigenous languages of the north-east coastal regions, the physical characteristics of the Malays and the magnificent stands of non native tamarind trees which grow along the coast of the Territory.

Much better documented, though always from the perspective of the victors, are the stories of European explorers, the Dutch, French, and English, who touched the coasts, or travelled overland within Australia and their sometimes friendly, at times hostile, dealings with the local inhabitants.

And then, of course, there is the history which is largely unknowable, what is, in effect, the story of the country we now know as Australia, and those who were the first colonisers—the people who became the Indigenous Australians. In attempting to flesh out this element of history it is important to note that they have a different view of their ancestry.

Their oral history is linked to the Dreamtime and according to that belief system, they have always inhabited this land.

The National Museum of Australia, in a 2020 article titled *Evidence of first peoples*, touched on this issue quoting an indigenous woman known as Auntie Val Coombs, a Quandamooka Elder, who, in 2012 said:

> Whitefellas like theorising we come from somewhere else other than Australia to lessen our connection to country. We are from here. Our knowledge of our history is embedded in our blood and our country. Whitefellas knowledge of our history is only as good as their technology.

For the amateur, especially one who is neither trained researcher nor anthropologist, it is difficult to know which of the experts one should give greatest credence to.

This is especially the case with regard to theories about the colonisation of the area which was known as Sahul, the name given to the geographic mass which, until relatively recently in geological terms, encompassed what are now the separate islands of Papua New Guinea, Australia and Tasmania.

Until relatively recently there seemed to be a generally accepted belief about the first colonisation: that it was an extension of the migratory push of the people who had progressively colonised what is now the

Indonesian Archipelago (or the Wallacean Archipelago), that it involved one or more sea crossings which, at the time, was probably at the limit of the experience of those making the voyage and that it probably ended geographically close to what is now the Kimberley or western Northern Territory region.

The time frame for such voyages was thought to have probably been between 50 000 and 60 000 years before the present era (BPE) during times of lowest sea levels and thus the shortest distances needing to be traversed by sea craft. The probable method of transport was a bamboo craft of some description. Even at these times of lowest sea levels a journey of 100 km would still need to have been made, an incredible achievement for the time.

Credible evidence, presented in the journal *Nature* and reported in *The Conversation* has recently emerged indicating a site called Madjedbebe near Jabiru could date from 65 000 years BPE which would make it the earliest known occupation date.

Western science indicates these people probably arrived by some sort of watercraft on deliberately made voyages from either Timor/Roti into northern Australia, the southern route, or from the Moluccas to north west Papua New Guinea, the northern route.

Once they reached Sahul, whether by the northern or southern route and wherever they arrived, evidence is that they moved rapidly to populate most of the continent over the next five to ten thousand years.

At the end of April 2021 the ABC reported that new research from the Australian Research Council Centre of Excellence for Australian Biodiversity and Heritage showed the paths that were likely trodden by the ancient Aboriginal people as they moved across the continent of Sahul. Significantly they posit the starting point for those journeys being in the Kimberley.

In their wakes

In early 1998 my friend the maritime adventurer, Bob Hobman, sought to demonstrate the southern route hypothesis by building a huge bamboo raft on the Indonesian island of Roti, the most southern part of Asia, and

Nale Tasih 1, sails up but going nowhere. Photo, Peter Rogers.

sailing it more or less due east to land somewhere on the northern, or north-west coast of Australia. He called it the *Nale Tasih* expedition

I was fortunate to be included among the 12 Europeans and Indonesians chosen to attempt the voyage. After months of construction the vessel, thought to weigh about 11 tonnes, and made up of several accommodation modules on a bamboo platform mounted on five bamboo pontoons, was towed offshore, the two hand woven grass mat sails mounted on tripod masts were raised and we were cast adrift.

It was a complete debacle. Even with a favourable current of one knot there was insufficient wind to move us any faster; manoeuvring the huge beast with a steering oar nearly five metres long was difficult and, in the end, I was the only able bodied male capable of this task.

The most experienced sailor aboard, a veteran of numerous Sydney to Hobart yacht races, had exposed himself to the elements so much in the three weeks before we left, that he was badly sunburnt and unable to venture into the sunshine, even fully clothed. Bob himself, also an experienced sailor, was suffering from a muscle wasting ailment and was unable to take the steering oar. That left me, assisted by one or two of the stronger women members of the crew, to do the steering, or more correctly the sculling by which we attempted to move forward.

51

Nale Tasih 2, *beached on Melville Island, but showing how a prehistoric voyage to Australia was possible. Author photo.*

Given the twelve crew and weight we were carrying in fresh water, stored in hollowed out tree trunks, the firewood which would fuel our traditional stone based cooking hearth and the bamboo containers holding our rations which included pre-cooked goat meat preserved in palm sugar syrup, it should not really have been a surprise that as we left, one of our decks was ankle-deep below sea-level.

It took just 24 hours for the decision to be made to turn back and when a bitterly disappointed Bob Hobman and his then partner Silvia Shliekelmann, who had to a large extent funded the project, hauled the huge vessel ashore at the village of Oeselli which had been the base for the attempt, the bamboo pontoons were found to be riddled with borers despite the efforts Bob made to ensure the bamboos were free of the pest.

A year later in 1999, Bob made another attempt using a smaller raft, built and launched from near the West Timorese capital of Kupang.

A smaller crew of five, two Indonesians from the first *Nale Tasih* attempt; the self-taught anthropologist and self-proclaimed Aboriginal rock art specialist, Robert Bednarik, Peter Rogers, an Australian cameraman who had documented almost every aspect of the *Nale Tasih* project and Hobman himself, set out to use the tail end of the north-west monsoon to sail to Australia.

A cyclone threat forced them to abandon the raft in the Arafura Sea not far from Darwin where they were taken aboard a passing rig tender and deposited in Darwin, The raft fetched up on a beach on the southernmost coast of Melville Island, just north of the Territory mainland, thus demonstrating that such a voyage was indeed possible.

What should have been a triumph for Bob Hobman passed almost unnoticed for a variety of reasons and the final ignominy came when the raft was towed from its temporary resting place in a boat harbour in Darwin, across the harbour to a remote beach where it was burnt and destroyed by over-zealous Commonwealth Fisheries Department officers who, wrongly, identified the raft as the possible source of an infestation of predatory mussels which infected the marina at the time.

It made no difference to these officials that Bob Hobman was the only owner of a vessel in the marina at that time who could show that his vessel had been fumigated, a requirement of the Australian Department of Customs before the raft could actually be brought into the marina.

Almost a decade later, Hobman built yet another raft and, with a crew of Indonesians, paddled it from the Balinese coastal fishing village of Padang Bai across the much more difficult Lombok straits, to show how the first significant sea barrier for the earliest seafarers might have been overcome.

What we do know is that by the time Australia was formally annexed on behalf of Great Britain in 1788, there were believed to be as many as 750 000 Indigenous Australians in more than 640 language groups spread across Australia.

More recent explorations

What is now the coast of the Northern Territory was certainly visited by Dutch and French explorers and, some believe, may even have been visited by the Portuguese in the sixteenth century, a disputed contention, or the Chinese as early as the fifteenth century. As mentioned, Macassan traders from what is now the Indonesian Island of Sulawesi, made regular visits from the late 1700s but it was the English who were the main colonisers of the island we now call Australia and of the metropolis we now call Darwin.

Darwin, or Palmerston as it was first called, was actually the fifth attempt at settlement in the north of Australia with the first attempt, Fort Wellington on Melville island, though short lived at just four years (1824–28) making the Territory the third oldest Australian colony after New South Wales and Tasmania.

However each of those first four attempts at Fort Wellington, Fort Dundas at Raffles Bay (1827–29), Victoria at Port Essington, (1838–49) and Escape Cliffs at the mouth of the Adelaide River (1863–67) failed to gain a significant foothold, brought unstuck by poor choice of location, disease, conflict with Indigenous Australians, cyclone, or an inability by the mother country or the other colonies to maintain the necessary supply lines.

It was in 1839 while surveying the north coast that Captain John Lort Stokes, commanding the HMS *Beagle*, on which Charles Darwin had earlier sailed, landed to take sightings at the site which he named Escape Cliffs because of a confrontation with local Indigenous Australians. He went on to explore the harbour that was to become Port Darwin and the eventual site of the town of Palmerston.

Much early recorded knowledge about the Territory's landscape and vegetation came from the four attempts made by John McDouall Stuart to cross the continent from south to north a task at which he was finally successful reaching Chambers Bay on July 24, 1862.

But after those four epic attempts, said to have been successful only because he knew when to turn back, McDouall Stuart returned to England a blind, sick and broken man. He died two years later at the age of 50, having received his reward of 2000 pounds but never having taken up the two-thousand acres of land granted to him by a grateful South Australian Government.

Equally harrowing are the stories of some of the other explorers who travelled overland: Ludvig Leichhardt who, in 1845, arrived at Port Essington having taken a year to complete the first overland expedition to reach the north coast, and who subsequently died trying to go from east to west and John McKinlay whose terrible story of a wet season attempt to explore the coastal plains east of what is now Darwin is enough to turn the stomach, detailing as it does, his killing of horses and use of their hides to make a foul smelling boat which carried him and his surviving expedition members back to Escape Cliffs. The books of Derek Pugh about each settlement are required reading for those seeking more information.

Stuart's epic final journey proved that it was feasible for one particular ambition of the southern colonies to be achieved, construction of an overland telegraph line to Australia's northern coastline where it would join an undersea cable from Batavia (now Jakarta) in the Dutch East Indies and finally provide a direct telegraphic connection between London and those southern colonies of Australia.

Queensland was reportedly keen to provide that overland telegraph link but an upstart South Australia announced in 1870 that it intended to commission construction of an overland telegraph line that would follow Stuart's route but instead of Chambers Bay would end up at the newly named town of Palmerston, surveyed by the South Australian Surveyor General, George Goyder, in 1869. Palmerston, together with surveyed town sites at Southport, Virginia and Fred's Pass would provide the basis for the final, successful attempt to establish a permanent colony on Australia's north coast.

South Australia gave the task of constructing the line to its Postmaster General, Charles Todd, together with a sum of 120 000 pounds with the requirement that it be completed by January 1, 1872, a task many considered impossible. However by all accounts Todd was a practical and energetic man and within weeks he had divided the route into three sections, appointed leaders and equipped and victualled expeditions to construct the northern and central sections while he started north from Adelaide.

Ernestine Hill's accounts of the trials and privations of this epic undertaking exhaustively, colourfully and perhaps written with some license, provide a wonderful story of those times.

Todd completed the task a few months late and, at just under 480 000 pounds, more than four times the anticipated cost when the Overland Telegraph cable was eventually joined at Frew Ponds in the Northern Territory on August 23, 1872. Its lateness was immaterial though because the undersea cable from Batavia had broken and searches were underway to locate the breach and repair it, a task achieved two months later on October 30, 1872.

Despite the cost it was reported that within one year alone the cable had brought South Australia income of one million pounds.

The promise of Palmerston's future as the sea land link in what was known as the British Australasian Telegraph (BAT) was slow to reach fulfilment.

Development of the town was slow and not helped by the cyclone of 1897. The discovery of gold at several places along the new Overland Telegraph Line in 1871, then major finds at Pine Creek a year later, had prompted a start on the Palmerston to Pine Creek railway, created by an act of the South Australian parliament in 1883 with that link completed in 1889. Thousands of Indians, Singhalese and Chinese were imported as labourers for the railway.

Many of the Chinese labourers brought in to work on the railway left for the goldfields, some making their fortunes and many becoming wealthy enough to provide the basis for a Chinese population of shopkeepers, merchants and businessmen who with their wives and children, became one of the largest ethnic groups in Darwin and for many years the mainstay of commercial activity.

As for the railway, its planned extension south was delayed by the transition of the Northern Territory from South Australian to Commonwealth control taking place in the early 1900s so it wasn't until 1917 that it reached the north bank of the Katherine river. What turned out to be the final section, to Birdum, just south of Larrimah, was completed in 1929.

No taxation without representation

The Northern Territory's system of governance has evolved over time but as late as 1971, the Territory still operated under what some called the yoke and others the dead hand of Canberra and specifically the Department of the Interior.

As mentioned elsewhere the land now known as the Northern Territory had originally been annexed to New South Wales before being taken over in 1863 by the colony of South Australia. After Federation in 1901, and with South Australia finding it difficult financially to support the Northern Territory, negotiations began between the new

Commonwealth Government and South Australia for the surrender of the NT which finally occurred in 1911.

Before the surrender, however, the Northern Territory elected two members to the South Australian lower house, was recognised as a division for the election of members to the upper house (both established in 1856) and was included with South Australia in a single electorate to vote in the 1901 Commonwealth election.

After passage of the Northern Territory Acceptance Act in 1911 the Commonwealth began processes for the administration of the Territory, establishing the office of Administrator who would appoint and suspend magistrates and execute Crown Land leases and dispositions.

A council of advice of six members was to be appointed and a Supreme Court to be established. Two years later, in 1913, a public service was established.

However it was to be a long time before Northern Territorians enjoyed any local political representation, and even longer before that representation was more than tokenistic.

It was this seemingly contemptuous treatment which led to what became known as the Darwin Rebellion, colourfully and extensively covered by Ernestine Hill in *The Territory*.

The essence was that in 1918 the Administrator of the day, Dr John Anderson Gilruth, fell foul of the community by trying to clean up what he saw as a mostly lawless town, rife with unemployment, poverty, prostitution, gambling, opium smoking and other social evils, by issuing many often hasty and restrictive decrees.

At one stage, disgusted by the state of the town's hotels, he took them over and imposed restrictions on who could drink and how much. This high-handed action was met with strikes by the drinkers and caused open rebellion leading to him being heckled, threatened and ridiculed wherever he went. The situation was brought to a head when Gilruth, apparently intending to go south for Christmas, ordered that a ship bringing 700 cases of Melbourne Bitter beer for an almost dry community, be turned around and sent to Singapore without unloading.

On December 21 1918, the Singapore ship returned with the beer still on board but there was no indication it was going to be unloaded.

At midday a huge crowd of unionists from the Vesteys meatworks, led by the Australian Worker's Union's firebrand leader Harold Nelson marched to Government House and stormed the gates and fence, which being white-ant ridden collapsed before them.

There was a tense standoff with Nelson reading an indictment of the Administrator until, after several demands to show himself, Gilruth finally appeared to attempt to appease the crowd. Before he could speak a brawl broke out in the crowd, allegedly prompted by the legendary buffalo shooter, cattleman, farmer and Gilruth supporter, Paddy Cahill, sworn in as a special constable, wielding a shillelagh. The heat went out of the moment, both sides retired. Some injured went for medical treatment and not long afterwards Dr Gilruth and family were smuggled aboard the Naval Vessel, HMAS *Encounter*, sent in response to southern newspaper reports of the Darwin Revolution and the Administrator's peril, and sailed away.

Paddy Cahill had been one of the Territory's most famous and popular sons for his cattle droving, buff shooting and other exploits. He was a knowledgeable and sympathetic supporter of Aboriginal people and with their help had established a successful farm at Oenpelli (the present day Gunbalunya, or Karnbalanya). In 1912 he had been appointed a Protector of Aborigines and had been an important advisor to noted anthropologist, Sir Baldwin Spencer. He had also provided zoological specimens and a significant collection of bark paintings to the National Museum of Victoria.

On the night of the rebellion he had reportedly been intending to sail south with some rare specimens of Australian fauna destined for Sydney's Taronga Park Zoo but for his role with the shillelagh his luggage was declared black by unionists and then a local wag opened the specimen crates on the wharf reportedly creating a merry panic among the crowd as kangaroos, wallabies, pythons and frill-necked lizards bolted for freedom.

Shortly after Gilruth's departure the two most senior public servants, Carey and Evans, and the Supreme Court Judge Bevan, all left Darwin by ship due to the hostility of the locals.

A subsequent Royal Commission into the uprising, reportedly found strongly in favour of the people that neglect and self-interest on the part of the government had incited them to action. Their indignation was justified and their allegations, for the most part true. Cahill came in for mention as a 'decent man but sometimes careless'.

In 1919 Vestey's meatworks closed ending the promise of a viable and valuable beef industry and Darwin sank back into what might have been described as its customary torpor.

However, the Darwin Rebellion had laid the groundwork for a continuing campaign of political agitation demanding representation for the governed particularly by increasing the influence of the Australian Workers Union Secretary, Harold Nelson, described as a fiery orator, who refused to pay tax as part of his protests and was gaoled for it.

The campaign bore fruit when, in 1922, the Commonwealth legislated to provide for one elected member from the Northern Territory and Nelson was elected but it was a pyrrhic victory because he would have no voting right, would not be able to be elected as Speaker or chairman of committees and would not be counted in any quorum.

As Federal Member Nelson continued to campaign for greater expenditure on the Territory and self-government but with little success. He was defeated at an election in 1934 and moved with his family to Alice Springs.

Meanwhile, in 1926 the Commonwealth tried a short lived experiment of dividing the Territory along the 20th parallel of South Latitude into two separate territories of North Australia and Central Australia, each with its own Government Resident, Advisory Council and separate administration but this arrangement lasted only five years before the act setting it up was repealed in 1931.

In 1936 the NT's elected Federal member, at that time Adair McAlister Blain, had been given the right to speak in the house, take part in committee work and veto motions to disallow laws made for the Territory, an almost derisory situation that pertained until 1959.

While still an elected member, Blain joined up for World War 2, being captured by the Japanese and held prisoner-of-war for several years. Uniquely he was re-elected while still a POW.

From 1959, the Territory Member, by then Jock Nelson, son of the first Federal member, Harold, and like his father representing the Labor Party, had been granted the right to vote on matters relating to the Territory alone. Jock Nelson, in 1963 was the last NT member of the house to be elected unopposed and retired in 1966. He would later be appointed Administrator of the Northern Territory.

His successor as Federal member, the wartime flying ace, Stephen Edward (Sam) Calder, representing the Country Party, was given full voting rights two years later, in 1968. Some might see the earlier recalcitrance by the Menzies Liberal Government in granting those rights to the Territory member as payback for the election of a Labor representative for so long. Calder, later representing the Territory's new Country Liberal Party, would hold the seat until 1980.

In his authoritative *A Short History of the Legislative Council for the Northern Territory*, published in 1986, Fred Walker, the first Clerk of the NT Legislative Assembly wrote that a first attempt to get a Territory legislature was pursued by Harold Nelson in 1930:

> ... when he successfully moved for the inclusion in a Government bill of clauses providing for a Legislative Council to make ordinances for the Northern Territory but the Senate, then, as on most occasions since, was controlled by ultra-conservatives who removed the clauses and sent the bill back to the House of Representatives which was forced to drop the measure.

As Walker noted:

> ... the National Party, later the Country party, (and even later the National Party again) delayed by 18 years the introduction of the first Legislative Council.

With the bombing of Darwin by the Japanese in 1942, the Northern Territory had been placed under military administration, a situation which continued until 1946. Civilian administration was restored in 1947 with the establishment of the Northern Territory Legislative Council comprised of the Administrator as council chairman, seven appointed members, local heads of Commonwealth departments and six elected members. It had the power to make ordinances for the peace, order and good government of the Territory but these were subject to assent by the Administrator and provisions for disallowance by the Federal Government.

This latter power would create another significant political conflict in the NT a number of years later when it was used by a Victorian MP to have

Federal Parliament disallow Northern Territory legislation giving terminally ill patients the right and the means to have their lives legally terminated.

Electoral districts of Alice Springs, Batchelor, Stuart and Tennant Creek were established to elect a member to the Legislative Council with two members to be elected from Darwin. On December 13, 1947 just over 4440 enrolled citizens voted in the election. That first Council had as its president the Administrator, AR Driver with the elected members being RC (Dick) Ward representing Alice Springs, W Fulton, Batchelor; M Luke, representing the first Darwin seat and FC Hopkins, the second; Jock Nelson (son of Harold), representing Stuart and VH Webster, Tennant Creek.

The Official Members were the Director of Lands, Director of Mines, Crown Law Officer, Director of Native Affairs, Director of Works, and the Director of Health.

The first sitting of the new Council took place on 19 February 1948, coincidentally the sixth anniversary of the first wartime bombing of Darwin.

Walker writes that:

> While some were disappointed at the composition of the Council, Dick Ward recognised it as the foot in the door to self-government in that the establishment of a legislative body, notwithstanding a parliamentary minority for the people, amounted to the creation of a device for changing the constitution.

The first elected Legislative Council ran for only two years until November 1949. Over subsequent years a number of legislative changes by the Commonwealth included in 1959 increasing the number of elected members from six to eight, and the number of appointed members from seven to nine, at the same time creating eight new electoral districts.

In 1962 another change allowed the council to make ordinances relating to its powers and enabling Indigenous Australians to enrol and vote in Commonwealth elections.

From 1965 Council members were permitted to elect their own president and in 1968 the number of elected members increased to 11, while the number of appointed members was reduced to six, again providing for the creation of the appropriate electoral districts.

The last Legislative Council

Thus it was that at the time of the coming of television in August 1971, campaigning was already under way for an October election of what would turn out to be the last Northern Territory Legislative Council with a total of 25 338 people eligible to vote.

One of those electioneering the hardest was a feisty and determined young woman named Dawn Lawrie who, disillusioned with the representations of the sitting member, Harold Cooper, had decided to run for the seat of Nightcliff. She wasn't the only one disillusioned; in his *Short History of the Legislative Council*, former Clerk, Fred Walker, described Cooper's performance as 'unimpressive'.

Ms Lawrie had arrived in Alice Springs in the early '60s and worked with the regional airline, Connellan Airways, known as Connair, a private company which flew DC3 and other aircraft on a network of routes across the Territory's outback. She and a friend, also named Dawn, bought a Land rover for 50 pounds and drove to Darwin over a period of several weeks, camping out along the way.

By the time of the election she was employed by a local doctor as his evening receptionist. The other receptionist in the office was the endorsed Labor candidate she went on to defeat. According to Fred Walker:

> Lawrie had campaigned for a Labor candidate in another election and had hoped to get Labor pre-selection for the seat. Failing that, she stood as an independent going on to defeat not only her endorsed Labor opponent but also the incumbent.

One of the issues of the time was a proposal for a second access road to the expanding northern suburbs.

Given the notional name of the Palmerston Freeway, its need had been recognised since 1967 but Ms Lawrie was concerned that no money had been allocated in the Federal Budget for the new road yet $4.5 million had been allocated for development of new suburbs, Tiwi and Anula.

For an article in the *Northern Territory News* she produced vehicle numbers showing that, during the peak hour at 8 a.m. the two lane Bagot Road was already carrying more than its designed traffic load. Ms Lawrie said this meant it was taking half an hour to travel six miles on Bagot

Road, or 12 miles per hour. She said with new housing subdivisions under construction and new office blocks being built in the city (sic) whose workers would no doubt live in the northern suburbs, lack of action on a second road would worsen traffic chaos. (Drivers coming from Sydney or Melbourne where commutes of an hour were common, tended to laugh off the idea of a peak hour in Darwin)

One of the traffic problems was caused by a bottleneck at the intersection of Bagot Road with the Stuart Highway where morning traffic had to be controlled by a traffic police officer, there being no traffic lights.

Upon her election Lawrie joined two other Independents in that Eleventh Legislative Council: mining consultant, Joe Fisher (Fannie Bay) and former Crown Law officer and official member, Ron Withnall (Port Darwin).

The rest of the promised eleven elected members were Bernie Kilgariff, representing the electorate of Alice Springs (and later to be one of the Territory's first Senators); Rupert Kentish, Arnhem; Eric Marks, Barkly; Les MacFarlane, Elsey; Dick Ward, Ludmilla; Tom Bell, McMillan; Tony Greatorex, Stuart and Goff Letts, Victoria River. Greatorex was elected President, the first elected member to hold the position.

The Official members were the two Assistant Administrators, Martyn Finger and Harry Giese, who was also Director of Aboriginal Affairs; Crown Law Officer, Clem O'Sullivan; Director of Mines, Phil Purich; Director of Health, D B Travers; Director of Primary Industry, Barry Hart and Director of Local Government, Harry Plant.

Before the term ended Charles Gurd had become Director of Health replacing Travers who in turn had replaced Purich; Giese had been replaced by Ray McHenry who was in turn replaced by Creed Lovegrove but remained as an Assistant Administrator, Barry Hart had left, replaced by Director of Education, Hedley Beare while Director of Local Government, Harry Plant had also gone.

Fred Walker in his *Short History of the Legislative Council*, wrote that Dawn Lawrie, was the only member to unseat a sitting member but noted that Harold 'Tiger' Brennan, who had, over a long career represented several different electorates—Elsey, Batchelor and Victoria

River—had resigned before the election. His successor in Victoria River, Goff Letts, was a former Director of Primary Industries and had been an official member in a previous Legco, as it was known.

Letts immediately became leader of the Country Party members. The strength of the parties was Country Party five, Letts, Kilgariff, MacFarlane, Kentish and Greatorex; and Labor three, Ward, Marks and Bell and three independents, Withnall, Fisher and Lawrie.

Goff Letts was the second former Official Member to cross the chamber to become an elected member, the other being Ron Withnall, the former Crown Law Officer at that time the Independent member for Port Darwin.

Goff Letts had had a distinguished career in the Animal Industry Branch having arrived in 1957 with what he described 'as the task of helping to lift the cattle industry out of the 19th Century'. Among his many achievements was helping to eradicate the dreadful lung disease, *Pleuro Pneumonia* in cattle, and he played a significant role in the control of the feral buffalo then roaming wild in vast numbers across the coastal plains of the Top End.

Letts would turn out to have an astonishing number of old family, school or university friends who, at crucial moments, would prove to be unexpectedly valuable as his soon to be published memoir shows.

A tall rangy six footer with a shock of white hair, he was an accomplished horse rider, expert marksman and former joint winner with his father of the Queen's Prize for shooting. He was, according to our mutual friend, John Flynn, not only deeply interested in, but also knowledgeable about, every aspect of the Territory's history, geography, flora and fauna as well as having an abiding interest in Indigenous matters from his earliest days.

Letts himself explained that his interest in politics dated from his attendance at a meeting in 1966 to form an NT Branch of the Australian Country Party.

Several years later and by then both an official member of the Legislative Council as Director of Primary Industries and the head of an amalgamated Animal Industry and Agriculture Branch he wrote that he 'had had enough of the Bureaucratic Bulldust from Canberra so resigned from both his job and his Legco position and started what became a successful veterinary practice'. When Tiger Brennan retired in 1971 Letts saw what he called 'an opportunity to join the elected self government crusaders'.

The first sitting of the Eleventh Legislative Council took place on December 7, 1971 but its ceremonial opening was apparently not covered by the new ABC Television, there being very limited picture-taking capabilities at that time.

As will be seen, constitutional development of the Northern Territory would be a continuing story covered by our ABC TV newsroom.

How television news made it to air

The ABC management had maintained its austerity program towards the Darwin operation by providing what many regarded as the bare minimum staff required to provide such a service. What had been a small staff producing radio programs from six in the morning until midnight, seven days a week, was now going to also be required to produce television programming initially from four o'clock in the afternoon until 10.30 or eleven at night.

At that time the staff of what was then known as Radio 8DR consisted of a regional manager, Don Sanders, assistant manager, Ian Marshall, their secretary, Sandra Nicholson, a talks officer, Tom Wilkinson; rural officer, Peter Knudsen and several announcers: Alf Jervis, Richard Peach, Glenn Taylor and Rick Dowling. There was a sound librarian Mary Wilson who catalogued and ordered the collection of musical recordings used by the announcers to fill out their programs and a handful of technicians, some on secondment from the Postmaster General's Department (PMG) including Mike 'Father' Yates, Henry Anderssen, Jim Eustice and Don Geddes. The newsroom consisted of four journalists and a typist, a total staff of 19.

In his interview for the *NT News* previewing the coming of television, Sanders spoke of the staff increasing from five, but he had clearly forgotten or overlooked those with whom he had few dealings, including the newsroom and the announcers and technicians working on the lower floor of the Housing Commission building which had become the ABC's new radio studios and administrative centre. The new TV Studio building was under construction next door.

The advent of television saw a further 19 staff added, including two more journalists, extra announcers, another sound librarian, Esther Lang, two presentation officers, Adrian Payne and David Nordsvan; receptionist, Yuleen Payne (wife of Adrian); film assistant, Amanda Taylor; a second rural reporter, Alan Humphreys and of course the technical staff who would ensure the programs were actually broadcast from the new TV studio: Roger Burnard, Alf Amrein, Graeme Halprin, Jon Davey, Bruce Watson, Gerry Orrin, Bruce Black, plus a film librarian, Arthur Harris and graphics artist, Colin Martin. Amanda Taylor doubled as make-up artist for the on-air personalities: newsreaders, weather presenters and any studio guests.

For the first few months of television in Darwin, the news consisted of a five-minute slot at 7 p.m. when a slide of a Territory scene would be shown while an announcer read the radio news bulletin being put to air at the same time. This was followed by a 10-minute newsreel compiled in Adelaide.

The full daily program also came from Adelaide in the form of videotapes of the entire Adelaide program line-up, flown up the following day, so always at least a day late. Programs were also sent from Sydney on videotape.

In the first week of February 1972, full-length state-type news bulletins would begin going to air.

Until that time, with only radio news to worry about, the Darwin newsroom as noted above, had four journalists. They were led by the journalist in charge (JIC), Geoff Hughes who had been a cadet in Darwin several years earlier, had left to spend time in the Sydney newsroom, during which he married his wife, Elly, and had returned to Darwin to take charge. The others were, Mike Hayes who had worked on The *Age* newspaper in Melbourne before arriving in Darwin a year earlier, Bill Fletcher who had come to Darwin from Tasmania earlier that year and long-time local Dick Muddimer, employed as a casual or part-timer.

Added to the team by the time I arrived was Dave Molesworth, also a former *Age* journalist and colleague of Mike Hayes, who had arrived in Darwin on what was going to be a round Australia trip with his wife Diana, also a journalist, in their four wheel drive vehicle, a converted former army ambulance based on a Land Rover body.

Hairy ABC newsroom, 1972. (l to r) Bill Fletcher, Geoff Hughes (JIC),
Dick Muddimer, Author, Mike Hayes. Front David Molesworth.
Photo, Keith Bushnell, from the author's collection.

David and Diana were staying with Mike Hayes and his family when the newsroom was expanded ahead of the introduction of the (so called) full length bulletins. David had been doing some casual journalism shifts when Mike Hayes, acting JIC while Geoff was on leave, offered him a full time job which Dave took up on January 24, 1972.

My arrival on February 1, 1972 was the final appointment which would enable the newsroom to take on the task of producing not only radio but television news bulletins, seven days a week which was a fairly monumental task for such a small group of people.

I had begun my journalism as a cadet reporter on a group of suburban giveaway newspapers, *Standard News*, in the south eastern suburbs of Melbourne, completing three years of a routine four-year cadetship before being appointed to the, largely titular, position of Editor of one of the suburban weeklies with a circulation of 30 000 a week.

After a few months in this position and feeling the need for a change, in 1968 I relocated to Perth where, after some time doing casual work, I was given a C Grade journalist's position in the ABC newsroom. Over the next three years I spent a considerable amount of time as a relieving journalist, filling in for the regional journalists in Geraldton, Albany, Bunbury and Kalgoorlie while the incumbents took their five weeks annual leave.

Regional news reporting was a five day a week job requiring the writing and compilation of two seven-minute news bulletins, one going to air at seven minutes to seven each evening and a morning bulletin read twice during programs presented by the local rural officer. It was during this time that I met and married my wife, Patsy a teacher.

These periods of regional relief on a higher grading together with a fairly limited time learning scriptwriting, shot listing, production and other aspects of the use of moving pictures in a television news bulletin, became my qualifications for applying for the two-year posting in the Darwin newsroom when it was advertised in the *Official Bulletin* of the ABC.

When I was told my job application had been successful, we were given three weeks to pack up one life and move to Darwin for a new one. The staff people responsible for arranging our uplift had given me a small booklet providing limited information about the town, the way of life, dress requirements, and the climate—two seasons consisting of the Wet and the Dry. However they needed it returned as it was the only copy they had.

It was also emphasised to me that as Darwin was still regarded as a hardship post and it was generally accepted to be hard for wives, there would be understanding if my wife or I couldn't last the distance, but because of the expense of relocating us, it really would be appreciated if we could see out the two years.

Patsy, having won a Commonwealth scholarship to teachers college, had been bonded to the West Australian Education Department for three years. She had just worked out her bond and was able to transfer to the Commonwealth Teaching Service. Interestingly the person handling her transfer thought Darwin was up north in Western Australia. Remote indeed.

Thus it was that at 8.00 a.m. on February 1, 1972 Patsy and I arrived in Darwin for the start of what we expected to be a two-year posting.

We stepped out of the air conditioning of the MacRobertson Miller Airlines (MMA) Fokker Friendship into the humid aftermath of a rainstorm and the perfumed air of a tropical wet season morning and were immediately entranced.

What we were not ready for, however, was the grey uniformity of the housing which greeted us. New suburbs were being built at a fairly rapid rate by the Commonwealth Department of Housing and Construction, or 'Works and Jerks', as it was known. Their approach to constructing a new suburb was to selectively clear an area of several square kilometres.

Selective clearing meant bulldozing the entire area except for a few mature mineatas or Darwin woolybutts, the predominant local tree species in the prevailing tropical savanna landscape. These would be left to provide isolated patches of feeble shade and were often prone to falling branches because they were inevitably eaten out inside by the voracious local termite, *Mastotermes darwiniensis*.

The layer of topsoil left was generally shallow, because most of the northern suburbs are located on a layer of coffee-rock, and of poor quality. A virtually rainless dry followed by a humid build up period known as troppo time or suicide season and then the wet typified by an annual rainfall of between 1600 and 2600 millimetres took a harsh toll on the soil.

Senior Government officers' houses on Myilly Point. Photo, Old Darwin;
maybe NT Government Photographer.

On this selectively cleared area, sewerage lines would be laid, roads, gutters and footpaths would be constructed in a fairly uniform pattern. There would be a centrally located primary school to cater for the children of the families which would occupy the houses and a small area for a few shops which would provide amenities the inhabitants would otherwise have to travel into Darwin for.

The land would be divided into house lots of 1000 to 1200 square metres, each fenced with a low cyclone-mesh perimeter fence with gates and then housing construction would begin. The Department of Housing and Construction built the majority of the houses using either their own labourers or private contractors.

These houses were in one of several designs, with designated numbers such as C6, C19 or D3 but basically a rectangle of about sixty feet by thirty (roughly twenty metres by ten) of asbestos cement sheet on a timber frame lined with fibrous plaster or gyprock and elevated on steel or, later, concrete pillars about eight feet (2.4 metres) high.

There was usually a small balcony either at one end, or in the middle, depending on the design, while sets of stairs led to doors at the front and back.

The under floor area usually incorporated a concrete block store room and simple laundry with the idea being that this area would provide extra living space in the wet.

These houses were provided at a subsidised rental to those employed in the Commonwealth Public Service or Defence personnel accommodated in separate suburbs close to the airport and RAAF base, on the Coonawarra Naval Base which was inland and on the Larrakeyah Army Base which was on one of the prime pieces of waterfront land in Darwin yes that's right, navy inland, army by the water though this would change some years later with construction of a patrol boat base at Larrakeyah.

Another prime piece of waterfront, or rather clifftop, land was the area known as Myilly Point and it was on this highly desirable peninsula within a peninsula, that the senior public servants were housed in premises of similar design to, but generally a bit larger than, those of the general run of public servants.

These were the houses of the heads of the various Commonwealth Government Departments who were the *de facto* Government of the Northern Territory and included the official members of the Legislative Council.

The second tier of housing was provided by the Housing Commission and generally consisted of ground level houses, also rectangular in shape, built of red or grey concrete bricks and almost always with little concession to the climate of Darwin, although the (usually) poky rooms did have ceiling fans and louvre windows which could be opened when it wasn't raining.

These houses were available to people who were privately employed, or were day labour crews for building or other companies and these houses too had subsidised rents.

The Housing Commission also built a number of blocks of flats. Some early examples, in Parap for instance, were quite well designed with good flow through ventilation but for the most part they were multi-storey blocks which were destined to become ghettoes and havens for those of the lowest socio-economic demographic. In future years they would claim an inordinate amount of police time attending problems there until they were progressively demolished in the new century to be replaced by more pleasant accommodation.

Finally there were the few private dwellings built, usually by Greek or Italian contractors, for sale or rental to those not eligible for either form of subsidised housing.

Until the inquiry by Justice Else-Mitchell into the issue of land tenure in the Northern Territory in the early '70s, all land in the Territory was owned by the Crown and was leased out to pastoralists or others seeking land. In Darwin the Government held occasional land sales usually for about twenty blocks of land in one of the new subdivisions. These sales were actually auctions and there were two sections, restricted and open.

The blocks in the restricted section were available only to buyers who had not previously owned a house or land in the Territory while the open section as the name implies, was where the developers could bid, and as a result blocks which sold for a couple of thousand in the restricted section would fetch multiples more in the open section.

For those able, or needing, to buy a house there were options available. Real estate agents, some allied to major national groups but others formed locally, advertised both sales and rentals of houses and flats.

One of the better known independents was an eccentric woman named Stella Kirk who offered furnished one bedroom flats from $30 per week and two bedrooms for $40 or $50 a week. Action Real Estate was offering a brand new three-bedroom elevated house amidst private and government homes in Jingili with a full length bath, shower recess and separate toilet for $18 500 while another company had a five-bedroom elevated home in Alawa for $30 000. On the commercial side a one and a half acre corner site in inner-suburban Bishop Street, with a 4000 square foot warehouse and 4 bedroom residence with downstairs flat was on offer for $130 000.

Within the ABC there was also something of a hierarchy of residences. Some of those who had been recruited locally, had to find their own housing while those of us brought in from elsewhere were accommodated in versions of the above-ground houses, augmented by having the under-floor area concreted, not the norm for this type of housing.

This did contribute to making the under-floor area valuable clean extra living space as well as providing undercover parking for cars and a place where clothes could dry when the rain made the ubiquitous Hills Hoists unusable.

Another feature of Government housing unusual for the time is that almost every house had a solar hot water system, the storage tanks being housed in a curious tepee affair on the roof's ridge.

The ABC leased its houses from the NTA, in turn charging its employees a fairly modest rent compared with that asked for private houses.

The houses allocated to the ABC ranged from older style houses either in Darwin itself or in nearby suburbs such as Parap and Stuart Park.

The big influx of staff for TV meant the ABC had to seek houses in the newly developing northern suburbs such as Jingili and Moil. This was why some of us found ourselves in what became known as the ghetto, a cluster of about ten houses in Jingili, which meant that we were neighbours to a number of our workmates, an arrangement which generally worked well because it gave us a more or less instant community, with at least one shared interest.

Public service functional ugly

Meanwhile, back at the airport at eight o'clock on Tuesday February 1, 1972 we were met by the journalist in charge, Geoff Hughes, an amiable, bearded chap just a few years older than me. His first words were that he was pleased to see I had a beard, giving me to understand I would fit right into the newsroom where my other five colleagues had either beards, or in one case, a substantial soup-strainer moustache. Geoff was to become a good friend and proved a colourful companion.

His form of transport that day was a Volkswagen Beetle which was just barely capable of carrying the three of us and our luggage.

Later I would discover that his preferred form of travel was an ex-police BMW motor cycle which he would ride to various pubs at

The two surviving interior photographs of our house in Jingili, about 1974.
Ocker the cat leaping off the very substantial dutch cupboard I built.
Author photos.

the weekend accompanied by a former fellow university student, Hu Bradley, a lawyer who would many years later, and after a successful legal career, become Chief Magistrate.

The heavily loaded Beetle brought us at leisurely pace to our new home, one of the previously mentioned asbestos cement clad rectangular structures elevated on concrete piers. Our new house had highly polished Jarrah floors and was sparsely furnished in what I came to call the public service functional ugly style, square tubular metal frames for beds and tables, as well as the chairs which were upholstered in either vinyl or a coarsely woven fabric. Older houses were furnished with much more attractive bamboo furniture in several styles, a preferred alternative.

Our house had stairs leading up at one end to a small veranda about two metres wide and taking up half the width of the house, or about five metres.

It was matched in size by the enclosed small kitchen containing refrigerator, electric stove, sink some bench space and some cupboards, painted a utilitarian green.

A door from the veranda opened into the combined lounge/dining room which ran the full width of the house with banks of louvres at either end. A doorway led to a central hallway with floor to ceiling cupboards on one side and three bedrooms, the main being air conditioned, another ABC luxury.

A smaller hallway with bathroom on one side and toilet on the other led to a set of back stairs giving access to the downstairs laundry, an open area with washing machine and sink, and a lockable concrete block storeroom.

On the floor in the centre of the lounge-dining room there was a tea chest, a box made of thin plywood with metal corners of roughly a cubic metre capacity, which contained what we were told was the emergency kit, a collection of the absolute basics designed to get newcomers through the hiatus until their own goods arrived. It contained sheets, towels, table cloths, tea towels, a set of crockery, some cutlery and a basic pot and pan collection. It was, of course very useful because it was to be at least a fortnight before our own goods arrived by state ship and Patsy would be able to turn a bare box into a home.

Despite it being the wet, our house's surrounds were a dry mass of knee high weeds and scrubby grass. The house itself was only about three years old and, as we walked in, it appeared to be utterly soulless. There were no curtains on windows which had metal louvres from the floor to about three feet high and above that glass louvres which provided an unobstructed view to similar houses across the road and stretching seemingly into infinity.

As we pulled into the driveway, we noticed a neighbour who turned out to be one of the ABC's presentation officers, Dave Nordsvan, planting a fairly well developed tree, an activity I thought a bit unusual at that relatively early hour of the day. Sometime later, as we walked around our backyard with its two large survivors of the selective clearing process the only plant features, we kept stumbling into holes in the ground.

It was subsequently explained to us that our yard had been subject to a ritual occurrence: when tenants left the neighbours would come in and dig up any usable tree or shrub to enhance their own gardens. The tree being so assiduously planted by our neighbour was the last surviving relic of what had formerly been our garden.

Not to worry, Patsy was to become a keen gardener and with applications of topsoil, supplied by the ABC, and trees courtesy of a Department of Primary Industry plant give-away scheme, not to mention grass runners collected from all over the place she gradually developed a presentable garden.

On our first weekend in Darwin, we visited a distant relative of Patsy. She and her husband lived in the salubrious suburb of Fannie Bay in an elevated home they had occupied for some years and had then been able to buy under a particularly generous scheme the Federal Government used to try to encourage people to settle in the Territory. This scheme allowed public servants to buy their houses at cost less depreciation. This meant that those who lived in older houses, usually in the desirable inner suburbs like Larrakeyah, Stuart Park, Parap and Fannie Bay, could buy houses built some years earlier, and therefore more cheaply, and by also applying a depreciation element equivalent to a percentage of the value for each year of the house's age, could end up paying surprisingly low prices for houses which, on an open market, would have cost much more.

We came away from that visit with plants to re-establish our decimated garden. At that time aralias, a slender trunked shrub which grew prolifically and quickly, were the plant of choice to screen the under floor areas of elevated houses. You could cut the stems, stick them straight in the ground and with only water, they would grow and quite quickly provide a privacy screen. We left Pam and Terry's house with a stack of them sticking out through the Fiat Bambino's fold back sunroof and within a short time had a vegetation privacy screen at our new house.

One new addition we made to the house was the installation of a good sized above ground pool, bought from a fellow ABC employee. As we were installing it, the neighbour, Bob, leaned on the fence and opined that we probably wouldn't use it in the dry because it got too cold. We laughed at him and though we went on to have many good parties in and around the pool, eventually we realised Bob was right, and we sold it.

Much later we were to find that in the evenings it was possible to switch off the sound of the TV and still hear it from every neighbour and when a wet season storm was approaching there would be a burst of wind which was immediately followed by the *clack clack clack* sound of people closing louvres up and down the street. Our cats were to discover that an open louvre was a good place to lie to catch any breeze but we, and other cat lovers occasionally returned home to the bleating of a cat whose louvre had tipped, depositing it between glass and fly screen.

Another sound new to us was the soon to become familiar click-click of the house geckos.

Meanwhile Geoff, having shown us over our future home, said he would take me to work to introduce me around, but first he would take Patsy over to one of the other houses in the ghetto occupied by the wife of a mystery colleague I was destined never to meet.

This was Lani Hunter, an experienced television news producer from Sydney who had been sent to Darwin to train the local journalists in TV news production ahead of the introduction of full television news bulletins the following week, which was why I had been promoted to Darwin.

Lani had spent a couple of weeks training, had got the newsroom into a period of news dummy runs and had then disappeared, some suggested on a drinking binge. After some time his wife left Darwin and Lani himself was never seen in the newsroom again.

A cast of characters

It was late morning by the time we got to the newsroom and all of the journalists were on deck when Geoff brought me in to introduce me.

My new workmates were an eclectic bunch, all of about the same age as me. The exception was Dick Muddimer, who turned out to be the resident eccentric in a group I was to discover were all a bit eccentric in their own ways.

Mike Hayes had settled into the role of TV Line-up (TVL), the person responsible for actually compiling the news bulletin and, we were to discover, in Darwin, also directed the bulletin, a role which in other states was usually delegated to an assistant. The TVL position could be one of the most stressful jobs in TV, especially if there were technical glitches, and it required a particular temperament, calmness and confidence to do it well. Although he had no previous television experience Mike Hayes turned out to be a natural.

Standing over six feet tall, he was built like a brick shithouse and dressed in his own version of public service attire: baggy shorts, a blue denim work shirt with a special pocket for the fountain pens he favoured and which always had a stain of black ink where the pen leaked, RM Williams boots and socks worn around the tops of the boots.

Physically imposing, he had long, straight black hair down to his shoulders and an impressive black soup strainer moustache which hid his mouth.

Being a former journalist covering rural affairs for the *Melbourne Age*, he had brought his interest in issues agricultural with him and was already well known by many of the cattle station owners of the Top End. He was also a fine guitarist in the Bluegrass style and was part of a group known as Brown Sugar, the name chosen, he said, because its members were coarse and unrefined.

Mike was already a noted raconteur with a fund of stories about Territory characters, both of the present day, and of the past.

It was a skill which ensured that his television news stories, though rare, were always off beat and humorous, and it came as no surprise that in his later, post ABC years, he became famous for his *Prickle Farmer* books and radio programs which made his small property in the hamlet of Gunderoo outside Canberra and its cast of characters almost world famous. Mike was married at that time to Jill, mother of his two young children and a country singer in her own right who occasionally joined Mike and the band as singer.

The next journalist I met was Dick Muddimer, at that stage aged 46 and almost twenty years older than the rest of us. Dick was the permanent early morning journalist and our principal political reporter.

He was English and some claimed a remittance man, sent abroad to save embarrassing the family. In fact, Dick had begun his journalistic career on a range of English country newspapers in the Somerset district before deciding to try his hand in Australia.

He had fetched up in Sydney and very quickly gained work with one of the major daily newspapers but the hours didn't suit him and he was, anyway, attracted by all he had heard of the outback and planned to go to Alice Springs. As he told me many years later he had reached Threeways at the junction of the Barkly and Stuart Highways, and faced with the choice of going south or north, had flipped a coin and headed north which took him to Darwin.

Before he had managed to get his job as an ABC casual journalist he had worked on the Rum Jungle Uranium Mine, as a day labourer for the Darwin Town Council and a casual journalist on the *NT News*. He was an old-fashioned journalist but very thorough and well respected around the town.

He lived about 3 km out of town in Stuart Park and didn't have a car so walked into the office where he started work at 5.00 a.m., compiled the morning radio news bulletins, had a bowl of cornflakes at his desk for breakfast then spent a couple of hours as a general reporter, or covering the Legislative Council.

At twelve o'clock, when all of the preparation for the 12.30 news had been completed, he would fold his arms on his typewriter, lower his head and go to sleep until his official knock off time of one o'clock when he would set off to walk home. This regimen ensured he was very fit. He was also always well tanned courtesy of another claim to fame as a founding member of the Darwin Sun Club, in which capacity he was instrumental in helping have a section of the then remote Casuarina Beach declared a free beach or nude swimming area in the early 1970s.

Dick was very much a loner in the newsroom until I persuaded him to forgo his nap and join the rest of us for what became a daily habit, a counter lunch at the newly opened Post Bar at the rebuilt Don Hotel, a convenient 100 metres from the ABC. I was also later to sell him the first car he ever owned in Australia, a Mini Moke.

Dick wasn't known for his sartorial elegance having a small collection of much washed shirts, even fewer pairs of shorts and his long socks often had holes at the heels. On one occasion he was banned from the Post Bar because of his dress. It turned out to be a very short ban because the rest of us boycotted the Post Bar in protest and that cost them a substantial part of their weekly takings.

Dick was frugal in his habits, his only extravagance being his tins of Erinmore tobacco for the pipe he favoured.

In those days our fortnightly pay packets contained cash and Dick habitually threw his into the top drawer of a dressing table at home and, as he never locked his doors, would often be robbed. As far as I know he never registered a complaint with the police.

Moving on, I was introduced to David Molesworth, an experienced journalist who, like Mike Hayes, had worked for the *Melbourne Age*.

David had been a Geelong Grammarian, and was distantly related to a fellow student, Ranald McDonald, a member of the Syme family which owned the *Age* and who would become Managing Director fairly rapidly.

Dave had been competing with Mike Hayes for an *Age* cadetship. Mike got it, Dave didn't, but about five months later, courtesy of a distant relative known enigmatically as The Colonel, was advised to apply again. The Colonel was, in fact, Lieutenant Colonel EHB Neill, Chairman of David Syme and Co., Ranald's grandfather and a cousin of David's father, John.

He did and was accepted. He and Mike became great friends and, as he told me later, drinking companions.

They told some hilarious stories of jaunts into country Victoria to report on rural events such as field days, country fairs and agricultural shows with Mike there as a reporter and Dave filling in as photographer when an *Age* staff snapper wasn't available but also with an eye out for the opportunity to photograph an aeroplane because this was his true passion and one he pursues to this day. He says he was never paid for photographs of prize bulls but the outings were always enjoyable.

Their stories always involved references to heavy drinking and occasionally to fighting. Although neither Mike nor Dave had pugilistic inclinations they seemed to have been adept at finding a fight, or being close to where one took place.

Dave had been working for the *Age Radio News* which supplied a rip and read story service by telex to a number of commercial radio stations in metropolitan and country Victoria.

It was a job he had loved because it covered not only police rounds but state rounds which at that time meant attending the daily press conferences of the State's colourful and notorious leaders, Premier Sir Henry Bolte and Deputy Premier Arthur Rylah, journalistic opportunities Dave said he would never have been assigned to cover as a lowly cadet in the newspaper's newsroom.

Dave and his wife, Diana, who he had met on the *Age* had travelled fairly widely working as journalists in both New Zealand and Hong Kong before returning to Melbourne and the *Age* again for three years. Although I had come to Darwin from Perth, I was a Victorian and with a shared interest in Australian Rules football, via what was then the Victorian Football League (VFL). Dave and I became firm friends.

When the football season started in Victoria, the ABC produced a weekly compilation of games highlights which was flown to Darwin and replayed on the Wednesday night following. It became our habit to watch the program together over a Darwin Stubby, the famous but no longer marketed half gallon or sixty ounces of beer. In the early days, one of them would comfortably see us through the hour of outdated football.

The final journalist member of the newsroom was also its youngest, Bill Fletcher, a stocky blond-haired, blond-bearded former Tasmanian who had come to Darwin as a cadet journalist in early 1971 and with the forthcoming advent of TV News had been given a grading. His wife, Meri, a nurse would go on to a senior position in Territory Health before her untimely death.

The final members of that newsroom, and some would say the most important, were the two news typists, Betty Gadd and Kathy Palmer. Betty was an older woman who took on a mothering role over us younger staff but was tyrannical when it came to making us pay our weekly contributions for the morning coffee or tea and biscuits which she also supplied to us.

Kathy Palmer was a younger woman, closer in age to us journalists. An Englishwoman, mother of two young daughters and she liked to sunbathe, ensuring she always had a good tan which she liked to show off. She was a bright butterfly in that newsroom of mostly males.

I was not formally introduced to the other staff with whom I would work; I would learn their names as our working paths crossed. As for meeting the Branch Manager, Don Sanders, I don't remember ever being introduced to him, saw him only rarely since the TV studios were a foreign land to him and he never could differentiate between Dave Molesworth and me

But having been introduced to my immediate workmates, those who were able repaired to the new Don Hotel for lunch.

And so, to lunches long

The former Gordon's Don Hotel had been famous, or infamous, for its bamboo bar; a public bar which, as the name implies, was made of bamboo and had a sand floor. It was the roughest bar in the place and the one where most, though not all, of the fights took place.

The old Gordon's Don Hotel and infamous Bamboo Lounge.
Photo, Old Darwin.

The new Don was not only a pub but also a motel, and, though it made many concessions to modernity, with carpets on the floor of the Post Bar, at least it doffed its hat to the past with what was then known as the Gallery Bar at the rear of the building, behind the bottle shop. This most basic of bars had a tiled floor which sloped gently towards the centre, the better, it was said, to allow the spilt beer, blood and vomit to be hosed out as required.

The Post Bar opened soon after I arrived. It had been named in honour of the Postmaster General (PMG) which at that time was responsible for post, telephones and telegraphs, and also the transmitters used by the ABC. Indeed many of the ABC's employees across the nation were either former PMG employees, or were seconded from the PMG as technicians. The post bar was decorated with black and white prints of highlights of the construction of the overland telegraph line from South Australia to Darwin which would celebrate the centenary of its completion later in 1972.

Beer was served, as a matter of course, in handles a ten ounce pot with a handle which, the aficionados said, stopped the beer from getting warm when it was held in the hand.

Bill Fletcher at work. Bill Fletcher collection.

Most of us believed a beer should never last long enough to get warm whether held in the hand or by the handle. And although it was two cents a pot dearer than in the adjoining schooner bar the carpet on the floors and ready access to Becky's counter lunch kitchen made it the lunch venue of choice for us and at that stage you could still get five handles for a dollar.

Many long lunches, perhaps too many and certainly some too long, would be enjoyed at the Post Bar, especially when the regular wet season afternoon rains arrived and we were rained in.

The next day, I started work. The newsroom was a bare concrete block structure, built as the first storey of the new TV building.

It was originally designed to be the staff amenities room but with the increased number of News staff it had been commandeered as the newsroom, replacing a much smaller room in the adjoining Housing Commission building which now housed the radio studios, record library, technical areas and the managerial offices.

This newsroom had a small kitchenette with a big refrigerator which we came to ensure always had beer and cask wine, in case of visitors, of which there were a few.

There was also a solid lockable storeroom where stationery and other essentials were kept. The key was guarded by Betty.

Bill Fletcher reminds me that the ABC was so penny pinching that Betty had to make a requisition for paper, pens, notebooks, carbon paper, etc. and it would be supplied on the basis of what Adelaide thought we should be using.

He says reporters were often asked to return a used biro before a new one would be issued, a request which was universally ignored.

The newsroom later had a small cubicle with frosted glass panels added where the JIC, Geoff, subbed (that is, edited) the radio news bulletins and carried out his other duties. In what was more or less the centre of the room, four desks were placed together and occupied by the two typists, one for radio and one for TV, a desk for the TV Lineup, Mike Hayes, and one for the A/Lineup which was a role rotated between those who I called the hacks: Dave, Bill and me.

Along the side wall were three more desks—one for Dick as permanent early morning man, and one each for those of us who were not the A/Lineup.

Every desk had a second hand upright typewriter, usually handed to journalists after they had long outlived their lives with typists, the rationale being that you couldn't give heavy handed pounders like journalists a good typewriter as they would only wreck it. This is an attitude I have found everywhere I have worked with typewriters. It only changed when we switched to computers but that's a long way in the future.

There were three other desks, one holding the two constantly chattering Siemens Teleprinters or telexes, which were the main source of word stories and other communications from interstate, and a second used by a casual typist who came in at 5.00 p.m., to help with the late afternoon pressure generated by the demands of the approaching television news bulletin.

The room itself was gloomy having only three small windows covered in the metal mesh which shielded the whole building. One of the windows was partly obscured by one of several tall lockers which I never saw used. There was little by way of adornment apart from a Territory map showing all of the stations, towns, reserves and other points of interest. It was invaluable for a newcomer.

The room had one other feature, a door which led out onto the roof so that Techs could adjust aerials, tend to air-conditioners and do other tasks. Because air conditioning was required to keep all of the electronic equipment from overheating, the entire TV building was always cold so sometimes we would open the door to warm things up.

The problem was that the air conditioning downstairs compensated by becoming colder and the Techs would wander around wearing jumpers and complaining.

Television news stories were written on specially adapted electric typewriters capable of taking the sets which comprised a coloured cover sheet and seven flimsies or copies, separated by sheets of carbon paper. Radio news stories were typed on rough white paper with just one copy.

The final desk was the site of the last act of the day, separating the flimsies and compiling them into a set of scripts to be used by all those involved in the production of the news bulletin.

Bill Fletcher again reminds me that in the days before TV, the news typist only worked week days which meant journalists had to type their own weekend radio news bulletins.

One of the typists' duties in their spare time was to make up the sets. A green cover sheet represented a word story, a yellow cover sheet represented a story with either film or videotape. The newsreader got the original or coloured sheets.

The flimsies were distributed to the presentation officer or vision mixer; sound tech, lighting and camera operator, and videotape and telecine operators. The TV Lineup kept one and the A/Lineup had one. The last couple of flimsies were pretty hard to read.

In his comments about Darwin's new television regime, senior broadcast officer, Rodger Andrews, noted that we were expected to provide what was essentially a state type seven-day-a-week radio and television service, under conditions unheard of anywhere else in Australia.

As he wrote:

> A little known aspect of Darwin staffing was the greatly reduced numbers to provide similar program output to the BAPH stations. The total staffing for all, Technical, News, Production, Rural, Talks and Administration was only 32 [actually 35].

One way to improve efficiency was to combine the duties of radio and television staff while another was to use the now familiar multi-tasking with staff doing multiple jobs during their shift. Naturally, the Staff Association was not happy and some staff did in some cases react unfavourably but it was a case of 'do it this way or not at all' and eventually 'this way' of operation became the norm.

With the benefit of hindsight, and advanced age, I can now say that the ABC exploited us and imposed demands of performance not expected anywhere else in the network, but because we were almost all young and many of us were quite idealistic, we did things which were beyond the normal.

Sam's contributions

It has also been suggested the ABC was not ready to provide a state type operation in Darwin in 1971.

Glenn Taylor says the ABC had been holding out for the completion of the Broadband Microwave link from Mount Isa to Darwin, intending just to provide a relayed television service from Brisbane. However, the link's completion was several years away and the federal member, Sam Calder was, again according to Glenn, agitating on behalf of Territorians for television in Darwin and the rest of the Territory.

That a relayed service only was under consideration is borne out in one of Don Sanders' regional reports from August 1967. This memo was recovered by Graeme Halprin from a skip where it had been discarded, destined for the rubbish tip.

In it Don Sanders refers to a visit by three southerners, identified as Messrs Brownless of the Broadcasting Control Board, Beard of the PMG and Anderson from the ABC for the purpose of establishing possible sites for TV studios and transmitters.

Sanders wrote:

> This is the first sign of any activity concerning TV in Darwin and we trust that due consideration will be given, right from the outset, to Darwin's unique position and great rate of development.

DARWIN, N.T.   DRS: JLA: 22   31st August, 1967.

                        8 DR   DARWIN
                REGIONAL REPORT FOR PERIOD ENDING AUGUST, 67

TELEVISION:
            Darwin has been recently visited by Messrs. Brownless (B.C.B.), Board
(P.M.G.) and Anderson (A.P.C.) for the purpose of establishing possible sites for
T.V. Studios and transmitters.

            This is the first sign of any activity concerning T.V. in Darwin and
we trust that due consideration will be given, right from the outset, to Darwin's
unique position and great rate of development. Darwin should be considered as
the future capital of an independent Northern Territory State, and our thinking
should not be restricted to the extent that a T.V. Station here should be just
another relay station at the end of a micro-wave link. Development in this area
is being closely watched. It is to be hoped that any building associated with
this medium will be designed with our future development and expansion well in
mind.

*Don Sanders' 1967 memo about ABC Darwin being a possible relay
station. Graeme Halprin collection.*

Darwin should be considered as the future capital of an
independent Northern Territory state, and our thinking
should not be restricted to the extent that a TV station
should be just another relay station at the end of a microwave [sic.] link. Development of this area is being closely
watched. It is to be hoped that any building associated
with this medium will be designed with our future
development and expansion well in mind.

Just how much pressure Sam Calder applied on the government to
get television for the NT is captured in a response from the Parliamentary
Library to another former ABC colleague and friend, Senator Malarndirri
McCarthy ahead of this year's anniversary.

As far back as March 1968, Calder had told Parliament:

The people of the Northern Territory are young, vigorous
and determined to make a worthwhile life for themselves
in the most remote part of Australia.

They are dedicated to making their contribution to
the development of our nation and because of this
they deserve to be given every possible consideration
to make living in these remote regions as pleasant as
possible. The Government must give them special
consideration in providing facilities and amenities.
The people of Darwin and Alice Springs must have

television. I am determined that they will have television—not in the never never but as soon as possible. In consultation with experts I am preparing a workable plan to bring television to Darwin and Alice Springs and progressively to Katherine and Tennant Creek. I intend to present this proposal to the government in the near future.

In a somewhat obfuscatory response to another parliamentary question from Calder about extending television not only to Darwin but also the rest of the Territory, the Postmaster General, Alan Hulme, in August 1968 said he was considering a report received from the Australian Broadcasting Commission about the proposed Darwin television station and hoped a decision 'would not be too long delayed'.

Calder's rejoinder was to say that:

If the government is going to be slow in producing this amenity for people in the outback I strongly urge the Postmaster General to assist private enterprise to enter this field.

He also asked the PMG to provide stronger and better radio and television facilities in order to ease the burden of loneliness of people in the outback.

In April 1969, noting a recent announcement by the ABC that Darwin would receive television, an amenity for which he had been constantly asking, Calder again asked the Postmaster General for an approximate date.

Hulme responded that he understood the Darwin station would be brought on air in the early part of 1971.

On February 11, 1970 the *Canberra Times* reported that the Territory's first two television stations, one ABC and one commercial were expected to start transmissions in June the next year (1971) noting the awarding of a contract to construct the ABC studios had been let to a Queensland company for $347 415.

Then in October 1970, Calder told parliament the people in Darwin 'would be overjoyed when they hear the news that they will have a commercial television station', adding that he was certain the businessmen connected to the running of the stations (including one in Mount Isa) will make a success of them.

Federal Member, 'Sam' Calder, with daughter Diana, at the January, 2000 launch of his biography, Not so silent Sam, *at Government House, Darwin. Photo, possibly NT Government photographer collection, NT Library.*

Glenn Taylor claims the Liberal Country Party (LCP) Government, of which Calder was a Country Party member, leaned on the ABC for a more immediate response rather than waiting for the completion of the Microwave link and thus the somewhat hastily conceived and executed, and minimally staffed service begun in 1971.

It is worth considering the Broadband Microwave Network for a moment because it is now a largely abandoned and forgotten piece of communications technology which I believe should be regarded as one of the most significant technological achievements in Australian communications history.

The service was designed to take telephone and television services from the densely populated south eastern corner of the country, meaning the arc from Sydney to Adelaide, to the far flung centres of Perth, and on eventually to Broome, and later, to Darwin and Alice Springs as well as north from Townsville to Cairns.

The link from Mount Isa to Darwin via Tennant Creek was eventually completed in late 1974 just in time to play a significant communications role in Cyclone Tracy.

The service meant installing a repeater station approximately every forty kilometres running parallel with the main highways across the entire nation. In difficult terrain these distances could be as short as 10 km.

Each repeater station had a brick hut housing the equipment required to send the signal on, a power source, 24-volt battery, wind generator and, as back-up, a single cylinder diesel powered generator which (supposedly) started automatically when battery power fell below a certain level.

There was also a tower with receiving and sending dishes.

Because microwaves travelled by line of sight and due to the curvature of the earth and the 40 km between stations, the towers

Tower of a former Broadband Micrrowave repeater station near Coomalie, NT. While many have fallen into disrepair, this one has been re-purposed as a mobile phone tower. Author photo.

carrying the four-metre dishes had to be a minimum of 73 metres tall. Where appropriate some were built on higher ground. There could be no impediments in the way.

These services replaced fixed line transmissions made obsolete by the limited number of telephone services they could carry, usually about 100. Microwave Broadband services could carry up to 600 telephone lines, sometimes more, as well as television services, with a standby bearer offering a back up.

Hundreds of repeater stations were installed by the PMG, and its successors Telecom and Telstra, across Australia from 1959 until the Mobile Broadband system itself became obsolete and was replaced by fibre optic transmission in the late '80s. I have been unable to find out exactly how many repeater stations there were but estimates I have read range from 560 to 2200.

The full-length TV news

It is perhaps a misnomer to call our new TV bulletins full length because they were actually only 21 minutes in duration, compared to the 26 minutes (plus four minutes of weather) that made up the usual half hour of news elsewhere in the network.

I am not sure why our bulletins were initially only 21 minutes long but perhaps it was a recognition that our sources of visual material were severely limited and, after all, TV is about pictures.

The bulletin was followed by four minutes of weather presented by a rural officer.

The weather segment was usually pre-recorded and over the years the weather presenters included some colourful characters who often went rogue with their presentations.

On one occasion Alan Humphreys presented a wet season segment in yellow raincoat and sou'wester hat. It ended with a bucket of water being thrown over him. Technicians not amused. Monte Dwyer was a later presenter popular for his colourful weather sessions.

When the dry set in the cool nights would often be tipped to be two-dog or even three-dog nights, a reference to the habit of bushies sleeping with their dogs to keep warm.

Twenty-one minutes of news and four minutes of weather meant evening adult programs actually began five minutes earlier than the Broadcasting Control Board-stipulated 7.30 p.m. and a special dispensation was required.

At that time, news was followed by the new current affairs program, *Today Tonight*, recorded the previous night in Sydney and flown to Darwin on such flights as were available, not always daily at that time of two major domestic airlines.

As noted elsewhere in news, we were required to produce radio bulletins seven days a week with the first at 6.00 a.m. and the last just before midnight; and television news bulletins seven days a week. The shorter weekend bulletins were compiled by one journalist who also produced the radio bulletins until a casual journalist arrived at 3 p.m. to provide assistance, generate stories and compile the Saturday night and Sunday morning radio bulletins. Only one typist worked at weekends, typing both radio and TV stories.

The TV journalist thus not only produced the midday radio news bulletin, but subbed or wrote the TV news stories and even compiled those film stories available for the news into the play reel which involved splicing universal leaders in front of each film story and then splicing the stories together.

He, or we, then had to carry out the TVL role in producing the bulletin by instructing the presentation officer and all of those in subsidiary roles such as telecine or videotape.

Fortunately the weekend bulletins were shorter, usually of about ten minutes duration. But if you had required that sort of performance in a newsroom anywhere else in Australia you would have had a revolution, or at the least a union revolt.

The nuts and bolts of TV news

The way our newsroom worked was that one of us hacks worked a 9.30 to 6.30 general reporting shift five days a week, one worked Monday, Tuesday and Friday 2.00 to 11.00 with (usually) Wednesday and Thursday off, then the weekend shift of 10.30 to 7.30 while the third worked a 10.30 to 7.30 shift as general reporter and A/Lineup.

It was this latter shift that most of us preferred because the morning would be taken up with a TV job followed by supervising the editing of that story. By then it was time for lunch and then some general reporting before helping compile the TV News bulletin.

It quickly became apparent that the advent of TV News had spread the reporting staff thinner than was practical and a casual journalists was employed to work two half shifts on Saturday and Sunday.

One of these casuals was a journalist who was on a return visit to Darwin, having worked on the *NT News* some years before when he had met Geoff Hughes.

At this time he was trying to put together a project which involved building a traditional fishing vessel and sailing it around the Maldives.

Bringing this project to fruition involved lengthy telephone calls to London, some of which he made from home but some from the ABC's phones, once he was ensconced there, and that only occurred with his arrival about an hour later than rostered.

It was the job of the journalist on duty to give the casual a file of stories for follow up, in the hope of generating some of the copy needed to fill the voracious radio bulletins.

I had prepared such a file but immediately on his late arrival, for which he had the grace to apologise, my casual explained that he couldn't do the work required because of the planning demands of his project. He might have done some work for the news but, again with apologies, he left at 6 p.m., an hour before his shift nominally ended and without having compiled any of the required radio bulletins, because he was expecting an important telephone call from London.

Needless to say I was not impressed, because it meant I then had to also compile radio bulletins while working on a TV bulletin. I was even less impressed when there was a similar performance the following day and the following Monday I told Geoff in no uncertain terms that I wasn't prepared to work with this person again.

Dave says his experience of the particular casual was his becoming aware of the smell of marijuana drifting through the air-conditioning and finding him in a downstairs office on a phone call. Geoff didn't listen to me but when Bill and Dave had the same reaction after their experiences with the casual, he had no choice but to look for alternatives.

One alternative was Rex Clark formerly a cadet at the *NT News* under Jim Bowditch, who had transferred to Sydney's *Daily Mirror* for a few years before going overseas. Returning to Australia in 1971, he had been unable to find work down south so returned to Darwin on the promise a job with the *NT News* would be forthcoming, soon.

In the meantime, he became our casual for a short time.

When the full time *NT News* job eventuated Rex left and it was fortuitous that outside the Commonwealth Bank one day I happened to meet Kerry Doak, a diminutive woman journalist I had met at the *Albany Advertiser* a few years before.

Kerry had left the *Advertiser* and was working for a catering company on Finucane Island in the north-west until leaving there on the West Australian State Ship *Koolama*. She had arrived in Darwin with her friend and fellow worker, Cri Pas, who would later become our casual typist. On her first day in Darwin, after moving into one of the women's hostels, and looking for fun at the Vic Hotel she met Colin, the man who would later become her husband. It was not long after her arrival that I met her in the street.

Asked if she would care to take on the casual shifts at the ABC, by now extended to include the 2 to 11 shifts on Wednesdays and Thursdays, she showed interest and when I introduced her to Geoff she was immediately given the job.

She proved a reliable, willing, competent and pleasant co-worker until she went on leave two weeks before Cyclone Tracy. She returned two months later to find her home wrecked.

She got part time work at the *NT News* in 1975, held several positions with government agencies like the Conservation Commission until a couple of years later when she went to a full-time and long-term position at the *Northern Territory News*.

Perhaps it's worth noting that, like Patsy and me, and so many of our friends, Kerry's two-year term became a lifetime residency in Darwin and she went on to a successful freelance photo journalist career writing colour stories for a number of national publications.

Kerry's replacement for what turned out to be a very short lived job was Barbara James, a native of the American mid-western state of Nebraska and married to a well known Darwin lawyer, Geoff James. Apart from her later career as a historian, Barbara became famous for her dinner parties featuring interesting dishes from her home state with its heavy Scandinavian influence.

The early sources of vision available to us in news were limited and primitive. Apart from the very occasional film item shot by a stringer, a freelance cameraman, including sometimes our own Geoff Hughes, and which had to be sent south for processing and editing, the only other access we had to film stories was from a telerecording of the Melbourne news from either a day or, perhaps two, before and a specially produced newsreel from Adelaide. On at least one occasion the airline forgot to unload the Melbourne reel in Darwin and it continued on to London.

Have OB van, will travel

From early in 1972 we had an Outside Broadcast (OB) van, a Ford F250 with a big panel-van rear, the interior of which had been converted into a control room for a one-inch Ampex reel-to-reel videotape machine.

This machine, which was quite heavy, had to be manhandled between the OB van and Master Control, the studio control room where it was required for playback. As it was too heavy for one person to lift a trolley was eventually built to shuttle it between van and studio.

The OB van towed a trailer with what looked like an outback dunny fitted. Inside was a six-cylinder Ford engine driving a generator of about 5 kW to power the electronics and equipment and for some months this was our only source of moving pictures recorded outside the studio.

As his first job of the morning, the TVL would arrange an interview (hopefully in a location which would allow some background footage to be superimposed afterwards).

Then the Ampex video recorder would be installed in the OB van by two TV techs after which the TVL, a technician and the tech who would be cameraman, would take the OB van to the interview location to be met by the A/Lineup who would be doing the interview.

Two cables were required for the camera, another for headphones for the camera operator and a fourth cable was connected to the interviewer's microphone. Because the maximum length of the camera cables was only about 30 metres, it became a challenge to position the OB van and generator to provide the least possible noise interference.

In practice the most popular place for interviews became the gardens of Civic Park just opposite the ABC, being close and thus allowing relatively quick set up. The OB van, which was also used by other program producers, became a familiar sight on Darwin streets. It also became a familiar sight outside various pubs we just happened to be passing around lunchtime on our way back to the office.

Dave Molesworth recalls one of his memorable OB van interviews was with the well-known local charity worker, Auntie Billie Pitcheneder.

OB van goes bush—towed out of a washaway near the Darwin River Dam.
Photo, Bill Fletcher.

Billie was almost a fixture outside Woolworths on the Smith and Knuckey Streets corner where she would sit with her chair and card table selling raffle tickets in aid of almost any charity you could think of. A large and gregarious woman, she could talk the leg off a chair.

On this particular occasion Dave recalls her being ten minutes into an answer and he was unable to get a word in. Then the techs began rolling up cables and when Billie finally stopped talking they were in the van ready to go. The tape had long run out. I had a similar experience interviewing this warm-hearted but loquacious woman when she announced that she was finally retiring from fundraising activities. It was, perhaps surprisingly, a story big enough for ABC TV to cover because she was known to everybody.

There was limited opportunity to edit a story on the Ampex so it became the practice of the TVL to select a suitable grab of the interview and the cameraman would then be directed to shoot overlay which could be laid down over the interview, hopefully with pictures roughly appropriate to the subject matter.

Back at the ABC, the recorder would be manhandled back into the studio to be linked into the system and used to play back its one, and sometimes more, stories into the news bulletin.

The other, less frequently used source of local visuals was through a studio interview recorded onto two-inch videotape, which was the source of much of the regular programming, the rest being in the form of film.

The two-inch videotaped programs arrived in green boxes about 20 inches (50 cm) square and they became a familiar sight on luggage trolleys of the two domestic airlines, Trans Australia Airways (TAA) and Ansett, either arriving from Sydney or Adelaide, and occasionally other states, or being returned. The TAA building was next door to the ABC and there was a hatch from their drive through into the OB van garage where their freight person would post our tapes to save our film librarian having to collect them.

A studio interview was not popular with the already busy techs because it involved setting up a special interview area within the main TV studio, with attendant lighting and microphone requirements, and repositioning the two automatic studio cameras, the Nodding Neddies.

It was a time-consuming process, especially as it could only take place late in the afternoon and there had to be time for the cameras to be repositioned for both the weather recording and the regular news.

One particularly memorable studio interview I conducted arose out of an unfortunate incident involving an over enthusiastic scientist who had imported a dozen of the ugly cane toads then ubiquitous in Queensland but which had yet to spread to the Territory.

The live toads were imported for research purposes but they had somehow escaped and the institution in question desperately wanted them back so were planning to have radio stations broadcast the toads mating call and were asking the public to help in the search for the missing amphibians.

The interviewee duly arrived in the studio with a living toad, the first I had seen, and I learned about some of their lesser known attributes such as the fact that if you flipped them on their backs they became paralysed and that their skin when dried could be shredded and smoked as a hallucinogenic. These were not facts which we put to air.

My friend Peter Simon recently recalled the incident telling me his young children had responded to the call and gone out hunting the toads around their home at Nightcliff. They didn't find any toads but they returned home with a bedraggled kitten found in a drain and it became a much loved member of the family.

The public appeal for help was successful and the errant toads were all recovered.

Very occasionally one of the Nodding Neddies would suddenly and for no apparent reason, decide to droop, requiring prompt remedial action from a tech in Master Control, the actual nerve centre of all TV production and presentation, especially if the camera was in use at the time.

On more than one occasion the pre-emptive droop occurred during the weather and viewers would be treated to the sight of the presenter, usually Alan Humphreys, motioning the camera up while saying 'up boy', as the tech in Master Control returned it to its proper position.

As mentioned there were two of these automated cameras used for News. One held a fairly tight close-up of the newsreader, the other, at a slight angle, was a wider shot of the newsreader with a rear-projection (RP) screen behind and to one side.

This screen had a projector behind it with a collection of monochrome slides depicting scenes of the Territory including geographical features, significant buildings, wildlife and other animals including cattle and buffalo, and a selection of head shots of prominent people.

These RP's were an important element of illustration for stories without other visuals such as film or videotape. A further source of visual information was what is known as the caption scanner, which held cards with either photographs or other types of illustration. For example, some public relations companies would issue press releases accompanied by a ten by eight inch (10x8) photograph of some relevant aspect of the story they were promoting. They might be of a group of officials, or a piece of equipment.

If a story made it to air, it would occasionally be accompanied by a caption superimposed over the newsreader. The Royal Australia Air Force would often send glossy photographs of aircraft to accompany a media release and these would occasionally make it to air. Our graphic designer, Colin Martin, who occupied a hole-in-the-wall office at the extreme back of the building, would mount photographs or other visuals on a card, spray it with matt spray to reduce reflections and deliver them to the A/Lineup.

The reject aircraft photographs were consigned to the wastepaper basket from where, I discovered many years later, they were retrieved by my colleague, Dave Molesworth. Dave was an obsessive photographer of aircraft and collector of anything aircraft related.

At one time he had one of the biggest collections of photographs of Australian Aircraft then flying with an estimated 17 000 negatives.

One of the tasks of the journalist as A/Lineup was to gather any captions and slides listed in the news stories, and ensure they were in the right order and appropriate place, either the projector behind the newsreader or in the videotape room where the caption scanner was located.

As mentioned, there were multiple copies of the TV bulletin to be distributed.

The newsreader of the day would usually arrive in the newsroom an hour before news time, to pre-read the bulletin, check for any unusual pronunciations and occasionally, offer some corrections or gratuitous advice.

About 15 minutes before news time, the TVL would have his bulletin in order and work could begin on separating the flimsies and clipping them together for distribution. This was done by the A/Lineup and the casual typist.

The A/Lineup then distributed the various copies to the reader, by then in the studio for lighting and sound checks, the videotape and telecine operators, the presentation officer or vision mixer who would actually ensure the right vision sources were put to air, plus the sound and lighting technicians.

The Lineup, in the meantime, would be marking up his script with all of the instructions he needed to give as the director of the bulletin. This is one of the most exacting tasks in TV news production because timings are critical.

Both film and videotape machines needed run up time to allow their picture and sound to stabilise before they were put to air, hence the universal leaders.

For film this run up time is five seconds and for videotape, ten seconds.

Using the standard three words a second, this required a countback of either 15 or thirty words for when the order to roll film or roll video was given. As the picture stabilised, the instruction would be given to take film or video as appropriate.

All films had a system of what are called cue dots a small mark etched into a frame of film five seconds and two seconds before the film ends, and it is the task of the TVL to announce those dots as part of indicating the film is about to end, before instructing the vision mixer to take Camera One (or Two) and cue reader. As another visual item would be coming up the TVL had to warn either Telecine or Videotape of their next item so they could cue to the Universal Leader which preceded each visual item.

Elsewhere, Rodger Andrews has referred to the different types of film which were used in the industry at that time.

There were two types of what is generically called sound on film (SOF), composite optical or Comopt, where the sound is recorded as a series of bars on one edge of the 16 mm film and composite magnetic or Commag where sound could be recorded onto a narrow magnetic tape bonded to the film. Comopt was already becoming outdated because the more a Comopt film was copied, the more deterioration there was in sound quality so that sound could become fuzzy, while Commag could be copied numerous times with little deterioration in sound quality. In both cases the recording heads on a 16 mm film camera had to be located ahead of the point where pictures were recorded.

This meant that when sound films were edited to a picture, the sound would be leading the picture by either 25 or 26 frames, or about a second, while if you were editing for sound, the picture would trail the sound by a second, a quite visible disturbance which could occasionally be hidden by the use of overlaid pictures.

The final sound on film option was separate magnetic, or Sepmag, where the sound was recorded on a separate 16 mm sound tape (16 mm then being the standard width of film for news recording).

This system, requiring both a cameraman and sound recordist was only rarely used in news, being more popular for programs of longer duration. To play Sepmag, telecine machines required two reel-to-reel chains mechanically linked to run at the same speed. A story filmed on Sepmag would begin with a clapper board which contained the visual information—story title, date, reporter and cameraman's names and would be filmed as the clapper dropped making an audible noise. This recorded noise would be edited on to the head of the sound tape and synchronised to the two second mark on the universal leader ensuring that both sound and picture were in synch when put to air.

The universal leader, as the name implies, is used throughout the film industry to give a standard lead in to a film. It is a piece of film of a countdown from ten seconds to zero, with the last two seconds being black. This is so that if a director is a bit trigger happy and jumps the gun in putting a film to air, or if a TVL misses the roll cue, all that will be seen is a flash of black before the picture appears.

Universal Leader also has an audio warning at two seconds, a pip, which is used to cue the sound from the clapper board when Sepmag films are being played.

Give me a peg

In the first days of television news our film stories, all from interstate, and sometimes days old, were edited by our film librarian, Arthur Harris, or his assistant Amanda Taylor.

As film or videotape was received into the film library, the TVL would be shown what was available for him to use in his own bulletin. Some stories were continuing and therefore the pictures, even though a day or two old, could be used if updated with a different introduction, or a new peg.

At the time of which I am writing, the Vietnam War was a daily news story but the film was usually outdated by the time it reached us, so the day's new word story would be used as the intro, with a sometimes forced link to refer back to the outdated film about to be shown.

This was frequently the case also for news stories from interstate which we wanted to use, or needed to use but had to have a new peg from which to hang them. This led to some quite creative introductions being written for older visual items.

Meanwhile, back at the news bulletin the TVL had an additional crucial task, ensuring the bulletin ended in time for the following program to begin at its advertised time. This meant both counting back through the bulletin to select the notional point at which it would end and watching the clock for when that point would be reached while at the same time using a stopwatch to time each film/video story, call out rolls and takes and cues.

Although every item in the bulletin was timed according to its word count, there was a notional two words lost with the turn of each page of the script, so the number of stories could affect the actual length of a bulletin by several seconds.

We usually ended the bulletin with a 'must', a story selected because it was humorous, or particularly interesting and therefore a must read. Thus, to ensure the must was used, its duration had to be taken into consideration when determining the notional end of the bulletin.

A series of short word stories was usually included around the time of the notional end. This whole process coming at the end of a full day of work could be incredibly stressful and success at it required a particular type of temperament, not to mention the timing skills.

As I have mentioned, Mike Hayes turned out to be a natural, being calm and unexcitable. Dave Molesworth was also a natural and some years later, through force of circumstances, I was able to ensure he became the permanent TVL when he returned to work after a long illness. Bill tells me he never had any problems with directing either. Fortunately, the only times I directed a main bulletin were when Mike was either on leave, or relieving as JIC, at which times we three hacks would alternate through the job, and every third weekend when bulletins were much shorter.

I soon discovered that I did not have the right temperament for the job. It stressed me and for many years afterwards it was a subject of nightmares for me though recently Dave Molesworth admitted he still occasionally has lineup nightmares. I did not seem to be able to get my bulletins to fit into the time allotted.

Sometimes the presentation officers could cover for my timing problems by dropping a 'promo' for a forthcoming program, but on one notable occasion my must was too long. I had used up all of the extra time, and patience, of the presentation officer, Dave Nordsvan, and he was forced to cut out of the bulletin. We didn't even get the usual newsreader sign-off.

The worst of it was that the story I was using for my must was film of the great English runner, Sebastian Coe, setting a new world record for the mile, I think, and we cut out of him one hundred metres from the finish. I am told the switchboard ran hot with complaints but I had long since slunk off into the night.

Despite such issues, and given the demands placed on such a small staff, there were remarkably few technical or other problems with the presentation of news in those first years of television.

Rodger Andrews has already referred to the problem of maintaining the heads on the only videotape machine:

> One evening watching our infamous two-inch videotape machine going to air and cringing at the noise banding and the instability it was causing when suddenly a perfectly stable noise-free picture appeared on air. Immediately I rang the tape operator to find out why.
> The duty videotape technician, Roger Burnard, replied 'Well I didn't think I would do any harm and used methylated spirits on a cotton bud to clean the slip rings while the tape was running'. As Rodger Andrews noted: for weeks we had used Freon, the recognised cleaner for tape machines at the time but this was creating a build-

up rather than cleaning and so was actually causing our head problems. Suddenly like our Southern counterparts we were getting better than 100 hours per head. Roger Burnard you are a wizard.

Many years later, Rodger said the suggestion to use meths had actually come from another tech, Gerry Orrin, so credit where credit's due.

A year or so later another Ampex VTR 1100 was installed into the tape area and life became much easier.

A near disaster on our first day of broadcast of the long news identified a minor oversight which had the potential to create havoc.

Previous mention has been made of the, nominally portable, Ampex one-inch videotape machine used in the OB van as our one source of outside news stories. It happened that, as part of the preparations for the first full-length bulletin, four stories had been pre-recorded on this machine, including one very long, and possibly self-indulgent piece, by our JIC, Geoff Hughes about a so-called 'drug house' which everyone knew about but which was never closed down by authorities.

These four stories were interspersed with other film/video stories to allow time for each story from the one-inch machine to be laced up and cued.

The first story from the one-inch machine was introduced by the newsreader, Alf Jervis, but as it was switched to air, it became unstable, the picture rolling vertically and unviewable.

On the news reader's desk, sits an unobtrusive telephone, rarely used but on this occasion Mike Hayes as TVL called Alf, told him to apologise and go on with the next story. In the meantime there was consternation among the techs in Master Control but the next story on the Ampex had to be cued up. In due course the intro was read, the vision switched to air and again, instability, unacceptability.

The phone again. The apology, we have a slight technical problem, and the next story is introduced. In Master Control, more consternation as the third story is cued up, and appears to be stable. But, again, unstable on air, another phone call, another apology and another story.

In the meantime with Mike staring down the barrel of a dramatic shortage of visual content, as A/Lineup I was dispatched upstairs to the newsroom to comb through the rubbish bins for set stories, those typed onto sets but discarded, to fill at least some of the potentially lost time.

I got back to Master Control with a somewhat meagre collection of stories to find that the problem had been sorted, a technician had realized that a switch, essential for the one-inch machine to talk to the main internal system, had not been activated. The stories on the one-inch went to air without further dramas and later, as a feeling of relief spread over us at the successful start of proper news bulletins, Alf Jervis, unflappable Alf, was heard to say that had there been one more telephone call he would have 'told my wife to please stop calling me while I was at work'.

We get film

In April 1972 a significant breakthrough in our News facilities occurred with the arrival of our own film cameraman, Keith Bushnell. Keith was not actually an ABC employee but rather was employed by a Sydney film producer, Oscar Scherl, of Cinematic Services, who in 1971 was stringing for the ABC and had contracted to provide ABC Darwin with filming, processing and editing facilities.

Keith, who had arrived from England as a 12-year-old with his parents, brother and sister, still managed to sound like Terry McCann in the popular British TV series, *Minder*, despite having lived in Australia for 16 years.

This is how he remembers that arrival:

> July 1956. Family and I delivered to the migrant camp, Finsbury Hostel, in Adelaide. However the previous six weeks had been my grand introduction to a taste for travel. Starting with a short train ride out of conservative, suburban London my world changed from small screen black and white to widescreen colour as we boarded the 20,000-ton RMS *Otranto*. Two days out from Tilbury, before my 12-year-old eyes, the Rock of Gibraltar floated from below the horizon. I'd never been on a ship before. I don't think I'd ever seen a craft bigger than those which raced between Oxford and Cambridge, and seen from Putney Bridge. The *Otranto* also gave us a day at

Naples before passing through the Suez Canal, the last passenger ship to come that way before the canal was closed by the six-day war. We also managed to fit in Aden and Colombo before we all found ourselves in Western Australia and another Sunny-as-Hollywood day, riding a bus beside palm trees from Fremantle to Perth.

I'd been a year at Grammar school in England (mortarboards, black capes) before joining an Australian high school (sports jackets and cigarettes) and knew I was no longer interested in those classes but I had enough natural abilities with Maths, Physics and Chemistry to get by. About the time I was 15 and could legally leave school, television began in Adelaide and I applied for and got a job at commercial station, NWS-9 as office boy riding a push-bike, taking and delivering lunch orders.

All manner of professions and people met there and, seeing some magic in cameras, I found myself in the right place at the right time again, the film-operator left the station at short notice and as I already knew how to operate the 'Houston Fearless', a huge film processor, was frequently called upon to assist the cameraman, Brian Bosisto. I had learned enough to be the right person again when NWS-9 needed a second cameraman. I'd bought a much-used Bolex a wind-up (clockwork) hand-held 16 mm camera popular with both amateur and professional users, which allowed a lot of ambulance-chasing and weekend stringer work.

I was only being paid a teenager's wage but I volunteered for everything available: Thursday night wrestling, Friday night speedway, Saturday night trots which I would shoot, drive back to the station and process then cut the last lap-and-a-half of each race into the Sunday sports show.

When I was 18 I quit and took off for a year to the UK, Europe and Canada. I came back to Adelaide when I was broke and NWS-9 were needing another cameraman. By the time I was 21, and having completed my apprenticeship, I was an A-grade Cinematographer.

I was in London again for more of the swinging '60s, tried for work at the BBC (and others) but couldn't get

A young Keith Bushnell explains the Houston Fearless film processing unit to an NWS9 executive. Keith Bushnell collection.

around the union-controlled hiring system, so returned to Australia and a job in Sydney, shooting news at ATN-7. I was there only a year or so when I had a little more union-inspired unhappiness and chose to quit. While thinking I'd go to Canada again, I was approached by Oscar Scherl who had taken on the Darwin ABC contract but now couldn't do it so needed someone who could shoot, process and edit 16mm film, and somebody who had no particular plans for a year or two. He convinced me that Darwin was a great fun place and it was somewhere I'd not seen or even thought about.

The job started with the purchase of a new short-wheelbase Toyota Land Cruiser and a 15-foot caravan in which Keith would live. On the way to Darwin, Oscar and Keith stopped in North Queensland to buy a home made film processor from a cameraman/engineer.

That was how Keith Bushnell lobbed into town, the Land Cruiser now sporting a hefty bull bar and roof rack with four 20 litre jerry cans mounted across the front, each emblazoned with a big letter in white N-E-W-S, a plywood base on which he could mount tripod and camera, and towing the caravan.

Cameraman Keith Bushnell showing the sartorial style with which he arrived in Darwin ready for assignments. Keith Bushnell collection.

The caravan was soon ensconced under a huge mango tree in the yard at the rear of Lee Grover's Saddle Shed in Cavenagh Street, where it had access to a separate outside toilet bathroom and laundry. The van had a large bed at one end and wardrobe space but the usual dinette and second bed at the front had been removed to make way for the 16 mm black and white film processing unit which consisted of a series of rollers and baths through which the exposed film passed to be developed. A garden hose entered and exited the caravan and processor with the water fortunately always at 20 degrees Celsius, the recommended ideal temperature for processing. It was also the temperature of the shower.

It is appropriate here to describe the way Keith processed his film. Film magazines were capable of holding a reel of film of up to 400 feet (or 10 minutes 40 duration) though most jobs were done using 100 foot reels (2 minutes 40 of film). The magazines were detached from the camera and placed in a black lightproof bag with two armholes and sleeves which closed around the arms to exclude light.

The exposed film was then transferred in the bag to a lightproof container and stapled onto a tongue of film which was, in turn, stapled to the leader, a strip of old film which would be pulled from left to right through a series of baths, the first few in darkness, through a developer, then a stop bath, into the light for another developer bath, then a fixer and finally a hot air dryer before it reached the take up spool. The last frames of the developed film would be stapled to another leader which was pulled through after the shot film and ensured the machine was always threaded.

Three hundred yards up the road at the ABC, Keith inherited the small storeroom in the newsroom which became his editing suite. Equipped with a primitive sound reader and viewer with a miniature screen and two hand rollers, a razor blade and either glue or tape for cementing the joins, Keith was able to provide us with a complete film service. Allowing for an hour to process the film, edit, shot list and write the script, a story could be shot as late as 5 p.m. and included in the news at 7.00.

In real television editing suites an editor would have access to a free standing four or six plate Steenbeck, a state-of-the-art electric powered and much more sophisticated editing machine which also allowed the simultaneous editing of 16 mm sound tape when Sepmag was being edited. I believe there might have been a Steenbeck in the film library downstairs.

My brother John was a film editor in his younger days and I recall him explaining how editors using the simple winding system could wind sound film at speed and still understand what they were hearing. He told me editors developed Mickey Mouse ears which allowed them to understand high-pitched speech which sounded like the chipmunks to me.

I thought Keith arrived in Darwin equipped with one of the latest CP16 film cameras though he thinks his first camera was an Arriflex S which could be mated to a quarter inch reel-to-reel tape recorder for sound jobs. Soon after his arrival Keith did get one of the CP 16s, bought new in Hong Kong by Oscar Scherl and capable of also shooting sound on film, as referred to earlier, it gave us flexibility to match that of the states.

Three stories a week

One minor setback was that Keith was contracted to shoot only three stories a week for news, he supplemented his, and Oscar's, income by shooting for the TV programs of the talks, rural, and even sports, departments. On occasions, shooting for these other programs would make him unavailable for news and we had to fall back on the OB Van.

From November 1971, with film starting to be shot by stringers on a regular basis, a record needed to be kept of the jobs done and thus the *Moving Pitchers* journal was launched. A foolscap sized book, that is the same width but two inches (50 mm) longer than A4, it was the TVL's job to maintain the record by job number, date, subject, cameraman, footage shot, footage used and the date it went to air.

Recently exhumed from the vault in ABC Archives, Darwin, it is an evocative record of the stories covered in those years although the often single word subjects can be bafflingly uninformative. For example two film stories shot in November 1971 by long-forgotten stringers were identified as cable raising and YWCA building. I believe the latter might have alluded to a new women's hostel under construction which, in a subsequent ABC film story was erroneously referred to as the YMCA, and Dave has since told me cable raising almost certainly referred to the centenary celebrations associated with the commissioning of the undersea telegraph cable from Batavia to Darwin.

Between December 1971 and Keith Bushnell's first story, *Greek Easter*, shot on April 4, 1972 a total of just 25 film stories were shot, about half of them by Oscar Scherl, Keith's employer who appears to have spent about a week in Darwin in late 1971 working as a stringer.

And from that date onward, the record includes one extra notation listing how many jobs Keith was ahead of his contracted rate of three jobs a week. To those of us who worked there, those one- or two-word subject notations are an amazing memory jogger. Some of the stories appear in the following pages. Many are lost in the mists of time such as *Croc fishing, Motor cycles* or *Big boycott*.

Some require no explanation such as NTD8 (the launch), *Orbison arrives, Darwin bombing* (the annual commemoration) or *Concorde*, the arrival and departure of which caused intense interest both here and elsewhere. Dave, who had his own 16 mm Bolex movie camera shot film of the Concorde alongside Keith Bushnell who was shooting for several programs. Dave's film was used for the opening titles to the news and its processing and editing was cut so fine there was no time to put it on feed or take up reels so it was being fed into the telecine machine by hand, and running out onto the floor.

And from every page glows the black ink and untidy scrawl of Mike Hayes record keeping with, from July 1973, the footage used being replaced by a note of where else the story had been sent, either Sydney or Adelaide which still used a lot of Darwin stories.

Although *Greek Easter* is listed as his first story in Darwin, in fact Keith shot two stories while he and Oscar Scherl were on the road to Darwin. The first was the Renner Springs race meeting and the second, which surely must have been a must, was listed as 'Donkey in a garage', a slight misnomer.

As Keith tells it they had been told to look out for a place called 522 mile, or something similar.

> We watched for it for a couple of days before discovering
> it wasn't a place, but a distance to Darwin, and we were
> nearly there. The story was a beer-swilling donkey which

110

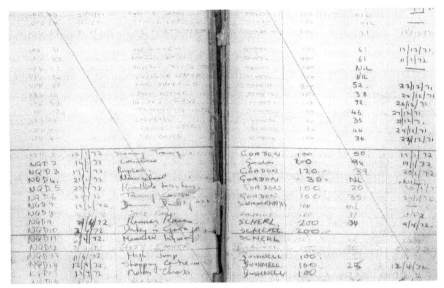

First page of the 'moving pitchers' book. Showing Bushnell's arrival.
Author photo.

lounged around a beer garden waiting for tourists to buy
him a stubby which he held in his teeth while throwing
his head back and emptying the bottle straight down his
throat.

A true Territory story and Keith hadn't even officially started work
yet.

A law unto itself

One of the interesting side aspects of being an ABC television reporter, was
the public notoriety it gave you. We suddenly became minor celebrities,
and people we didn't know would feel able to open conversations as if
we were friends.

An upside was that people who might previously have been
reluctant or not interested in talking to a journalist, suddenly found the
opportunity to be on camera attractive. And because, at that stage, the
ABC was the only local television station with a news bulletin everyone
watched.

One thing television didn't do was make reporting of the activities
of government, as distinct from Parliament, any easier.

At that time the Administration, as it was called, was a law unto itself. A journalist could not just ring a public servant or a departmental head for a response to a story of the day. Questions for the Administration had to be made in writing and submitted to the Public Relations Office, or the Information Office as it was then, and several days later a response would be received, occasionally a response which even contained some usable information.

With TV, it sometimes became much easier to get a response to a request for information, depending on whether that departmental head wanted the recognition which would be inevitable.

It has been mentioned elsewhere that radio news bulletins were voracious consumers of stories. Sometimes a story would be important or interesting enough to run over several bulletins, or even into the following morning but such stories were few and far between.

In the main, bulletins would be filled with stories from the police, the Court of Petty Sessions and the Supreme Court, from the Bureau of Statistics, from the many agricultural or mining interests, the unions, from the town council, the Legislative Council when it sat and, of course, the many individuals or groups which wanted to push their own particular barrows.

We had a fairly rudimentary and untidy system of filing stories but it worked and after each news bulletin the JIC, or a duty sub-editor, would look through the flimsy copy of each story to see if, when, and how it might be followed up. These flimsies would be filed for follow-up next day, next week, next month or any specific month, or next year.

Each day, the JIC would look at the stories in the today files, assess whether there was a likelihood of some advance and, if there was, assign it to a journalist. Each journalist would arrive at work to find on his or her desk, a stapled collection of flimsies, sometimes with other information like a newspaper clipping attached and would set out to work through the list and write follow up stories as appropriate.

On my first day at work I came up against the great public service wall referred to above. I had a story to chase which involved what was then known as Welfare, the branch which dealt with Aboriginal Affairs and which had been headed for many years by the crusty Harry Giese.

Having come from Perth where it was acceptable, if appropriate, to speak to anyone from a state minister down, and even at unsociable hours of the morning, I thought it natural to ring the Head of Department, so I called Mr Giese.

His secretary put me through and I explained what I wanted. Giese gave me the information I sought, something fairly innocuous, but knowing I was very new to the job, he asked that I pay him the courtesy of running my story past him before it went to air. As a qualified and, I felt, professional journalist of some years standing, this offended my estimate of self worth, but I agreed that being new to the subject of Indigenous affairs I would give him the opportunity to vet my copy.

Having written the story I called his office to find that he had gone to lunch. Feeling a bit narky and perhaps being petty, I insisted on dictating my quite short story for his secretary to type out and give to him. Sometime later I had a call from Giese telling me the story was accurately reported, however I could not use it. Why? I asked. Because all requests to the public service for information must be put in writing to the Information Office.

I binned the story, although, in hindsight I should have used it and copped whatever repercussions there might have been. This example of what I considered bureaucratic bullshit coloured my perception of Giese thereafter and, probably, his of me.

However we were quite quickly thrown together again when Giese flew to Maningrida 500 km east of Darwin to open a new Community Hall.

A place was provided for an ABC film crew and I drew the short straw. Our cameraman, Keith Bushnell was also included. It represented a number of firsts for me. It was my first flight in a light aircraft, it was my first visit to an Indigenous community and it would be the first time I ate the famous mud crab.

Maningrida was a former trading post established in 1949 by Syd Kyle-Little, a patrol officer in the newly formed Native Affairs Department. His idea was to create a self-sufficient Aboriginal community independent of welfare support, but the trading post was closed in 1950 after a change of administration in Darwin. Kyle-Little was said to have resigned in disgust, his dream of a series of independent trading posts in the region not realised. Seven years later, former missionaries David and Ingrid Drysdale established a new settlement, sponsored by the Commonwealth Government, the first non-mission settlement in Arnhemland.

By 1972, Maningrida was a thriving community but, in what would become an almost constant refrain, was said to be under the control of too many Balanda (white people) who took the majority of managerial and supervisory positions.

It was also a meeting place for many different clans which did not always get on with each other so there were often inter tribal tensions and even occasional outbreaks of violence.

Our host on that 1972 visit was the white Superintendent who lived in an aboveground house with a commanding view over the coast and it was on his veranda that we lunched on mud crabs.

This, however, was only after the formal hall opening and a tour of a thriving plant nursery, brickworks, timber milling operation and other enterprises and, Keith reminds me, a tribal Emu Dance, which impressed us.

Later we were taken to an outstation at Cadell River where a young employee of the Commonwealth Scientific and Industrial Research Organisation (CSIRO) was on secondment supervising a significant market garden development. This was a young Bob Collins who some years later would go on to be the Labor Opposition Leader in the NT's Legislative Assembly before being elected an NT Senator and ultimately a Minister in the Hawke/Keating Labor Government, no mean feat for a non-factionally aligned Labor politician, a Senator and a Territorian.

Flying back from Maningrida late in the afternoon our small plane was bounced around as the pilot dodged a succession of late wet season thunderstorms and I was very glad to land.

Creating a sock

The voraciousness of the radio bulletins was a constant dilemma for the journalist who would be working the weekend shifts and we became adept at creating what we called a 'sock', a stash of timeless stories which could be held until the following weekend. Each Monday this journalist would be given a pile of flimsies of stories requiring follow up from the

Administration. We would type a series of questions arising from each flimsy and submit that typed list of questions to the Information Office.

When the replies were received, a few days later, they were given to the weekend reporter to be matched to the original stories and any additional information would be written into a new story suitable, at least, for padding out an obscure weekend radio news bulletin.

Even a reply of 'No' or 'Not yet' could be turned into a story of several lines and, just occasionally, a reply would contain some real information generating a real story.

The system of measuring the length of stories varied between radio and television. Radio stories were measured in lines with 15 lines taking a minute to read and thus a five-minute news bulletin being 75 lines. Stories averaged eight to 12 lines. Television stories were timed in minutes and seconds based on the accepted reading standard of three words a second for ABC announcers.

ABC radio had seven news bulletins a day, five minutes long at 6.10 and 7.25 in the morning, the 12.30 midday bulletin and two evening bulletins at 7.10 and 9.40. Then there were two shorter bulletins at 10.40 and two minutes to midnight. All followed a ten minute national news bulletin. This meant we needed to find 31 minutes, 465 lines of copy or about 60 stories each day, hence the use of the word voracious.

I have already referred to Darwin's isolation from the rest of Australia in terms of communications. Telephone services via what was known as fixed wire meant limited phone lines. Until Subscriber Trunk Dialling was introduced, beginning in 1971, long distance or trunk calls could only be made by phoning 011, the trunk services where an operator would connect you. When I arrived, Darwin telephone numbers had only three or four digits. If you wanted to talk to someone on a station or some other remote location, you had to call VJY or Outpost Radio where conversations required you to say 'over' allowing the person you were calling to respond and end their segment with 'over', the end of a conversation was signalled by use of 'over and out'. It made conversations stilted and conducting an interview difficult, especially as there was frequently interference or crossed lines.

A regular caller was the Member for Elsey, Les MacFarlane who owned Moroak Station east of Katherine, close to the Arnhemland border. Les was an old style pastoralist who had Aboriginal ringers and their families living on his property. He was one of many pastoralists who were concerned at the growing Land Rights movement and increasing demands for Aboriginal workers to be paid the same as white employees, one of the big issues arising from the Wave Hill walk off.

Often I would get a weekend call from Les wanting to comment on some aspect of these movements, often from a somewhat outrageous perspective. At a personal level I liked Les and on occasion would suggest that if I was to report him accurately he would be crucified. 'Well', he would say, 'you know what I want to say, you write it'. So I would compose a suitably anodyne story which, while still generating a response of outrage in some quarters, would be less confrontational.

Never once did Les walk away from something I had written on his behalf. This sort of interventionism would probably appal some present-day reporters but this was a different time.

Land Rights pushback

As the Land Rights movement gathered pace Les, who had become the Speaker in the Legislative Assembly, became prominent in a reactionary organisation initially called Rights for Whites but subsequently given the less incendiary name of Rights for Territorians.

Also prominent in the movement was June Tapp, wife of Bill Tapp of Killarney Station southwest of Katherine. June was a petite but feisty woman, self-confident, assertive and very vocal on the issue.

I covered a street march organised by the group in Katherine which was followed by a public meeting attended by about 400 people, most opposed to Aboriginal Land Rights and the excision of living areas on pastoral properties.

Such was the level of national interest aroused by the movement that the ABC's premier interview program, *Monday Conference*, hosted by Robert Moore, came to Darwin to record a program with June Tapp and Jim Bowditch, a well-known supporter of Aboriginal advancement, squaring off in our TV studio. Naturally the producer of the program was hugely experienced and many of the ABC staff gathered outside Master Control or in other parts of the building to watch the fiery interview as it was being recorded for replay later, there being no way to send the program south live.

Some time afterwards I interviewed Les MacFarlane on the subject and asked him. Les, are you a racist?'. He took a very long time to reply before saying, 'No, I don't think so'. When I got back to the office, I told Dave Molesworth, who was TVL at that time, that he might need to edit, or shorten, the pause. However, he decided to leave all 13 seconds of it in because it was so compelling.

The advent of a real TV news ensured that we began getting many more visitors to the newsroom including some local characters but actually getting to the newsroom was not easy. Visitors had to pass the receptionist, walk down a long corridor flanked by the Presentation Office, Master-Control and a technical store on one side and the film library, telecine and videotape suites on the other; then mount some stairs to the Newsroom.

The flamboyant and personable Member for Nightcliff, Dawn Lawrie, an active and engaged local member, became a regular visitor promoting her electoral issues. Another flamboyant woman visitor was Sandra LeBrun Holmes who wore big hats, lots of perfume, scarves and flowing long-sleeved dresses to protect her sensitive skin. Sandra had become the champion of an Aboriginal artist named Yirawala from the Maningrida area. Not only did she collect his bark paintings but she promoted him as a significant talent. More, she was helping him and some of his people pursue a Land Rights claim to an area identified to us as Marlgoorlidba, between the Liverpool and Goomadeer rivers in Arnhemland. She, like Jim Bowditch, was one of a number of people becoming thorns in the side of the Director of Aboriginal Affairs, Harry Giese, who had significant powers of control over access to, and happenings on, Aboriginal lands.

In his (as yet) unpublished book about Jim Bowditch, Peter Simon writes of a meeting of pastoralists and others Giese addressed in Alice Springs soon after his appointment as Director of Welfare in 1954.

Simon quotes Bowditch as being impressed with Giese's stated attitudes towards those who would be his charges and his hints that big changes were coming for pastoralists who, it was felt by many, exploited those Indigenous Australians who worked on their stations. Simon reports Bowditch saying Giese's attitudes were to change over the years and he often wondered why.

In my limited interactions with him, I found Giese stiff, stern and aloof. I don't think he liked journalists. As Dawn Lawrie was to tell me, he certainly didn't like to have his actions questioned and he had tried to give her a hard time when she first appeared in the Legislative Council. She says she was speaking about secondary and tertiary education for Aboriginal students and looked forward to a time when there would be doctors, teachers, lawyers and other Indigenous professionals. Dawn said Giese commented, 'What would she know about it?', which drew rebukes from both CLP and Labor Leaders, Goff Letts and Dick Ward.

Land Rights as a movement had been given a huge national profile with the 1966 walk-off from Wave Hill Station by the Gurindji people led by Vincent Lingiari, with the support of unionists and some notable southern activists including the author, Frank Hardy.

A later slightly less famous campaign was that mounted by the Yolŋu people of the Gove Peninsula seeking compensation from the giant Nabalco Company proposing to mine and process Bauxite.

The case, *Milirrpum v Nabalco Pty Ltd*, or the *Gove Land Rights Case*, was the first litigation on native title in Australia and the first significant legal case for Aboriginal Land Rights in Australia. In 1971, Justice Richard Blackburn, found against the claimants, rejecting the doctrine of Aboriginal title, instead finding British colonisation had given the Crown the power to extinguish native title, if it existed.

This doctrine, known as Terra Nullius, was not corrected until 1992 when the High Court overturned the Blackburn ruling in what became the celebrated Mabo Case.

Aboriginal Land Rights would be one of the significant continuing stories covered by our Newsroom and other media over the ensuing years. Indeed in 1971, the *Northern Territory News* ran a story headlined New 'black power' bid reporting a 'roneoed' news sheet with apparent 'black power' leanings was circulating among Aborigines in Darwin and at Bagot settlement. Called *Bunji*, the sheet was written in English so all the Aboriginal tribes in the area could understand it.

The pamphlet urged support for the Aboriginal activist, Bobby Secretary, in his fight to help the Larrakia tribe get land rights over

Kulaluk land which encompassed the Bagot Aboriginal Settlement close to Darwin. *Bunji* was written by Bill Day, then an anthropology student, who was doing fieldwork in what he called the Aboriginal fringe camps around Darwin for a PhD thesis. He became active in supporting what became known as the 'Gwalwa Daraniki' (or 'Our Land') movement which began demanding land rights for the Aboriginal Larrakia, Wagait and Brinkin groups.

Bunji had other advice for Aboriginal people including an injunction to always plead Not Guilty if they went to court. In 1994, the story of the Gwalwa Daraniki movement was told in Day's book, also called *Bunji*.

Another regular newsroom visitor was Allan Stewart, operator of the very popular White Hunter Safaris from a camp he had established at Nourlangie on the Jim Jim Creek but apparently due to a surveying error was in the middle of the Woolwonga Aboriginal Reserve and Wildlife Reserve established in 1964. Hunting and fishing being banned in the reserve. Allan, whose livelihood depended on those activities, was often at war with officialdom over permits. With a gammy leg, big hat and prominent moustache, he would limp into the newsroom on a walking stick to deliver his latest diatribe of criticism of the government. Deciding to contest the federal election of late 1972, he changed his name by deed poll to Alexander Allan-Stewart, thus ensuring his name would be first on the ballot paper and garner the so-called donkey vote.

It didn't work and Stephen Edward (Sam) Calder, known as 'Silent Sam' by his detractors, was re-elected for a third term. Another unsuccessful candidate at that election was John Waters, a lawyer and son of the mayor of the time, Ken Waters.

John Waters would go on to be involved in a number of celebrated legal cases while also being a serial contender for Labor at elections and long-time president of the party. He would also become a lifetime friend.

Have spear, will travel

Socially, being an ABC staffer was fun. With around 35 staff, wives or partners and an extended circle of friends there was a ready-made community until outside friendships formed or strengthened, as they inevitably did. It was also easy to enter the drinking culture that prevailed at the time. Almost every weekend someone in the ABC had a party at which an 18 gallon keg of beer would be the centrepiece and, of course, all were invited. One of the radio technicians, 'Father' Yates, ensured he was invited to every party because he owned a spear, the mechanism whereby a keg was tapped.

There were other social occasions which one was expected to attend. Soon after the arrival from Perth of my own car, a Torana GTR, I was commanded to attend a Sunday social cricket match to be played against one of the rugby clubs on one of the Gardens Ovals, a concrete pitch which is still visible in the Gardens Park Golf Course.

I arrived with a six pack of beer, thinking that was a good day's drinking but quickly discovered that, under the rules of engagement, it was inadequate.

Before the game even got underway, several cans had been consumed and with a compulsory drinks break every few overs, plus taking a can onto the field, by the time the game ended in the late afternoon, everyone was either mildly or heavily alcohol affected. I don't remember much of the game, I was almost certainly out for a duck having never played cricket.

I drove home in the direction of Jingili along Gilruth Avenue, a new route for me, and as I moved into the right lane to turn into Goyder Road, found myself in the same lane as an oncoming police car. I quickly swerved into my own lane and as I made the right turn into Goyder road looked into the rear view mirror to see the police car turning around to come after me. I hung a hard left into Seale Street, powered down to the end, made another left, reached East Point Road and by exceeding the speed limit was able to turn back into Goyder Road in time to see the police car just reaching the far end of Seale Street. I drove home very discreetly.

It was not the last narrow squeak I had but I am able to say, though not with pride, that I have never lost my driver's license in all my years in Darwin.

Having arrived at the peak of the wet we quickly came to enjoy the wonderful lightning displays, a reflection of Darwin's claim to one of the highest levels of iso-keraunic (lightning) activity in the world. From our little balcony we had clear views to the north where most of the storm activity seemed to occur. These storms were often seen most spectacularly when the power failures they caused left us in the dark which was often.

My colleague, Dave Molesworth, reminds me that some of these blackouts, or what the industry called outages, were short but others could last for hours. He recalled one which lasted for four hours during which stories for the TV news were being typed by torchlight.

This was before a large generator was installed for TV so no power meant no TV. Dave says that particular news bulletin finally went to air at 8 p.m. when power was restored.

But come the dry we joined fellow journalists Dave and Geoff, and their wives, Diana and Elly and sometimes Mike, Jill and kids, on regular weekend camping trips to explore the creeks, rivers and other waterways of the Top End.

Tumbling Waters, UDP Falls (now Gunlom), Mary River, Katherine Gorge (now Nitmiluk), the Katherine low level, Butterfly Gorge and the Douglas Hot Springs, Daly River Crossing, the South and East Alligator Rivers, Lost Lagoon and of course, closer to home, Howard and Berry Springs. At that time, because crocodile shooting had just been made illegal after decades of legal and widespread hunting, crocodile numbers were at historic lows and posed nothing like the risk they do today. We often camped on the Mary River where you could sit on a sandbank up to your neck in water, can of beer in hand, and unable to see your body for the turbidity of the water. Early on, Patsy and I paddled up the Daly River in a canoe borrowed from technician Jim Eustice, and camped on a sand spit beside the water. In the night we heard the bark of crocodiles but didn't see any.

This experience persuaded me I needed a boat of my own but I couldn't afford the tinny and outboard combos then popular so I decided to build my own. I commandeered the small front verandah of our house in Jingili and built a small eight-foot dinghy in a 'Pram' design in plywood. We fitted it with a two-horsepower Seagull outboard motor—the smallest, lightest, least powerful outboard it was possible to buy. For a couple of years this pathetically small, underpowered, frequently ridiculously-overloaded craft took us on some remarkable river adventures.

No 4WD here—my Torana fording the South Alligator River, 1972. Photo, Patsy Creswick.

During our first dry season Patsy's mother visited and we decided to take her camping at points of interest along the Arnhemland escarpment. That my vehicle, the Torana mentioned above, a two-door sports car, was completely unsuitable for the task worried us not a bit. Our first night we camped at the South Alligator River on the old Jim Jim road, waking the next morning to discover tracks indicating that our campsite had been visited by several buffalo during the night.

The unsuitability of the Torana for the type of travel was highlighted when it proved too low to negotiate the rutted track into Jim Jim falls and we were forced to turn back. It did, later, take us to UDP Falls, now Gunlom.

Two other camping trips were to prove interesting. In 1973, Patsy's mother Elva, visited us again, this time bringing Patsy's youngest brother, Robert. By this time I was driving a Mini Moke without side curtains but with a rack built by my friend, Harry, to carry our little dinghy.

We set off for a weekend camp on the Mary River taking as much, or little, camping gear as the moke could carry in addition to the boat, outboard and four people.

We motored down the Mary until we got to a favourite camping spot, a nice sandy bank with shade. This was one of the occasions when the boat was ridiculously overloaded and we had motored down on calm water with freeboard of about two inches. This time we had taken no shelter, just sleeping bags and a small mozzie net for Patsy and her mum. We 'men' were going to tough it out but we hadn't reckoned with the ferocity of the mosquitoes and tried to squeeze in under the women's net.

However, much to our surprise during the night it started to rain and being without shelter we packed up and motored back up the river in tropical rain so heavy Robert had to bail constantly as we were in danger of capsizing. Our relatives had never seen rain so heavy the drops were bouncing back off the surface of the river. Back at the parking area the bank had been turned into a slippery mud slide so getting our gear up and loaded and the boat on the rack was slow and we were all thoroughly wet and muddy by the time we set off on the long, cold journey home.

The other occasion featured yet another vehicle completely unsuitable for the task, this time an MGB which had only a hardtop, which we left at home and a tonneau cover. This time Patsy and I were going to camp at a nice secluded little lagoon on our friends, the Withnall's, Marrakai Station.

Going in we crossed a shallow creek and set up a tarp and our mossie net before we had a float in the shallow tepid water of the lagoon and dinner cooked over a campfire. Once again, without warning, it started to rain, again heavily and I became worried about the creek we had crossed. In the dark, we broke camp once again, loaded the gear and set off home with Patsy sheltering under her half of the tonneau cover. Being the driver, I had to accept the rain. It turned out to be the right decision because in just a short time the creek had risen a foot (30cm) and was going up. Suffice to say it was a miserable drive home.

We did have many other camps where the weather was clement and we were better equipped and much later when we and our friends had children we allowed them to play without any concern for crocs. It would not be long before that changed but in the meantime it was as if crocodiles didn't exist.

Patsy, in the meantime, was firmly embedded in the education system as a teacher at Millner School and was making her own circle of friends and exploring a developing interest in more child-centred methods of education.

The Border Staw and beyond

Meanwhile the flexibility Keith offered, and his professionalism as a cameraman and editor, meant he was very soon doing more than three stories a week for us and allowing us to range further afield for stories.

One was a trip to the Arnhemland border with the previously mentioned Sandra Holmes who was to meet Yirawala and some other elders at the Border Staw as it was then called, close to the East Alligator River and the famous Cahill's Crossing.

This would be an overnight trip meaning a camp at Cooinda, a former trading post and then a primitive motel and camping ground operated by Tom and Judy Opitz.

Theirs had been the first wayside store in that part of the world since the early '60s when the couple met at Allan Stewart's White Hunter Safaris camp at nearby Nourlangie.

Judy, whose real name was June, and Tom were to become well known across the Territory and she wrote a couple of books on her early Territory experiences.

Sandra, who was married to a film producer, Cecil Holmes, was accompanied in her old Land Rover by her young son and daughter.

It should, perhaps, be noted that I was doing the story on my two midweek days off, the sort of thing one did in those days of limited staffing when a journalist could not be spared for that length of time for a single story.

The next day after breaking camp, we went to the Border Staw for the meeting which, if I remember, was a wash out as the elders failed to turn up. One of the Border Staw's claims to fame, apart from being the last shop, and source of alcohol, before Arnhemland was the mountain of beer cans out the back. In those days before aluminium beer cans became ubiquitous, we hypothesised this steel mountain being mined at some time in the future.

Keith and I, having little to show for the exercise, drove the short distance to the East Alligator River where a lawyer and amateur cameraman mate of his, John Withnall, was camping with his father, Ron, the former Crown Law Officer and now independent MLC, and another official Legco member, Director of Primary Industries, Barry Hart.

This extended camp was an annual ritual and apart from a very large tent, creature comforts included a large refrigerator, lying on its back in a trailer, powered by a generator and designed to hold the fish, and some beer, though Bundaburg Rum was the drink of choice for bushies because it didn't require cooling. Having caught my first barramundi in the famous East Alligator River, Keith and I headed back to Darwin in time for me to go back to work.

One of Keith's first contributions to the newsroom was a good quality pig's-bristle dart board which was set up on the notice board and soon we all had our own darts with an in-office competition that became quite fierce. Keith and I did a lot of jobs together and became good mates.

In later years we had a freelance film production and public relations company together for a couple of years and he remains a mate to this day.

Familiarity doesn't count

In April 1972, soon after Keith's arrival, the flexibility of having a cameraman was proven again when a RAAF Mirage crashed at Holmes Jungle, 12 nautical miles east of Darwin, though getting the story was not without its dramas.

I was enjoying the usual counter lunch at the Don when I was paged to the Hotel's telephone for a call from JIC, Geoff Hughes, to be advised of the crash and telling me to meet up with Keith and we would then go to Berrimah where we would be met by someone with horses who would guide us to the wreck site which was in bushland and otherwise inaccessible.

We got to Berrimah, found a public phone booth to call the office, only to be told the horse riding plan was off, a relief to both of us because neither of us were horse riders, and we should return to Darwin for further instructions. On the way back we passed the entrance to the

Darwin RAAF Base with its entry flanked by two Bristol Bloodhound surface to air missiles rampant.

Keith reckoned that, given the coverage we had been giving the RAAF for its forthcoming air exercise Top Limit a few weeks hence, they should be willing to help us get footage of the crash site. However rather than stopping to get permission to enter the base, Keith relied on his very recognisable vehicle to get us in so we sailed past the guards and went to HQ.

We weren't even out of the vehicle before the base second-in-command, Wing Commander Alf Jones, incandescent with rage, told us to *fuck off* out of his base and if we ever pulled such a stunt again he would have us in the brig, or threats to that effect.

Tails between our legs, we headed off base and made another public phone booth call to the office. This time Geoff told us he had organised a helicopter and we should go to the Light Aircraft section where a chopper would be waiting. It was, but unfortunately that's what we did too. The pilot had sought clearance for our flight but the RAAF delayed flight approval for more than an hour, probably payback for our stunt. We were finally cleared for take off about half past five and with daylight fading fast, had time for only two or three circuits of the crash site, the pilot rigidly observing no fly zone instructions.

It was later confirmed the crash was the result of a bird strike on take off. The pilot, Flying Officer R Perry, ejected at 900 feet and his parachute was caught in a tree. He suffered minor injuries and was rescued by RAAF helicopter shortly afterwards.

At the site we were able to film the red and white parachute, still hanging in the tree, a significant scar in the earth and some sheared off trees where the single engine and fuselage had ploughed a furrow and a few pieces of wreckage, the largest of which was about the size of a car bonnet. Then it was back to the airport.

By now it was close to 6 p.m. and Keith would really have to move to get the film processed and edited, so he took off in his vehicle leaving me to do the paperwork and find my own way back to the office where I would have to gather the information and write the film script. We were able to slip the script to the newsreader and the edited film to telecine within the first half of the bulletin, and sat back to contemplate a job well done.

Not long afterwards we gave extensive coverage to the Top Limit event. More than 50 aircraft took part including Vulcan bombers from the Royal Air Force, Skyhawks from the New Zealand Air Force as well as Australia's Mirage, Phantom, Neptune, Hercules and Caribou aircraft. No hard feelings anywhere.

Thirteen years later, in 1985 another Mirage crashed near Darwin. This one was on final approach to the Airport when it suffered an engine failure, the pilot to avoid the risk of damage to housing, turned the aircraft around and ditched it in mudflats offshore from Ludmilla from where it was subsequently retrieved showing very little damage. The pilot also ejected safely.

One other memorable job was a shoot of the Administrator of the day, Fred Chaney, a former Federal Liberal politician and Minister, presenting various honours at an awards ceremony at Government House.

Because it was to be filmed inside, Keith had come prepared with high powered lights which he plugged into wall sockets in the room where the ceremony was to take place. As soon as he switched on the lights the overhead chandeliers and other lights went out leaving the place otherwise in darkness.

Mayor Harold 'Tiger' Brennan with the Administrator, Fred Chaney and Mrs Chaney. Photo, Gavin Carpenter, Old Darwin.

127

When the Administrator was informed of the issue he said he would be taking it up with those responsible for maintenance because the Government had only just spent $50 000 fixing the electrics in the historic old building. A long extension cord to another set of power points fixed the problem for us.

Give us the fluff

One of the interesting things we were to find as reporters trying to provide a good news service, up to ABC standards, under less than perfect circumstances was the attitude towards us from our southern counterparts.

Few of those with whom we dealt had much of an understanding of the Territory and much of what they did know came from publications which preferred colourful stories to real news.

Thus we found it difficult to interest Nationals as Sydney was known, in serious stories such as the work being done by politicians like Dick Ward, Ron Withnall, Goff Letts and others to advance the constitutional development of the Territory.

They preferred stories about crocodiles, outback characters and the offbeat, of which there were obviously many.

One story I wrote which went far and wide, was the result of the usual police check when I was working a weekend. The story was that three men, drunk in the Berrimah Pub the previous night (a Saturday), had been approached by an Aboriginal man offering to sell them a supposedly harmless snake in a hessian sack. The men bought the snake and proceeded to play with it, passing it around, putting its head in their mouths and other silly stunts.

It being close to closing time, and one of the men having a pregnant wife about to give birth in the old Darwin Hospital, they decided it would be a lark to take the snake in to show her. Naturally the night duty nursing staff resisted any attempt to share the snake with the pregnant wife so the drunks, thinking the fun was over, threw the snake into the bush behind the hospital.

One man set off home but the other two confessed to feeling unwell and when one started to vomit black, the nurses diagnosed snake bite and administered antivenin. Police were called to track down the third man who was found unconscious in his car in the driveway of his house and he too was admitted for treatment. It was assumed that all the handling had weakened the snake's venom so that none of the men died.

To check this story I tracked the policeman involved to the annual beer can regatta where he was on crowd control duties. He confirmed the story which I sent off to nationals. My colleague, Dave Molesworth, travelling overseas at the time told me subsequently he heard the story on BBC Radio in Wales.

But serious stories did still require our attention. In June, 1972 the Prime Minister of the day, William McMahon, was in Darwin to open the newly completed Darwin River Dam. Built at a cost of $9 million it was said to hold about half the equivalent water of Sydney Harbour and was eleven times bigger than Manton Dam, which it replaced as the town's principal water source.

If his speech opening the dam sounded a lot like an election campaign speech it may well have been because his Government was due to go to the polls later that year and McMahon would lose both the election and his leadership of the Liberal Party. The Prime Minister noted that he had been to the Gove Peninsula to inspect the new Nabalco Bauxite and Alumina project and to talk to the Aborigines of Yirrkala (who had strenuously opposed the excision of the land for the project, and the town of Nhulunbuy being built to support it).

Speaking of the need to balance necessary mining developments with preserving the natural environment McMahon said the government would be irresponsible if it failed to develop recently discovered uranium deposits but he said it was not interested in development for development's sake, being concerned about conservation of the natural environment and preservation for posterity of unique features of the ecology. This speech presaged yet another bitter and long running debate between miners and developers and conservationists—uranium mining.

Because he was a Prime Minister unpopular with his own colleagues as well as the people generally, some of his achievements, particularly in relation to Aboriginal Land Rights, have been overlooked in favour of some of his successors but McMahon had begun discussing the issue as far back as 1967.

He had established the Gibb Committee in 1971 to look into the issue of Aboriginal employment and living conditions in the pastoral industry and had appointed the first Minister for Aboriginal Affairs, William Wentworth, with a junior Minister assisting, Peter Howson.

It was also McMahon who, after discussions with Lord Vestey, owner of Wave Hill Station, announced he had accepted the offer to release 35 square miles from the Wave Hill lease as a living area for the Gurindji.

In a press release issued on October 12 1972 he said:

> The offer by Lord Vestey has been taken up in the context of the government's acceptance of the recommendations of the Gibb Committee that a policy be developed to enable community living areas for Aborigines to be established on land in pastoral properties and under control of the Aborigines themselves.

McMahon said he was:

> Pleased that a number of other pastoralists in the Northern Territory had also agreed in principle to the release of land for living areas for resident Aboriginal communities. These pastoralists have responded to the Government's acceptance of the Gibb Committee recommendations.
>
> Further discussions on the recommendations of the Gibb Committee would take place at a meeting of the Pastoral Lessees Association in Katherine next month (November, 1972).

Ironically it would be Gough Whitlam who, in a powerfully symbolic gesture, poured earth into the hand of Vincent Lingiari at a formal handover of the land in 1975.

Although both the Prime Minister and the Opposition Leader, had promised the withdrawal of Australian forces from the quagmire of Vietnam, the war was still being reported daily in our news bulletins and was one of the stories previously referred to as requiring a peg from which to hang the outdated footage.

War stories

Opposition to the War had even reached as far as the Northern Territory where an agronomist in the Primary Industries Branch, Rob Wesley-Smith was making a name for himself as an anti-war activist.

He claims to have organised the first Moratorium in 1970 which, on a *pro rata* population basis, drew a bigger crowd than any seen elsewhere, and that was at a time when the Victorian Moratorium March, led by future deputy Prime Minister, Dr Jim Cairns, drew 100 000 participants.

Wes, as he is known, recently reminded me that he was the first person I interviewed for TV on my arrival in Darwin. He contends that I asked him if he was a communist. Wes says he gave a non-committal reply but says his response caused considerable criticism of him so he asked me to interview him again a few days later and ask the same question so he could give a stronger answer. He says I did.

Wes was a friend of *NT News* Editor, Jim Bowditch, as well as Waterside Workers Federation President, Brian Manning.

Manning, along with the author Frank Hardy, had given considerable assistance to Vincent Lingiari, Mick Rangiari and the other Gurindji people both during and after their 1966 walk-off from the Vesteys owned Wave Hill station to traditional lands at Wattie Creek, later to be known as Dargaragu. Manning, Bowditch and others would continue to support the Gurindji and Wes became one of those supporters to the point where, at one stage, he bought a small herd of cattle which he kept on a property at Noonamah until they could be given to the Gurindji.

Wes was also to become a supporter of the ABC announcer, Glenn Taylor, when he fell foul of the Department of Labour and National Service. Glenn had been unlucky in one of the ballots by which young men were conscripted for service in Vietnam.

In this ballot numbered marbles were drawn corresponding to dates in a given month and if your birthday fell on one of the drawn dates, you were called up for service.

I had been in the second ballot in 1966 and escaped the call up. Glenn was not so lucky. His marble had been drawn and he had been called up but because he was at university was able to defer for several years. Then having graduated, but without accepting his degree, he joined the ABC, married and became a father so he had no interest in going to Vietnam and when the Department caught up with him in Darwin he told them he was a conscientious objector.

According to Glenn, for some days he became the story. The Department prosecuted him for desertion and was represented by a young Alice Springs lawyer named Paul Everingham, later to become Chief Minister of the Northern Territory. Taylor was represented by Dick Ward, a noted Labor Lawyer and Legislative Council member often called in to defend difficult human rights and other cases.

Taylor says he was subsequently found by the magistrate to have a satisfactory conscientious objection to war. He says his story was written up in the *NT News* under the headline 'ABC man says no'.

Taylor says he and his wife, Raelene, 'copped a lot of shit' over the phone with threats of violence from offended members of the public and Raelene returned to Adelaide to get away from the odium.

Royals' television first

In October 1972 both television and radio resources of the ABC were severely tested when the Royal couple, Princess Margaret and Lord Snowdon paid a two-day visit to Darwin. The couple were met at the airport by the Administrator, Fred Chaney, a twenty-one gun salute and the ABC's OB van which was to follow the couple relentlessly over the next two days.

While announcer Alf Jervis described the Royals arrival live for radio listeners across the Territory, Assistant Manager, Ian Marshall was recording a description for television viewers who would see it at 7.25 that night after the news and weather.

The following day, the couple's first appointment was at the ABC Television studio where Princess Margaret was to talk to children from two outback stations, Delamere and Croker Island. This exchange involved a complex arrangement of radio links with the session being broadcast live not only to ABC stations but also on commercial stations 8DN in Darwin and 8HA Alice Springs as well as through the outback shortwave radio network.

Putting Princes Margaret in the TV studio meant the segment could be videotaped using the Nodding Neddies with a clip being included in that evening's news. Meanwhile the OB van was set up at Kormilda College, the residential college for Aboriginal students at Berrimah, to capture the arrival of the Royal couple.

A tour of classrooms was covered by film cameraman Keith Bushnell, allowing the OB van to be moved to a new location where

and meets a Princess

ON their visit to Darwin, Princess Margaret and Lord Snowdon were met at the airport by the Administrator, Mr. Fred Chaney, a 21-gun salute (at close range) and the ABC Outside Broadcast unit.

With limited staff and facilities, ABC Radio and ABC-TV put maximum effort into coverage of the two-day visit.

Live on radio

Alf Jervis, Announcer, described the arrival live on radio for listeners from Alice Springs to Darwin, and Ian Marshall, Assistant Regional Manager, recorded a description for TV viewers, which could not be shown live because there is no TV link equipment in Darwin. It was recorded at 5 p.m. and replayed after the news and weather at 7.25 p.m.

After an overnight stay at

Government House the Royal Couple's first appointment next morning was with radio listeners in the Territory, not only through the ABC Network but also through two commercial stations (8DN Darwin, and 8HA Alice Springs), as well as the outback shortwave radio network.

Princess Margaret was met at the entrance to the television building by the Regional Manager, Don Sanders, and ushered through the double doors which were neatly opened by Yuleen Payne, Regional Assistant, and Amanda Taylor, Film Clerk. The TV studio was used so that Princess Margaret, as well as speaking on radio, could be seen to be speaking on radio by courtesy of the ABC's 1100 videotape much . This was shown during the TV news that evening.

The radio broadcast went as planned despite a fairly complex system which was set up to enable the double doors with replies to her address from four outback stations, Delamere Station and Croker Island. The man at the control desk on this occasion was Jim Eustice.

Meanwhile, 12 miles away the OB van was waiting for Princess Margaret and Lord Snowdon to arrive at Kormilda College, a residential high school for Aboriginal children.

Cameraman Bruce Black captured the arrival which made the first segment for broadcast at 7.25 that evening.

The Royal Couple were then escorted on a tour of several classroom areas, where students were (in all intents and purposes) at work; this period was covered on film, and during this time (15 minutes) the OB van was moved to a new location beside the swimming pool where Technical Officers Bruce Watson and Roger Burnard plugged it into a pre-cabled rig.

Princess Margaret and Lord Snowdon arrived "on cue" and watched a display of trampoline work. Also typical dancing and listened to the school song. While the Royal visitors enjoyed some refreshments the crew was busy surreptitiously changing camera positions for a presentation of Aboriginal art work to Princess Margaret from one of the senior girl students.

After this the Princess proclaimed the rest of the day a holiday. But for the crew, the day had just begun. It took four hours to edit and assemble a 20-minute programme for use that evening. Almost every step of the day was covered, with only

Don Sanders (Regional Manager, Darwin) with Princess Margaret in Studio 81, Darwin, just before her broadcast through radio networks in the Northern Territory. Picture courtesy Bill Bettison (official tour photographer) via N.T. News and Information Services.

three microphones, one camera, three technical members of staff, one Producer (Adrian Payne), a Commentator (Ian Marshall) and a stringer Cameraman (Keith Bushnell), who also covered the requirements for National and Territory news broadcasts.

AMBASSADOR PRESS—30536

Radio Active report of Princess Margaret and Lord Snowdon visit. Don Sanders and Princess in the TV studio. Photo, Graeme Halprin.

it was connected to a pre-wired camera rig for coverage of a display of trampoline work, Aboriginal dancing and song.

While the guests enjoyed refreshments the OB van was relocated yet again to record a presentation of Aboriginal artwork by one of the senior students to the princess.

A report in the ABC house journal, *Radio Active* noted that the princess proclaimed the rest of the day a holiday, but for the ABC's crew the work had just begun. It took four hours to edit and assemble a twenty-minute program for airing after that evening's news.

Almost every step of the Royal couple's visit had been covered with three microphones, one videotape camera, three technical staff Bruce Black, Bruce Watson and Roger Burnard, radio tech Jim Eustice, a producer, Adrian Payne, commentator, Ian Marshall and a film cameraman, Keith Bushnell, who also filed for national and Territory news broadcasts. The article neglected to mention the role of Alf Jervis.

It was another graphic reminder of how remote and under resourced Darwin was yet how people would rise to an occasion when required.

A little known sidelight to Princess Margaret's visit was revealed many years later when evidence emerged that the Larrakia Aboriginal claimants to land at Kulaluk had attempted to present a petition to the Princess.

A letter signed by five Kulaluk claimants, Robert (Bobby) Secretary, Fred Fogarty, David Daniels, Peter Mundine and Harry Adam, accompanying a petition signed by 1000 Aboriginal people of Australia was sent to the Queen on October 17 1972, explaining several attempts to present the petition to Princess Margaret had been frustrated by aides and police.

The typewritten petition read:

> GWALWA DARANIKI. THIS IS OUR LAND. The British settlers took our land. No treaties were signed with the tribes. Today we are REFUGEES. Refugees in the country of our ancestors. We live in REFUGEE CAMPS without land, without employment, without justice. The British Crown signed TREATIES with the Maoris in New Zealand and the Indians in North America. We appeal to the Queen to help us, the Aboriginal people of Australia. We need land rights and political representation now.

It was signed by many people but also included fingerprints of many others.

The covering letter is date-stamped as having been received in the Private Secretary's Office, Buckingham Palace, 3 November 1972 with a copy forwarded to GG (Governor-General) Australia.

The Kulaluk claim was a long-running story well summarised in Dr David Ritchie's 2015 report for the Northern Territory Heritage Council and titled *Review of the Assessment Process Carried Out in Relation to the Kulaluk Lease Area*.

It wasn't until 1979 that the Kulaluk claim was finally settled with the handover of title by Chief Minister, Paul Everingham, who became the first Australian head of government to grant title to land within a city to the original Aboriginal owners. This was despite his government's trenchant opposition to every future land claim.

Constitutional development meets bureaucratic recalcitrance

In the meantime, constitutional development, according to Fred Walker, 'had continued to make little or no advance against the entrenched resistance of the public service'. But he noted that after a conference in March 1972 it appeared the Commonwealth seemed agreeable to some executive power being vested in a Territory legislature and would consider reducing the number and possibly the voting power of the official members.

However:

> An insidious element noticed in the Government's proposals was that there should be a trade-off for any powers granted to the Council by the removal of some of the legislative powers already held.

Dick Ward and Ron Withnall, both lawyers, recognised the danger in this proposition and at the Legislative Council sittings in June 1972, a resolution was sent to the Government:

> Expressing dissatisfaction with the extent of the constitutional changes being offered and seeking a firm offer of the changes in form of the Government of the Northern Territory and of any other progressive proposals to which it is prepared to commit itself.
>
> ... this induced Minister Ralph Hunt to produce in parliament on 25 October 1972 a paper entitled 'Outline of the transfer of a range of functions to the Northern Territory legislature and Executive'.
>
> A little over a week later [actually it was over a month] the Government had been bundled out of office, the LCP's reign of 23 years ended by the election of the Gough Whitlam Labor government on 2 December 1972.

Meanwhile, stories demanding television coverage kept happening. In November 1972, we were able to film the aftermath of a Commonwealth Railways, or North Australian Railways, train carrying iron ore from the Frances Creek Iron Ore Mine (FIMCO) which was derailed when it ran away and collided with a mixed goods train close to the railway station situated just below McMinn Street. One report said 33 wagons and three of the newly delivered 70-ton diesel locomotives were written off in the accident and this event was thought to be instrumental in the decision, a few years later, to shut down the North Australia Railway. Frances Creek Mine, the biggest user of the line, by that time had already closed down.

Train wreck, Darwin November 1972. Christa Roderick
Collection, NT Library.

Keith and I also covered the biggest funeral ever seen in the town which followed the death of Michael Paspalis, reputedly the richest man in Darwin.

The funeral followed a Greek tradition of having the cortege pass all the properties owned by the deceased and in Mick Paspalis's case they were many, so the long train of cars crisscrossed the city, watched by large crowds of people.

One of the community activities we covered was the annual *NT News* Walkabout, which started from a point along the Stuart Highway and proceeded into the city to end at the Esplanade after covering 15 miles (24 km). A bloke known as Walking Jimmy Wadsworth had supposedly been the inspiration for the event and although it was meant to be a social event, it was keenly contested by the fitter residents of the town, male and female. One of the regular participants until very late in her life was Shotgun Nellie Flynn, also known as Walkabout Nellie, an Indigenous woman who became notorious after threatening vandals with a shotgun at her Batchelor property. She died in 1982 aged 101, having taken part in the Walkabout until only a few years before.

The ABC's own Dick Muddimer was also a regular and in the 1972 event the entire newsroom competed as Team Fred, in homage to the

NOVEMBER, 1972 📻 RADIO ACTIVE

Graeme Halprin (left) and Jim Eustice crossing the line.

Assembled walkers (at back, from left): Colin Martin, Alan Kilpatrick, Glenn Taylor, Graeme Halprin, David Nordsvan, Garry Orrin (head turned) and Chris Dart. Front row (from left): Jon Davey, Bruce Watson and Jim Eustice.

Darwin walks a race...

THE Northern Territory Walkabout, an annual dose of tropical insanity, struck in epidemic proportions this year.

That is how Radio Active's Darwin correspondent Adrian Payne saw the event. Adrian adds:

It caused more than 800 Darwin people to arrive at a point 151 miles down 'the track' (Stuart Highway) from the city, at six one morning — this for the express purpose of enjoying the stroll back to town.

Jim Eustice, Broadcasting Technician, again organised the ABC entries. For months before the event Jim could be seen hiking around the northern suburbs at very uncivilised hours of the day — and soon many who came in contact with Jim became afflicted.

Fifteen staff members took part, mainly in three teams, Auntie's Adventurers, Big Birds and Sole Music. The walkers were decked out in the ABC colours — blue T shirts with silk screening of ABC symbols, done by our lady walker, Alison Black, wife of Bruce of

the-same-name (Technical Operator, TV).

Also 15 miles from town at six o'clock on the morning of the race was the OB van, staffed by bleary eyed folk who quite rightly thought that they (not being on foot) were the only sensible people in the area. Their job was to produce a special edition of This Week in Darwin.

With barely enough light for reasonable pictures the walk was on, and during the early stages the walkers were still smiling. A station-wagon proudly flying a large "house flag", and manned by Mike Yates, Technical Operator, sped up and down the road with water for those on the way to recovery (that is, those not taking the thing too seriously).

Alongside the moving OB van walked Ian Marshall, microphone in hand, interviewing competitors on the move. This meant that between edits the van needed to travel up and down the road to get a good cross section of interviews. Cueing up a videotape

machine at 25 mph is not easy.

At about 10 a.m. the first walker crossed the line and soon afterwards Graeme Halprin and Jim Eustice arrived together, having completed the course in two hours 55 minutes. They were both members of Auntie's Adventurers and their performance did much to secure third place in the team event, with team mates Alan Kilpatrick, David Nordsvan and Bruce Watson gaining the rest of the necessary points. Their only prize was $10 worth of beer from a Radio Australia team.

Alison Black did extremely well in her section, and other staff also suffered agony in the name of fitness and to put the ABC more in the public eye, were Alan Humphries, Garry Orrin, Colin Martin, Chris Dart, Jon Davey, Glenn Taylor, David Moleswort, and Dick Muddimer.

At the finishing line every body seemed completely cured of the walkabout malady, and Graeme Halprin's first remark when his breath was reasonably recovered was "Hell! Never again."

Words of encouragement from Assistant Regional Manager Ian Marshall to (from left) David Nordsvan, Graeme Halprin and Chris Dart.

ABC technicians and presentation teams in the NT News *Walkabout 1972 as reported in Radio Active. Photo, Graeme Halprin collection.*

popular Administrator, Fred Chaney, all wearing t-shirts sporting a caricature of His Honour.

This might have been because we had developed a friendly relationship with the Administrator but might also have been because Keith was going out with the Administrator's secretary at the time.

The ABC's technical staff were also well represented as (again) *Radio Active* quoted its Darwin correspondent, presentation officer Adrian Payne, reporting that 'an annual dose of tropical insanity struck in epidemic proportions'. Fifteen staff members, organised by radio tech Jim Eustice, represented the ABC in three teams.

The event began at 6 a.m. and there at the start was the OB van on hand to record the event for a special edition of the weekly current affairs program, *This Week in Darwin*.

A later newsroom team in a later walkabout. The t-shirt design, adapted from an NT News *cartoon by the author proclaims 'not the 7 o'clock News' a reference to the news being presented at 6.30 after Cyclone Tracy. (l to r) Chris Clark, the author, David Molesworth, Neil Naessens, Bill Fletcher. Photo, ABC Archives.*

While recording was taking place inside the moving van, outside Ian Marshall was walking alongside, microphone in hand, interviewing competitors on the move with the interviews being shot from a camera mounted on the OB van's roof.

It was noted that editing videotape in a van moving at 25 mph as it relocated to find a new group of competitors, was a technical challenge. Various wives of both the presentation/tech teams and the newsroom team kept up a steady supply of fluids, both soft and hard, the choice depending on the level of dedication shown by the participants.

At the end of 1972, our journalist-in-charge and good mate, Geoff Hughes, announced that he had won an overseas posting of two years as foreign correspondent in the capital of Malaysia, Kuala Lumpur.

For some of us it was a shock and we were sad to see him go. Geoff went to Sydney and then, with Elly and his son Gavin, to KL where, as it happened, I would catch up with him two years later, of which more anon.

However, prior to his departure, we newsroom newcomers were introduced to what would, for a few years, become a tradition, the newsroom Christmas party.

For a year or two the South Australian news editor, had given the newsroom about $50 with which to provide a modest supply of beer, a couple of flagons of wine and some snacks. This apparently measly amount, but the equivalent of half a week's wages, was supplemented, I found, by a levy imposed on us journalists. We invited the people, politicians and others, with whom we had dealt in the previous year.

The gathering took place in the newsroom just as Mike Hayes was finalising his bulletin, a little unfair really. Surprisingly, I was to find out about another tradition, the cod or goof reel, a compilation of taped or filmed gaffes made either by us reporters or the talent who had fluffed their interviews. It is a long-standing tradition in southern newsrooms but because it was our first we didn't have a lot of material so those making the reel had included some soft core pornography which didn't go down too well.

Subsequent cod reels ensured our newsroom parties were a must-attend event.

A new Administration

Within days of his December 1972 election win, Gough Whitlam announced radical changes to the administrative arrangements within the Territory, including the replacement of the Department of the Interior and, with it, the NT Administration, by the creation of the Department of the Northern Territory (DONT) which would have its administrative headquarters and departmental head in Darwin. The first departmental head was Allan O'Brien who, while initially stationed in Darwin, was later transferred to Canberra.

While this and some other changes were welcomed other changed administrative arrangements were less popular, with a number of locally administered functions being transferred to Commonwealth control including Aboriginal Welfare being taken over by the newly created Department of Aboriginal Affairs, Police taken over by the Attorney-General and some surveying and drafting functions of the Lands Branch transferred to a new Commonwealth Department of Services and Property.

For us at the ABC, the change meant our weekly list of questions to the public service became DONT questions, a change in name but no difference in practical terms, for a while anyway.

As the year progressed the Legislative Council was, according to Fred Walker:

> Having difficulty dealing with the new Minister for the Northern Territory, Keppel (Kep) Enderby, who was also Minister for the Australian Capital Territory and seemed to think there were similarities between the two territories and that administrative arrangements for one could be applied to the other. This would continue to be a bone of contention between the Territory and the Commonwealth.

Strategic alliances

The composition of the Legco from 1971 to the election of the Labor Government, had seen the five elected Country Party members join with six official members to form a bloc of 11 (conservative) votes, with the three Labor members and the three independents notionally forming an opposition of six (though this was not always the case for the independents).

The change of Government had one significant effect in that it changed the composition of the official membership of the Legislative Council where Harry Giese, the longest serving member of the Council (1954–73), was replaced by Ray McHenry but only for nine months until his place was taken by Creed Lovegrove, a long-time Territorian, as head of the Department of Aboriginal Affairs. By 1974, Barry Hart and Phil Purich had also gone, replaced by Charles Gurd and Hedley Beare.

Only Martyn Finger, Assistant Administrator, and Clem O'Sullivan, Crown Law Officer, remained from the original appointed Legco members.

Labor's election also meant the political complexion of the Legco changed, with the three elected Labor members and the six official members forming a bloc of nine votes against the notional eight of the Country Party/Independents, though in practice the Nightcliff Independent, Dawn Lawrie, tended to vote with Labor more often than the other way.

Although Harry Giese remained a senior public servant, he had no defined role or official position.

Given an office without a job, he threw himself into a range of community activities including Carpentaria Disability Services of which he was foundation president, the Marriage Guidance Council, now Relationships Australia, the NT Historical Society, the Royal Lifesaving Society and he became a founding member of the Board of Governors of the Menzies School of Health Research.

In 1978, with the advent of self government dominated by the CLP, he was appointed the Territory's first Ombudsman.

In 1965 he was made Member of the Order of the British Empire (MBE) for his public service and in 1997, in recognition of his services to Territory Health, he was made a Member of the Order of Australia (AM). He died in 2000 aged 83.

In a tribute following his death, then Senator Grant Tambling noted that Giese's time as Director of Welfare from his appointment in 1954 was one of great and rapid changes with advances in Aboriginal health, education and housing helping to lift many of the restrictions which applied to Aboriginal people. Senator Tambling said Giese weathered much criticism and resistance to some of the policies he was implementing.

To his critics, Giese had overseen a long period of malaise when Aboriginal people should have been guided and encouraged to take on more responsibilities for their own management.

This was a process accelerated when the Whitlam government appointed HC 'Nugget' Coombs to control of Aboriginal Affairs nationally.

Strange bedfellows—national parks and uranium mining

As another of his pre-election promises, Gough Whitlam had proposed the development of a network of national parks which would ultimately include two in the Northern Territory, one based on the Alligator Rivers wetlands area and the other on Ayers Rock.

They would eventually become Kakadu and Uluru National Parks. However there was a sticking point as Kakadu also covered an area rich in uranium which it was proposed should be mined.

Ultimately, given the controversy surrounding that proposal, in 1975, Whitlam appointed Justice Russell Fox to head an inquiry into the proposed Ranger Uranium Mine, Aboriginal Land Rights and the national park.

In the meantime, a spin off was the announcement of grants to the states and territories for the formation of environmental organisations.

In Darwin the nucleus of such a group had come together to oppose the destruction of mangroves by the construction of the proposed Palmerston freeway, and known as People Against Palmerston Freeway (PAPF) led by environmentalists Peter and Pam Garton, Bill Walsh (who would later change his name to Strider in a nod to the enigmatic character from Tolkein's *Lord of the Rings*), lawyer, Lex Silvester and architect, John Wilkins.

They decided to apply for a grant to form the Environment Council (NT) which Peter Garton told me he envisaged as a peak body representing existing NT organisations with an interest in the environment.

These groups then included the Amateur Fishermen's Association, the Land Rover Club, Keep Australia Beautiful, the CSIRO, Federal Department of Forestry, the Darwin Conservation Society and Institute of Architects among others.

There was something of a mix up when a cheque for the grant eventually arrived at the Conservation Commission which, unaware of the proposed Environment Council, returned it with a note 'not known here'. The issue was eventually sorted out and the organisation came into being in 1974.

Like so many organisations, its activities were disrupted by Cyclone Tracy but, in 1975, its Executive Officer would be none other than another local environmental activist, author and historian, Barbara James, who until then had been the last casual journalist at the ABC.

The ECNT went on to play an active role in protests against Uranium mining in the proposed national park, sponsoring major conferences of environmentalists and organising inspection tours of the proposed mine sites at Koongarra, Jabiluka and Ranger.

Close involvement with local CSIRO scientist Dr Mike Ridpath allowed the ECNT to highlight the conservation values of the proposed Kakadu National Park.

Peter Garton recalls the challenging logistics of transporting, accommodating and feeding the visitors in tent encampments set up at different locations of the proposed mines.

Among those who took part were heads of all Australian state environment centres including the well-known New South Wales activist Milo Dunphy and Queenslander, Robert Tickner, who would go on to be a Minister for Aboriginal Affairs in the next Labor Government, led by Bob Hawke from 1983.

Legislative councillor, Dawn Lawrie, and the colourful Council Parks and Gardens supervisor, later Lord Mayor, George Brown were also among opponents of uranium mining in national parks who supported protests organised by the ECNT.

The Fox Inquiry into Uranium Mining was ultimately set up in 1975, issuing reports in 1976 and 1977 recommending that mining should go ahead within the proposed national park area but with stringent safety and environmental guidelines with a comprehensive system of environmental monitoring and research overseen by a co-ordinating committee chaired by a supervising scientist. It also recommended granting of Aboriginal title to a substantial part of the region and the creation of a national park.

Internal movements

The relocation of Geoff Hughes left the newsroom in a bit of limbo for several months as the South Australian News Editor, Mark LeNevez, provided a couple of brief replacement JIC's until March 1973 when Geoff's new full time replacement, John Milbank, arrived.

John had worked for the ABC in both Papua New Guinea and Melbourne before his appointment to Darwin.

A very different person from the laid back Geoff Hughes, John was tall and fit—a squash player. He was highly organised and as one of his first tasks set out to completely and definitively organise a new filing system to replace the rather haphazard system he inherited. It was efficient and comprehensive and, for the first time, allowed us to look at the history of stories we were reporting on. To his credit, John also tried to rein in the rampant long lunch regime we had fallen into. When he wanted us back in the office, one or other of us would be paged by name with the instruction 'your mother wants you'.

It must be said that for some of us, to our shame, he was only partly successful.

This was because lunches were more than just an opportunity to eat and drink. Often one or other of the town's many characters could be found hoping to earn a drink in return for a tall tale or two. One such was Cowboy Bill Garrison.

A gravelly voiced former stockman who propped up the bar at the Vic hotel or the Green Room at the Darwin Hotel and spoke of stockmen, fighters, croc and buffalo shooters and many more. It was easy to while away a couple of hours listening to these stories and filling his beer as it emptied.

Cowboy Bill was always sure that, at some time his ship would come in and when it did he would be 'fetlock deep in sovereigns and drinking schooners of Drambuie'. Naturally it was anticipated that we would all share in that eventual good fortune. It didn't happen and when, in later years and another career, I had an office in the centre of the city, Bill would often call in to borrow a tenner to see him through to pension day. When he died I wrote a eulogy for the *NT News* and was honoured to be one of his pall-bearers.

High-handed actions

1973 saw another big administrative change with the appointment by the Whitlam Labor government of Jock Nelson as Administrator, replacing the affable Fred Chaney Senior. Jock had been the Federal Member for the Territory before the position gained any significant powers, and was a staunch Labor man.

At a Territory level, the Legislative Council was having trouble getting the Minister for the Northern Territory, Kep Enderby, to commit to what it thought had been agreed with the previous government, a fully elected Legislative Assembly and a path to statehood.

Enderby was, apparently, perfectly willing to meet with the Legislative Council but that was all. Then in July 1973, Enderby announced the government would be compulsorily acquiring an area of land just outside

Darwin which became known as the 32 square mile acquisition area. The land was occupied by several significant businesses including a brickworks, a piggery and a caravan park for which compensation would be paid.

The announcement was greeted with outrage, both by the businesses affected and by the Legislative Council. The majority leader, Goff Letts, was delegated to travel to Canberra to see if he could persuade the Senate to disallow the acquisition Bill. It would become another occasion where a family connection turned out to be fortuitous. Letts was able to persuade the leader of the balance-holding Democratic Labor Party, Senator Vince Gair, that in ensuring the Bill was rejected he would be helping a relative of one of Gair's long-term acquaintances.

The Bill was duly rejected and although the businesses had long since accepted compensation, Enderby's unpopularity, and that of the Whitlam Government, was entrenched.

Letts makes the point that this high-handed action, carried out without consultation with locals, probably contributed to a disastrous result for Labor locally at the next year's (1974) election which he, as a leader of the Country Party, and Tom Lawler, a Liberal Party stalwart, and husband of a later Mayor of Darwin, Ella Stack, were planning to contest under the banner of the soon to be formed, Country Liberal Party (CLP).

Plenty of fodder there for the ABC's reporters.

Australia's first international yacht race

Since 1969 a small but active group of trailer-sailor owners operating as the Darwin Cruising Yacht Association of the NT (CYANT) had been running regular short races as family fun affairs but by the early '70s the fleet was expanding to include keel boats and multi hulls so talk turned to more ambitious races starting with a Bathurst Island event which proved a success.

In late 1972 planning began for what would become the first international yacht race in Australia, a 545 nautical mile sail to Dili in East Timor. Committees were established in both Darwin and Dili, where the Portuguese government administration welcomed the event.

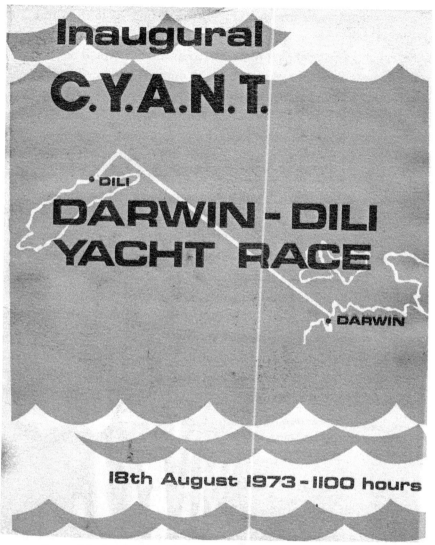

Cover of the brochure issued for the inaugural Darwin–Dili yacht race.
Collection of Bill Fletcher, author photo.

On 18 July 1973, the first Darwin to Dili race with six competing yachts was flagged off. It was a great success with the 25 foot trimaran *Bindi Borega* winning in a time of 96 hours and 17 minutes. A second race in 1974 drew an entry of 24 yachts, attesting to its success as an event. The winning yacht, *Kingo*, covered the distance in 91 hours 37 minutes.

146

Plans were well in hand for the 1975 event with 60 entries received when first Cyclone Tracy and then political events in East Timor intervened. It wasn't until 2010 that the event resumed.

In the meantime the Darwin Ambon race was created in 1976 to fill the sailing void with six yachts starting in the first year.

Coincidentally, from soon after my arrival in Darwin, I had entertained the idea of going sailing, something I had not broached with Patsy. I took to reading every available yachting magazine, and as many books on the subject as I could, starting with what was then regarded as the absolute bible, Captain Joshua Slocum's *Sailing Alone Around the World*.

Taking this dream even further and still without giving Patsy the opportunity to object, in 1973 I bought a steel hull built by Peter Buckley, another of the town's characters. Buckley was married to a wild Irish woman named Eve and had two young children.

He had started boat building at Nightcliff but when Patsy and I were introduced to him and Eve by our JIC, Geoff Hughes, he had set up business in Winnellie where he and his family lived in a caravan surrounded by a lawn, garden and a white picket fence.

Buckley had the rights to build the 34-foot, hard-chine, steel 'Temptress' design in either centre- or rear-cockpit layout and it was one of these craft that he campaigned in the first Darwin-Dili race.

Meanwhile, for $6900, mostly borrowed from the bank, I gained a finished hull, sand blasted and primed in grey.

A truck and crane installed it in the relatively narrow space between house and fence where it sat receiving only sporadic attention for almost a year, though when painted white it naturally became known in the district as the white elephant.

Along the way I bought an almost obsolete single sideband (SSB) radio at auction and Patsy and I studied for and gained our third-class radio operators' licences, essential for radio communications at sea. Our friend, Harry Maschke, owner of a steel fabrication business, made two galvanized metal tanks and with Dave's help I fitted perspex porthole covers.

However it soon became clear that I did not have anything like the skills required for such a major fitting out project and though by now I knew my leech from my luff, and port from starboard, I had absolutely no sailing experience.

At the same time I made no effort to actually gain sailing experience, a failure which frustrated Patsy and contributed to her lack of enthusiasm for the proposed venture. She was even less impressed with stories about yachting disasters and sailors surviving by drinking seagulls' blood.

But I did have some boating experience. In my childhood the family bought a small row boat in which we had a lot of fun for several years.

However, it was fortuitous when, one Sunday morning, Harry arrived with a nicely sand blasted slab of Oregon timber for me to turn into a coffee table and asked if Patsy would like to go to Germany with him the following year? Still keen to travel overseas and aware the boat would take too many years to be ready, she replied that it sounded interesting and she turned to me and asked if I would like to come too? Decision time.

Fairly soon the hull was sold and the small amount remaining after paying back the bank loan contributed to our airfares when, in June 1974, we went overseas with Harry, of which more later.

By this time Wagaman Primary School had opened as the Territory's first Open Education school where the Principal, Alan Dunstan, supervised an innovative, child focused and directed teaching and learning program. This had become an area of interest to Patsy and she had been selected as one of the teachers. Her friend, Lyn Maschke, wife of Harry, was teacher/librarian.

In one of the 1973 school holidays, Patsy and Lyn went on holiday to the Portuguese colony of East Timor, about an hour's flight north of Darwin which was then serviced by regular flights of Indonesia's Merpati Nusantara Airline. It was cheap to fly there and was developing as a popular tourist destination for Territorians as well as being one of the previously mentioned starting points for the hippie trail.

East Timor was one of four colonies of Portugal, the others being Angola, Mozambique and Guinea-Bissau. There was an independence movement developing but where similar movements in the African colonies had become increasingly violent, East Timor was regarded as a peaceful billet.

Because of its remoteness, Portuguese rule had been benign but ineffectual with the result that East Timor was relatively under developed. It was also the place the wealthy Portuguese could arrange for their sons to do their compulsory National Service, being assured of a peaceful posting.

Although Dili was the colony's capital, the flights from Darwin landed in the second largest town of Baucau. From there Patsy and Lyn travelled extensively throughout East Timor using limited local transport or hitching rides on army vehicles, riding with the troops. They found the young Portuguese soldiers to be generally well educated, polite and keen to talk English.

The lack of development under Portuguese rule was particularly noticeable in rural areas where the lack of infrastructure such as sealed roads and bridges was evident.

Patsy recalled one narrow but very deep ravine which required the driver of their vehicle to adjust a series of loose planks to the width of the vehicle's track before they could cross, a hair-raising experience.

Patsy returned from that trip eager for the further overseas travel that was to come.

More Aboriginal Land Rights action

As one of his election promises, Gough Whitlam had pledged if elected to legislate for Aboriginal Land Rights in the Northern Territory (the only part of Australia where the Federal Government could legally make such laws). In 1973, he appointed Justice Edward Woodward of the Federal Court to inquire into appropriate ways to recognise those rights.

Justice Woodward had been one of the lawyers for the Milirrpum people in their case against Nabalco on the Gove Peninsula. Over 1973 and 1974, he conducted hearings resulting in two reports, the first in 1973 recommending the formation of Land Councils to represent the interests of Aboriginal people and the second in 1974, which made recommendations on which land rights would be based.

One of the hearings held by Woodward occurred on a Saturday when I was rostered to work and involved a visit to the Kulaluk area at Bagot Reserve which was being claimed by the Gwalwa Daraniki group.

Filmed by Keith, this led to the unusual, some would say unprecedented, sight of a Royal Commissioner in casual dress and his attendant officials, sitting in chairs under a mango tree while others sat in a circle on the ground with the Aboriginal claimants, Bobby and Topsy Secretary, among others. Dave says he also covered this Woodward hearing, possibly for nationals.

Once again, however, it was not the originator of those proceedings, Gough Whitlam, but his successor, Malcolm Fraser whose government, in 1976, passed the Aboriginal Land Rights Act (NT) allowing Aboriginal people to claim land to which they could show traditional ties.

In September 1973, an Aboriginal issue of another complexion occurred which was to become something of a *cause celebre* according to the ABC's Glenn Taylor. He was referring to the Nola Bambiana affair in which an Aboriginal girl whose mother had died and who had subsequently been adopted by a white family in Darwin was suddenly, at the age of seven, taken from them and returned to her father at Maningrida. Taylor says southern activists were behind what he saw as the girl's kidnapping one of them being a well-known, but sometimes misguided, local agitator for Aboriginal rights, John Tomlinson.

Taylor says he interviewed the adoptive parents who were distraught at losing Nola. They gave him a pillow case full of her dolls and other toys which he delivered to the girl at Maningrida. He said she seemed like an alien in what should have been her home community and very sad. He also said there was a suggestion her father had promised the girl in marriage to another person.

Kim Lockwood also reported the case for the *Melbourne Herald* and says his picture of Nola sitting in her father's lap made page one as well as generating international interest. He also suggested that Gwen Cairns, wife of the Deputy Prime Minister, Jim Cairns, had become involved in the matter. It was also the sort of case that would interest former *NT News* editor, Jim Bowditch. Lockwood says that as he flew out to Maningrida in a light plane, another passed 1000 feet below returning from Maningrida.

He says his pilot indicated the plane below was carrying Jim Bowditch. Glenn Taylor says his piece was used on the national ABC current affairs program, *Today Tonight*, and led to the offer of a position

Royal Commissioner Justice Edward Woodward holds a land rights hearing at Kulaluk, 1973. David Molesworth collection.

on that program which in turn led to his departure from Darwin not long afterwards. Records show our newsroom generated at least three stories about the incident.

We bury Doc Dudson

On 15 May 1974, Keith Bushnell and I were once again called on for funeral duty for another legendary Territorian, Dr Keith Dudson. Doc Dudson, as he was known, had been a giant in the Northern Territory's buffalo domestication and meat program.

In 1957 he had taken out the lease on Marrakai Station between the Adelaide and Mary Rivers which was believed to have 20 000 head of wild buffalo which he thought he could domesticate.

Goff Letts described him as a close family friend from university days, unorthodox but a man of vision. In 1958, Dudson and a former buffalo shooter, began a program of domestication which became highly successful.

He built the Wild Boar buffalo abattoir on Marrakai and his efforts with buffalo eventually led to the establishment of seven small abattoirs and opened up a multi million dollar export market for the Territory.

In his later years the Doc had been joined in partnership by Ron Withnall, independent member of the Legislative Council.

Keith Bushnell and I had become friends with Ron's son John and with or without them, Patsy and I had enjoyed many camping trips to various parts of the property.

It was Ron who took control of arrangements for Doc Dudson's burial which would take place near the northern boundary of the property a couple of hundred kilometres from Darwin.

The funeral began with a well attended service in the small stone Christ Church Cathedral following which the cortege would travel down Smith Street, along Daly Street and the Stuart and Arnhem Highways and thus out to the picturesque burial site. Keith and I, in his Land Cruiser, left ahead of the cortege and filmed it at several recognisable locations, the first being the Smith and Daly street intersections where Jack Haritos's shop gave us the opportunity to pick up a six pack of VB to see us on the way.

Overtaking the cortege we filmed it again at the Arnhem Highway intersection and passing the famous Humpty Doo Hotel, where, since our first beers had been consumed, we bought another six pack for the rest of the journey which included a lengthy traversal of the property on a dirt track.

The burial site was in a clearing on a small hill with a magnificent view out over the floodplains to the east. There was a short service with some colourful tributes to the deceased then the festivities, suitably subdued, began. Ron Withnall had arranged a magnificent spread of food and there were ample supplies of beer, wine and of course, Bundy Rum.

Having eaten and drunk, it was time for us to return to Darwin to process, edit and script the film but Ron wouldn't let us go without loading us up with an armful of cans of cold beer.

Unfortunately by the time we reached the Humpty Doo Hotel again, the remaining cans were warm, so we stopped in there for a cold beer and a game of pool.

By this time it was mid afternoon and for fun Keith proposed a wager on whether or not he could get to Berrimah, about 25 km without touching either clutch, brake or accelerator. I was prepared to bet twenty cents he couldn't.

His Toyota Land Cruiser being equipped with a hand throttle we set off in top gear and by judicious use of the hand throttle managed to get through the Arnhem/Stuart Highways intersection without bothering any traffic and at the Berrimah Hotel and another cold beer stop, I handed over the twenty cents.

How does one admit without embarrassment that when it came time to write the script, I could not type so had to dictate the words to a typist from a prone position underneath my desk, from where, having done so, I was told to go home? The fact that Keith not only processed the film but also edited it into a story indicates his higher tolerance for alcohol than mine or perhaps his more judicious consumption.

The next day, somewhat the worse for wear but more embarrassed about what I might have written, it turned out that between us, Keith and I had crafted a colourful but sensitive story about what had been a most unusual event.

Bring on the beer can boats

Popular legend has it that Darwin's unique boating event, the long running Beer Can Regatta, started in 1975 as part of clean up efforts after Cyclone Tracy. However the event's historian, Des Gellert, assured me that while it was an endeavour to clean up Darwin's empty beer can litter, it actually began on the Queen's Birthday holiday weekend in June 1974.

In those days before Clean up Australia, Keep Australia Beautiful (KAB) and similar anti-litter campaigns, road journeys were often measured in how many cans of beer they took to drink, with the empty cans generally being thrown out of the window to twinkle in car headlights like stars in the night.

The origins of the event are both unclear and disputed. Des Gellert says the concept was attributed to a Darwin used-car dealer, Lutz Frankenfeld, working with a journalist, Paul Rice-Chapman, who had links to the Darwin Regional Tourist Promotion Association (DRTPA).

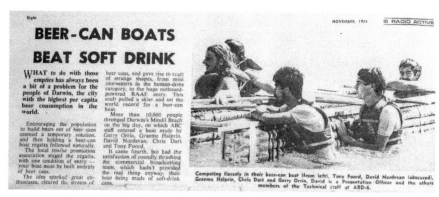

Radio Active report of ABC technicians' Beercan Regatta entry, 1974.
Photo Graeme Halprin.

The ABC's Glenn Taylor claims he came up with the idea while interviewing a member of the DRTPA, though he couldn't remember a name. The truth is lost in the mists of time and early records were lost in Cyclone Tracy.

Keith Bushnell has no doubts that Lutz Frankenfeld was indeed the originator as he filmed him in relation to the event a number of times.

What is known is that early organisers were the Darwin Ski Club or Darwin Power Boat Club with the Darwin event annually going on to attract dozens of strangely designed vessels using a variety of empty containers, not just beer cans, and attended by tens of thousands of people. It has spawned similar events in Canada and the United States and almost every year there has been a colourful story to guarantee its newsworthiness.

Naturally the ABC was interested in the original event, both as a news story and as a potential fun social event. We journalists decided we would enter a boat and began collecting our empty beer cans which were stored under my house in Jingili. When we thought we had enough cans I organised a working bee to build the thing, which was to be a simple raft of long lengths of cans taped together with gaffer tape.

It proved to be slow going and our lack of design skills showed when our gaffer tape refused to hold the cans together. Perhaps not too sadly the newsroom abandoned its efforts.

The ABC's technicians had more gumption, and more skills. The November 1974 edition of the ABC's then in-house newspaper, *Radio*

Keith Bushnell and friend, Dugan Petrie, trial the beercan canoe entry from Canada. Photo, Bob McAdorey.

Active, featured a photo of presentation officer, David Nordsvan, and TV technicians Tony Foord, Graeme Halprin, Chris Dart and Gerry Orrin with their boat in the water.

Known as the Darwin Lions Beer Can Regatta since 1978, it has now been running without interruption for 47 years, not even disrupted by Cyclone Tracy or the 2020 Corona Virus pandemic, though that year's event was much smaller and restricted to just a few craft made from milk cartons rather than beer cans.

Keith reminded me that when he decamped to Canada for five years after Cyclone Tracy, he and Bob McAdorey, the journalist he worked with at Toronto's Global Television Network, in 1977 talked the local Molson's brewery and Qantas airline into part-funding their holiday trip to Darwin to enter the Beer Can Regatta. They brought with them a Canadian canoe covered in cans from the beer company sponsor but Keith says it sank as soon as it hit the water.

He still has the plaque awarded as a special prize presented by the DRTPA to Canada as the regatta's first international entry.

These days it's a much more family orientated event with activities for children such as sand castle building, running races, thong throwing and teams events.

Federal Government shenanigans

While the citizens of Darwin were enjoying the annual dry season with its loaded calendar of social, sporting and other events, the Labor Government of Gough Whitlam was enduring obstruction from the Senate where the balance of power was held by five members of the Democratic Labor Party (DLP) which, despite its name, usually voted with the Coalition and three independents.

Frustrated by repeated refusals to pass some of the government's bills, Whitlam eventually asked the Governor-General for a Double Dissolution, hoping to win a Senate majority at an election in May 1974, less than halfway through its three-year term.

It didn't work out that way. While Labor won the House of Representatives with a reduced majority, numbers in the Senate remained tied at 29 each with two independents. Whitlam might have seen off the hated DLP but still didn't have the majority he needed which would have repercussions the following year, especially as Whitlam, in July 1974 appointed Sir John Kerr as Governor-General.

In November 1973, Glenn Taylor had accepted an invitation to join the *Today Tonight* current affairs program and was replaced as talks officer

Talks officer, Trevor Watson on the set of Today '74. *Photo, Trevor Watson.*

by Trevor Watson who presented several radio programs each week and on television, a five minute segment at the end of the seven o'clock news called *Today '74*, Trevor would remain until February 1975 when he took up the position of radio current affairs reporter in Adelaide.

Like so many of us, Trevor concedes his memory of the times is fading though some people he interviewed stand out including Victoria River MLA Goff Letts, who led the CLP to a whitewash in the first Legislative Assembly election.

Another was cattleman Bill Tapp of Killarney Station who was head of the NT Cattlemen's Council and was interviewed frequently on issues in the cattle industry.

He recalls doing a piece on Australia's first woman wharfie, a story which went national though details are now forgotten. He also reported an abortive push by local business and political leaders to have Darwin declared a free port.

Several aircraft-related stories included a piece on Qantas using Darwin as a training centre for its new Boeing 747 Jumbo jets, and with cameraman Keith Bushnell, flew in an RAAF Dakota to film an Air Force F111 on a bombing exercise in the Timor Sea.

Dave Molesworth was on the same flight for news and recalls leaning out of the Dakota's side door in a harness taking photos while Keith filmed beside him. Trevor recalls another film job inside the Air Force's top secret battle room at Darwin Airport.

Mayor, 'Tiger' Brennan and local businessman Lutz Frankenfeld, probably pushing the beer can regatta, were memorable regular guests on his radio programs.

Visitors were also interviewed, among them Slim Dusty, and Trevor recalls returning from lunch one day to find the legendary Buddy Williams waiting in the hope of an interview.

Adventures abroad

As it happened, I missed the first beer can regatta because Patsy and I had decided to accept Harry Maschke's invitation to visit Germany.

It was my first overseas trip and so I acquired my first passport, Patsy already having obtained one for her visit to East Timor. Our plan was to travel to Istanbul with Harry, who would then go on to visit his mother, sister and brother and their families in Germany while Patsy and I explored Turkey's west coast, several Greek Islands, Athens, Corfu and various must-see places in Italy and France before joining him in Germany.

First, however, we had to pass through Kuala Lumpur for a four-day stay with our friend and former Darwin colleague, Geoff Hughes and his wife Elly which was an eye opener for someone who had never been outside Australia. A highlight of that brief visit was a trip to the Cameroon Highlands and one of the hill stations where the English grandees of the Raj once retired for the wet season. I remember little English style cottages with picket fences and rose gardens.

Because we had taken three months' leave, a full school term without pay for Patsy, we travelled at a fairly leisurely pace enjoying historic cities and monuments largely free of the crowds of today.

Of interest, for a couple of non Catholics, was being blessed by the Pope in St Peters square then coming face to face with him in the Basilica where he was preaching the service. Some years later I had another Papal experience when, in 1986, I was delegated to set up a media centre for the brief two hour Darwin visit of Pope John Paul II.

Rome, Florence, Venice and Pisa were all on the agenda before we reached Germany and were treated like family by Harry's relatives. He then returned home and we went on with our trip.

An unsettling experience occurred when we were in Amsterdam. We had bought a Eurailpass which gave us free first-class travel for a month, although we had to pay if we wanted a sleeper. We had arrived in Amsterdam to such miserable weather that we decided not to stay, instead choosing to take a sleeper to Geneva where we were to catch up with relatives of Patsy.

It was a late-evening departure and we shared our compartment with two young men who were very busy in and out of the compartment. Patsy had retired as soon as we left Amsterdam.

Crossing the border into Germany at our first stop there was a lengthy delay and our two companions were brought back under escort to collect their belongings.

One of them spent quite a long time messing around with his pack which, like ours, was stored on a shelf above the bunks. When I asked him what was happening, he said quietly 'Polizei' and I watched from the window as the two were escorted along the platform by men in plain clothes.

Finally the train continued its journey but as the car attendant passed our compartment, I asked him what was going on. He indicated that the police had been watching the two men who, it transpired, were transporting several kilograms of hashish somewhere.

Apparently the police had recovered four one-kilo packs of hashish from hiding places behind panels concealing toilet cisterns in several carriages.

Suspicious about the length of time the man had taken retrieving his pack, I climbed up to check out my pack and was not particularly surprised to find what I took to be a kilo of hash, wrapped in muslin in the top of my pack. Leaving it there I went to find the car attendant, inviting him to inspect my pack. He too seemed unsurprised to find the package and took charge of it. I asked him about changing compartments which he agreed to, so I woke Patsy, told her the tale and we relocated to another compartment.

Perhaps I was too cautious but I had a clear conscience when we went through border checks entering Switzerland and we also broke our journey at Basel just in case. Some of my friends, hearing this story, have expressed regret that it wasn't them who had briefly been in possession of such a valuable commodity and it occurs that the car attendant might have enjoyed an unexpected bonus.

After a few days of sightseeing in Geneva, and fine dining with Patsy's diplomat uncle and aunt, we went on to Barcelona, Granada, Madrid, San Sebastian (where we saw a street parade by Basque separatists and were advised to stay off the street in case violence erupted), then Paris, London, Dublin and back to London where we stayed with another journalist friend from my Albany days, Alan Kennedy and his wife Kerrie Lee, and spent too much money on books at Foyles. These we sent home by surface mail, to have them arrive in time to be destroyed by Cyclone Tracy a few months later.

Nearly not all about drinking

Not all of our social activities in Darwin revolved around parties and drinking. Patsy had developed an active interest in spinning, weaving and other crafts so it was natural that we join in successful efforts to form a craft association. The ABC's assistant manager, Ian Marshall and his wife Pam, were also formation members.

The group, once officially formed, was given access to former Health Department premises in corrugated iron buildings in Mitchell Street. A number of fund raising events followed One effort I remember was a wine bottling. One of the members had links to a South Australian winery and had obtained a large keg of wine which we spent a very wine soaked afternoon sampling and bottling for potential sale. I do not remember any being sold but perhaps it was yet another victim of Cyclone Tracy.

Patsy reminds me of another successful event, a weekend craft activity at Jingili Primary School where group members led a variety of activities relating to their specialties. Patsy participated in weaving workshops using the weighted warp technique where two-litre juice containers were used to tension the warp threads.

I had followed my mate Dave into some amateur dramatics. Our first production together was a play called *Life Ceremony* where David was the patient, bandaged from head to toe and in a wheelchair for the entire (fortunately short) play.

As the doctor I was required to show more interest in the workings of the wheelchair than in the patient with the result that every night, Dave ended up being tipped out of the wheelchair and onto the floor.

It was a weird play but directed by a young aspiring producer named Eric Dowsett who, by day, worked for one of the big insurance companies. As a result of this confluence of events, Eric moved into our spare room as a paying guest and so was able to look after our house and three cats while we went off on our European grand tour. We had barely returned from that in September when Eric took off for England to visit his parents and birthplace.

One big step forward

I had returned from our overseas journey to the news that the Federal Labor Government had finally granted the Territory the fully elected legislature it had been seeking for so long, still against entrenched bureaucratic pushback, according to Fred Walker. Representation would also be expanded to nineteen members, two more than the final Legislative Council.

The election took place on Saturday 19 October 1974 and, for the first time, ABC television was able to broadcast the vote count over three special program inserts across the evening.

I had been given the task of anchoring the three segments and had as my expert party commentators Rex Jettner from the Country Liberal Party and John Waters from the Labor Party.

Both major parties had fielded large teams and there were many independent candidates.

From very early in the count it became apparent that the CLP was going to triumph and it would be a bad night for Labor. Ultimately the new CLP won seventeen of the nineteen seats, taking 49 per cent of the vote with the Independents Dawn Lawrie in Nightcliff and Ron Withnall in Port Darwin retaining their seats.

Although Labor won 30 per cent of the vote, not only did it not win any seats, it lost the three seats it had held in the previous Legislative Council. It had been a depressing night for John Waters but he was quick to capitalise when, in something of a faux pas, I ended the night by saying that brought us to the end of the ALP's Election Coverage. 'Thank you Richard', said John, before I could correct myself.

Commentators subsequently put much of the blame for Labor's poor performance on the Whitlam Government which was becoming electorally unpopular nationally for a series of poor decisions and scandals but Kep Enderby's abortive attempt at alienating the 32-square-mile acquisition area had clearly not been forgotten.

In 1973, Enderby had been replaced by Dr Rex Patterson, the Minister for Northern Development who also became Minister for the Northern Territory.

Patterson, being the Member for the North Queensland seat of Dawson was a much more acceptable Minister for Territory politician, particularly as he had made an early announcement of the much desired move to self government for the Territory.

In his capacity as both Minister for Northern Australia and Minister for the Northern Territory he was to fly into Darwin on Christmas Day 1974 to take responsibility for rebuilding the city wiped out by Cyclone Tracy.

Goff Letts retained leadership of what was now the CLP team and with the Territory firmly on the march towards self government, he took the post of Majority Leader heading up a seven-member Executive.

Not all seriousness

Naturally, given that ABD6 was run mostly by young people, there were opportunities for some light hearted activities.

Tech Graeme Halprin reminds me that April Fool's day for at least three years provided the opportunity for some fun and, of course, I was involved in all of them.

One purported to be an announcement by the NT Administration that all future government houses would, instead of ceiling fans, be fitted with punkahs, hanging strips of material which wafted back and forth creating a gentle breeze.

The purported rationale for the change was the extra employment it would provide if each house also required a punkah wallah, the person who operated the punkahs. The breakfast room at the Darwin Hotel featured punkahs so we filmed them in operation then dressed our Indonesian TV Tech, Alf Amrein, in a sarong and had him sitting outside with a string tied to his toe and disappearing into the house. Skilful editing made it look like he was operating the punkahs.

In another scenario, I was filmed in mask and snorkel swimming in Rapid Creek as a member of the newly formed but very successful Bunyip Taggers Association while the third warned viewers to look out for the wire-eating worm which was running rampant in Darwin eating electrical wires. We had an illustration of the worm drawn by our graphic artist, Colin Martin, a witchetty grub like creature swallowing a piece of three core flex. The idea was to lose the sound partway through my piece to camera leaving me goldfishing (talking without sound) to hint that the worm had eaten one of my wires. Juvenile but fun.

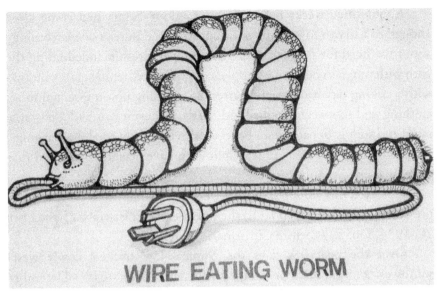

Graphic artist Colin Martin's depiction of the wire eating worm.
Author photo.

Cyclone Tracy

In November 1974 another event took place which would reverberate across Darwin. I reported a meeting of a range of national and state emergency service organisations, fortuitously being held in Darwin, at which the formation was agreed of the Natural Disasters Organisation within the Defence Department with Major-General Alan Stretton being nominated as its first head.

Within a very short time his services would be called on and severely tested.

The story of Cyclone Tracy, at that time Australia's worst natural disaster, has been well-canvassed elsewhere and rehashed many times. However I offer an ABC perspective and couple of personal stories.

It is now well known that two previous destructive cyclones in 1897 and 1937 had caused considerable damage to a town which was, on both occasions, recovering from other events. There had also been a couple of less destructive cyclones. However, it having been 37 years since the last cyclone and thus outside most citizens' memories, there was little experience to draw on in response to such a threat.

About three weeks before Tracy, Cyclone Selma had come close enough to Darwin to prompt warnings from the Bureau of Meteorology about the need for preparations. These preparations included filling the bath with water, in case water supplies were affected, taping glass windows with masking tape to prevent shattering, stocking up on essential food, clothing and footwear supplies and, lastly, ensuring you had a portable radio and supply of batteries. I believe many people heeded the warnings. I know we did, and some of us might even have been disappointed that Selma passed without impact.

However, this coloured our reactions somewhat when a tropical low pressure system developed far to the north-east of Darwin on December 20, 1974, four days before Christmas.

Over the next few days the tropical low tracked slowly west-southwest and gradually intensified with satellite photos on December 21 indicating the system had become a cyclone. At 10 p.m. that night, the Tropical Cyclone Warning Centre named it Tracy and issued the first warning for coastal communities between Goulburn and Bathurst Islands. The cyclone was then 200 km north northeast of Cape Don.

By midnight on December 23 it was clear Tracy was moving south and at 3.00 a.m. on December 24, it had rounded Cape Fourcroy on the southwest tip of Bathurst Island with winds measured at 120km/h. At midday on Christmas Eve the cyclone was seen to have changed to a south easterly course and was heading for Darwin.

At 12.30 p.m. a top priority warning was issued advising that Tracy was moving closer to Darwin, very destructive winds of 120 km/h with gusts to 150 km/h were expected in the Darwin area that night and the following Christmas day.

Some reports claim Darwin was already experiencing wild weather by late afternoon, but my memory and it was confirmed by the Bureau of Meteorology, was that conditions for most of the afternoon were relatively calm, almost eerily calm, overcast and drizzling.

The cyclone had been slow moving, only 3 to 4 km per hour, and when the first big wind gusts were felt, about 11 p.m. the eye was still 40 km west of Darwin.

Forecasters were predicting, and the ABC was broadcasting, that the cyclone would cross the coast at Shoal Bay, north of Darwin at 6.00 a.m.

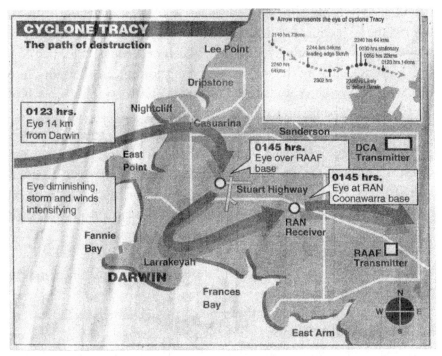

Graphic showing suggested track of Cyclone Tracy. The Australian.

As Tracy approached Darwin, the system narrowed and intensified further until the eye was reported to be less than 12 km in diameter. Details are imprecise but Tracy was said to have crossed the coast at Coconut Grove about 1 a.m.

Reports about the cyclone's movements vary but at least one depiction of her path looked like a huge paintbrush had taken a looping path from west to east, as if designed to create the greatest damage possible. It is why parts of inner Darwin were being severely damaged while in the northern suburbs less wild conditions were being experienced.

What is known is that the Met Bureau's wind speed recorder, or anemometer, broke with a peak gust of 217 km/h, though later winds might have reached 240km/h or even 260km/h. Even in 2021, debate continues within some online forums about the wind strengths of Cyclone Tracy.

For large numbers of those interviewed subsequently, the most notable element of Cyclone Tracy was the noise of the wind. It was described as howling, shrieking, a banshee wail, a scream that was almost beyond the level of human hearing. My own description is of white noise a sustained overwhelmingly loud hiss, which occasionally dropped to a shriek, punctuated by the crashes and bangs of objects smashing into the house, the crash of walls being torn away, or the rending screech of corrugated iron being ripped from the roof.

Very early on Christmas morning, a number of the senior leadership group including Police Commissioner, Bill McLaren, Housing and Construction head, George Redmond, the Director of Emergency Services, later disasters coordinator, Ray McHenry, had met at Police Headquarters to plan a course of action. Goff Letts would have been there but was down south on holidays, returning on an early RAAF flight.

Based on reports that there was already a big exodus of people leaving by road, it was decided there should be an evacuation to reduce the population to manageable proportions.

Later, the head of the recently formed Natural Disasters Organisation, Major-General Alan Stretton, who arrived in Darwin about 9.30 p.m. on Christmas night, would claim that it had been on his orders that the evacuation of more than 20 000 people took place.

Within days just over 25 000, mostly women and children, but some men, had been flown out of Darwin on any available aircraft military or civilian, including a Qantas 747 Jumbo which set a record for taking more than 600 passengers.

It was the biggest peacetime evacuation in Australia's history. A further 10 000 had left by road and the population was reduced to just over 10 600.

Stretton would later say that he exercised enormous discretion in his orders for the people of Darwin without knowing whether he had the legal powers to do so. He also clashed with the local leadership a number of times including barging into a court session then later having to apologise.

Although there is no doubt that Stretton, an active and media savvy operator, did mobilise the Army, Navy and Air Force in a massive relief and reconstruction effort which included the Navy bringing hundreds of tons of corrugated iron used in a huge re-roofing effort, he rubbed a lot of people the wrong way.

PM Gough Whitlam and head of the Natural Disasters Organisation, Major-General Alan Stretton in what the photographers billed as a confrontation. 'You may be in charge, but I'm the Prime Minister'. Photo, Baz Ledwidge/ Beat Erismann collection.

Within a week he announced that his job was done and he would be leaving on January the second. However, his goose was cooked when he issued an edict that New Year's Eve would be alcohol free and would be celebrated two days later. There was uproar and Stretton left that night.

The permits issue

One of the earliest edicts issued by Stretton was that permits would be required for those entering, or re-entering Darwin, and establishing police roadblocks for that purpose. This outraged many people, including the outspoken independent member for Nightcliff, Dawn Lawrie, re-elected in the first fully elected Legislative Assembly only months before.

As one of the most outraged and most vocal opponents she refused to play along. Early in 1975, required to attend a National Estate conference down south, she left without obtaining a permit. When she flew back into Darwin a few days later, the Commonwealth Police attempted to deny her entry because she didn't have the required exit/ entry permit. She stood her ground and was finally allowed to leave the airport to be met by a large and vocal crowd of supporters.

Ms Lawrie was to write later that with what she believed to be an act of almost criminal stupidity, the Australian Government and Northern

Territory Legislative Assembly had passed an infamous ordinance requiring that citizens obtain a permit to return to Darwin. She regards it as a shameful page in Australia's history noting that in the event of such a disaster, naturally, a percentage of people would want to leave and they should be assisted, but those wishing to stay should be able to and not be required to leave as happened with the mass evacuations.

Although electricity took some time to reach outer areas, water and sewerage services were quite quickly restored so it would have been feasible for more people to stay.

She says there were tales in southern newspapers about Darwin being no place for a woman or children. Her response:

> Lies and damned lies. There was no threat to the women left in the town, nor any threat to children other than the obvious hazard of debris, broken glass etc. For a few weeks Darwin was virtually a town without children. A town without children is a dead town and officialdom nearly accomplished what Cyclone Tracy could not do and that was to kill Darwin.

Darwin's mayor at the time of Cyclone Tracy was the colourful and eccentric but popular, Harold 'Tiger' Brennan. He had been a member of the Legislative Council for several terms, representing the electorates of Elsey, Batchelor and most recently Victoria River, which he did not re-contest at the 1971 Legco election. He had announced his intention to run for mayor at a local government election due in 1972 and was elected, succeeding Ken Waters whose short mayoralty had resulted from a by-election caused by the resignation and subsequent death of Lucius 'Bill' Richardson in November 1971.

Brennan, a portly Churchillian figure with a clipped moustache and dark-rimmed glasses, wore a pith helmet, smoked cigars and was known to like a whiskey. The story, possibly apocryphal, is that he slept through Cyclone Tracy and awoke to be surprised by what had happened to his town.

I can remember nothing significant from his term of office although Bill Fletcher says he was responsible for the installation of Darwin's first set of traffic lights at the intersection of Smith and Knuckey Streets.

Bill says after covering this event he offered 'Tiger' a lift back to the council chambers and the mayor insisted they drive through the newly commissioned traffic lights to see them in action.

In a council election later in 1975 he was succeeded by Dr Ella Stack, who would become a major force in guiding the reconstruction of Darwin through her membership of the Darwin Reconstruction Commission and, in 1979, became the first Lord Mayor of the city of Darwin.

My Cyclone Tracy

By Christmas 1974, school had broken up and Patsy was in Bali with her friend, Lyn Maschke. I couldn't go to Bali because I had used all my available leave and as a result would be working over the Christmas holidays. Eric and I were planning to have a Christmas night party and as a result our refrigerator was full. We had a ham, a turkey, substantial quantities of other food, beer, and several casks of wine on hand in preparation. Eric was to do the cooking because I was rostered to work from 10.30 a.m. to 7.30 p.m.

At that time I was producer of TV News because our regular TV Line-up, Mike Hayes, was acting Chief-of-Staff (COS), as the JIC position was now known, the regular COS, John Milbank, being on leave though still in Darwin.

Many windows still had the masking tape on them from the warnings about Cyclone Selma three weeks before, but it would be fair to say many people were a bit blasé about the threat from Tracy after Selma proved a fizzer.

Because it was Christmas and because the Bureau of Meteorology was telling us Tracy would pass to the northeast of Darwin, over Shoal Bay, about six o'clock on Christmas morning, we at ABC TV were asked not to over-dramatise the danger. As a result, while it was my lead TV news story, it was fairly low key.

As Cyclone Tracy approached, the weather took on what are now recognised as typical pre-cyclone conditions, relatively little wind, indeed sometimes eerie stillness, grey skies and almost constant drizzle. As usual, most of the members of the newsroom spent lunch at the Post Bar at the Don Hotel.

There were a variety of late afternoon business Christmas parties and I was invited to one such function, drinks from 3 o'clock at QBE Insurance where Eric was acting Manager, his boss being away on Christmas leave. I was one of the first to arrive at Eric's office, upstairs in what was then the Burns Philp building on the corner of Knuckey and Smith streets.

At one point Eric went to get extra beer from a tea room and a man came up to the office seeking to double the insurance cover on his suburban fish and chip shop. As a joke, I pretended to be the officer in charge and told him I'd be happy to make the necessary arrangements. However, I said that if any cyclone damage occurred within 24 hours, the increased insurance cover would not take effect.

He was nonplussed but before I could explain the joke, Eric came back and sent me away. He then increased the man's cover as requested. I have been told such a 24-hour period is now a standard caveat for insurance companies.

In due course, I returned to the ABC, put the news bulletin to air and then drove out to a friend's house in Jingili, not far from home, where there was to be a party.

At that time I had an MGB and I think I drove home sometime before midnight through very heavy rain, gusty winds and water on the road that was up to the door sills. I was probably inebriated and would probably have exceeded legal blood alcohol limits had they been in force at that time.

Ours was the third house in Newell Crescent with a low-level Housing Commission house on the corner, then a block where our neighbour, Bob, was in the process of building a big A-frame house. On the other side our immediate neighbour was Alf Amrein, a TV technician who had a wife and two very young sons; beyond him was Gerry Orrin, another TV Tech with a wife and several children. Directly opposite us was Bill DeVries, a Radio Technician, fairly newly arrived from Papua-New Guinea and next to him, in a block which adjoined a small park, was David Nordsvan, a presentation officer with his wife, Yvonne, young daughter and 13-day-old baby. He also had his parents and fortunately his brother, Ted, visiting.

With the rain getting heavier and the weather becoming wilder I got undressed though kept my jocks on, and went straight to bed not really concerned about the cyclone.

By this time Eric had come home. When the power inevitably failed, as it did frequently in Darwin's wet season storms, Eric was getting a bit worried so I suggested he stretch out on the double bed next to me.

It needs to be noted that during the wet many of us normally slept naked with only a sheet for cover and the overhead fans creating enough breeze to make sleep possible. And despite the storm raging outside, it was quite warm inside, at least until much later.

As the wind increased, the shaking of the house, again a normal occurrence for such houses in even mild winds, got worse and there were crashing noises as flying debris began hitting the house. Later, considering how the destruction occurred, it seems probable that the disintegration of our house began when the roof trusses for Bob's new house only delivered a day or two before and not fixed, took to the air under the force of the wind.

By the light of lightning flashes, which were virtually constant, Eric pointed to a sheet of corrugated iron hanging from the roof and swinging back and forth across the window of his bedroom. At that time we decided to retire to the bathroom which we had been told was the strongest room in the house because of its plumbing.

We had three cats which normally came and went through a window beside the front door from where I'd removed one of the metal louvres. It wasn't very good security but that didn't matter much in Darwin at that time, it being unusual to lock the doors. Patsy and I were both very attached to the cats and as one of my cyclone preparations I had replaced the missing louvre to keep the cats inside and that night had made sure they were all inside.

I went to collect the three cats from their various hiding places, gave them to Eric in the bathroom and collected a dozen cans of beer to see us through what we now expected to be a windy and noisy night.

We weren't able to talk because the wind's tempo had increased to the point where it was just a wild howling and shrieking noise added to by the sound of the house disintegrating. At some stage the window in the bathroom exploded inwards showering us with broken glass. We had spread towels over the floor because it was cold on the tiled floor.

With the roof clearly gone and the open window, rain was pouring in and the towels quickly became saturated and impregnated with broken glass.

Even though we were getting cold, the beer quickly became too warm to drink so I decided to go out to the lounge room for a bottle of Courvoisier brandy Eric had bought duty-free coming back from England. When I got to the lounge all of the glass windows were broken and rain was blowing horizontally the full length of the room. I slithered across the floor on my stomach to get the brandy from the sideboard, and returned the same way. I didn't know what was flying over my head apart from the rain. When I got back, Eric was angry with me for being so foolhardy. I don't know how long I was gone but under those circumstances it probably seemed a long time to Eric, particularly as the three cats were quite distressed and making the wailing noise they do when scared.

The cold increased and I proposed to Eric that I would make another foray out to my bedroom to get whatever warm clothes I could lay my hands on. I opened the bathroom door and started outside but it was horrifically windy and in the light of a flash of lightning I saw there were no longer any bedrooms, only the floor remained.

I had been sitting with my back to the bathroom door and my feet against the side of the bath, holding the door closed against the wind because the door catch didn't hold.

After seeing the extent of the damage to the house, I wanted to move away from the door conscious of how thin it was and how little protection it offered, so I tied the door handle to the towel rail using my Jocks. I wrapped one of the wet, cold, clammy and very scratchy towels around me to preserve my modesty. But virtually immediately the door blew open and ripped the towel rail off the wall destroying my underpants in the process. I again put my back to the door but fortunately, soon afterwards, the ceiling of the bathroom, a sheet of plaster, collapsed onto the hand basin and that served to hold the door closed. At that stage I climbed into the bath where Eric had been sitting for most of the time with the three cats. It was while we were sitting huddled in the bath, bowed down under the plaster sheet, that Eric decided I should teach him the words of *Waltzing Matilda*, which I did, or tried to, conscious that it was all a bit bizarre.

Gradually the storm abated, dawn broke and not long after this we were able to push aside the plaster to look out onto the scene of devastation which showed we were not alone in the damage we'd suffered. It was still quite windy and drizzling rain, those trees still standing were only trunks and the back yard was a sea of water littered with household wreckage that made it look like a rubbish dump.

Hiroshima and Nagasaki came to mind as I looked at what was left of the neighbouring houses. I went out to the lounge room where there was a substantial Dutch cupboard which I had made from cypress tongue and groove planks. It weighed a ton and had taken four people to carry it upstairs.

I knew my camera had been on a corner of the bench and remarkably it was still there. Although there was no longer a roof, the ceiling strangely had not fallen in although the wall from the spare bedroom had blown in and was folded down over the brick and plank bookcase which also held the TV and Stereo (Both subsequently worked with a spray of CRC but the books were all unsalvageable).

I don't know why, but I went back to the bathroom and took about three photos from the window, took three photos of ABC houses across the road then Eric and I went downstairs to climb into my MG in the hope that we would be able to warm up a bit.

The MG had a fibreglass hardtop but although the rear window had been broken by some flying debris it was otherwise undamaged. I have two photographs taken through the rear window of Eric, in leopard-print Jocks with armfuls of his sodden clothes gathered from his chest-of-drawers which was lying smashed in the mud of the front yard.

At that time, Eric was driving the office vehicle, a Ford Falcon, and it was parked in the driveway behind my car and surprisingly survived with only superficial damage.

A length of 4 x 2 timber had speared in under the bonnet, hit the rocker cover, and come out the other side between bonnet and mudguard forming a perfect V shape. Damage was minor but the distortion made it difficult to open the car's bonnet.

Not long after we moved downstairs, a person from the Emergency Services Organisation came through our block and asked us how many people were in the house? Were we alright? Did we have any injuries?

He advised that if we needed help we should go to either the nearby Casuarina High School (now Casuarina Secondary College) or the

Post cyclone photos:
Above: ABC houses across
the road with boat belonging
to newcomer, Bill De Vries.
Nordsvan house on left.

Left: From the bathroom
window: flooded rubbish tip.
Author photos.

Marrara Hotel, both of which were local rallying points. In retrospect this is a truly remarkable tribute to the Emergency Services personnel of the time.

Shortly after that and still well before eight o'clock, David Nordsvan, the ABC presentation officer from over the road came to see us. He was distressed because his family had spent a very rough night, not least because of the new baby. His house was a mirror image of mine. Where our bedrooms were at the western end, his were at the eastern end. In our house the doorway from bedrooms to lounge was pushed closed by the wind. In his case, the lounge room and kitchen were blown away and they would also have lost the bedrooms had not he and his brother Ted held the door closed, which given my own door experience must have been a nightmare few hours.

Just after sunrise on Christmas morning, Eric in jocks with an armful of sodden clothes. Author photo.

Having received the same advice from the Emergency Services person, he had tried to start his car, been unsuccessful, and wondered if Eric's car would be available to take his family to Casuarina High. We managed to remove the piece of wood and, surprisingly to us at the time, the car started immediately, so Eric took them up to the school. While Eric was away I poked around in the mud of the back yard and found my wallet, which had a very few dollars in it, and some other odds and ends.

When Eric returned, we decided we should see how friends had survived. The first were another Theatre Group member and her family who lived nearby. Their house was a ground-level brick Housing Commission house and it was virtually undamaged. Although they didn't have power, none of us did, they could make hot coffee and were also able to provide us with dry shorts and shirts, enabling me to get rid of the towel I was still wearing like a loin cloth.

Both Eric and I were smokers but had lost our cigarettes. Our friends were non smokers so I thought I would walk down to my local Jingili supermarket to get some cigarettes and a few things I thought were going to be essentials: toilet paper, soap and cat food. When I got there, the doors were open, the front windows were smashed and people were going through the shop pushing shopping trolleys and collecting food.

Montage of cyclone damage shots. Photos, Terry Fletcher.

There was a man standing near the entrance and, thinking he was somehow connected, though I didn't recognise him, I told him what I wanted. 'Help yourself', he said, 'Everyone else is'. When I collected our cigarettes, soap, toilet paper, and cat food I offered to pay. The bloke just laughed and waved his hand at the other people who were taking much more than me.

Two views by John Milbank of his and other ABC houses in Stuart Park after Cyclone Tracy.

By that time I was starting to think that as I was on duty that day, I should report to work. I walked home and started up the MG. I think I only got about 100 metres before debris on the road ripped the exhaust off the car. I climbed out, wrenched it free (it was being held by a small piece of metal) and burning my hands in the process pushed it through the missing rear window and over the front passenger seat.

I don't know how long it took to get into town, a distance of about eight miles (13 km) which normally took 15 minutes, but as I drove down Rothdale Road, a divided road, mine was the only car on the road.

Because of the debris I was forced to go from side to side, crossing and recrossing the median strip and dodging fallen power lines, steel power and light poles which were bent over, in some cases to the point where they touched the road, sheets of roofing iron and a mass of other household wreckage.

What struck me, apart from the total devastation was how difficult it was to navigate with the buildings and other signposts either destroyed or severely damaged. It made me realise how much visual cues guided me as I drove and when those visual cues disappeared or were altered, it became very confusing.

I remember driving down McMinn Street and being impressed that a huge front end loader from Housing and Construction was already out clearing debris from the road.

I arrived at the ABC sometime after 10.30 feeling guilty because I was late but also feeling I could justify being late because of the cyclone and road conditions. Who would have chastised me anyway?

John Milbank, although technically on leave, had gathered with all the other journalists at the ABC studios. It is a source of some mirth now, but indicated the degree to which I particularly, though obviously not alone, was affected by the events, that I asked him whether he thought I would have to put a TV bulletin to air that night.

I don't know how that could possibly have happened, but for me it was a serious question. Give John his due, he had a dry sense of humour so didn't answer immediately but took a long look around, a sort of wide sweep of the devastation, then said, 'I don't think so Richard'. I remember being enormously relieved.

My recollections of events over the following days are vague and non-sequential. Really just a disconnected series of events which stood out.

Early on, I found myself at a house in Edmunds Street which would later become Squires Tavern. It was occupied by media acquaintances Baz Ledwidge, photographer with the Australian Information Service, Beat Erismann, *NT News* snapper and his partner Dee and a sailing acquaintance of his, Rob Davy and his partner, Mo. Mo was a nurse and had been dispensing tetanus injections to all and sundry, so I received a shot in the arm as well.

The house had already attracted a motley collection of characters, some of them visiting media from interstate, others people whose suburban homes had been destroyed and who needed a dry place to doss for a while.

It was a situation to continue for some weeks. The house even featured obliquely in a pot boiler thriller written soon afterwards by one of the media visitors.

Dave Molesworth had a former ABC News typist, Kathy Palmer, and her two daughters, staying with him at his ABC house in Jingili. Like Eric they had also returned from England only a few days before.

The four of them went to the Marrara Hotel from where Dave was driven to hospital. He had been injured when a sheet of corrugated roofing iron flew in through a bedroom window and hit him in the side. Actually it was almost miraculous that he wasn't more severely injured. He'd been driven to the (then) Darwin Hospital to seek treatment but said when he saw the floor flooded with blood stained water and mud and the many others with injuries he considered much worse than his own, he decided to press on to the ABC.

He was walking up Mitchell St, when he was picked up by our very new casual typist a woman named Elaine who we remember chiefly because she drove a high powered panel van and had a huge Doberman.

Kathy and her girls were subsequently evacuated with the ABC wives and children.

There are two things worthy of note here.

It was the ABC's early morning journalist, Dick Muddimer who, although not rostered to work, just after dawn walked to the ABC

Photographers Beat Erismann and Baz Ledwidge outside the Edmunds Street house they shared with Rob and Mo. Photo from Ledwidge/Erismann collection.

through the tail end of the cyclone to try to get out a story about Darwin's devastation.

Finding the ABC off air, he tried Police Headquarters and the Overseas Telecommunications Commission (OTC) which operated short wave communications services to shipping. Both were also off air.

He finally walked the couple of kilometres to Blake Street, site of the television transmitters where he found the technician on duty was holding open the standby microwave bearer to Queensland for a planned Christmas Eve, in Italy, live broadcast of Pope Paul VI opening the Holy Door a Papal jubilee event dating back centuries and held every 25 to 33 years.

Dick persuaded the technician to reverse the line and allow him to get a message to the ABC in Sydney with the immortal line of one who knew, 'Darwin is a blitzed city'.

Other claims have been made since about communications with the outside world by ham radio operators, including one of the ABC's own techs, Henry Anderssen, but I believe Dick's was the first news story about the devastation of Cyclone Tracy.

Meanwhile, our film Cameraman, Keith Bushnell, had by now moved to a top floor unit in Stuart Park. He and Toni Joyce a long time friend who was staying with him at the time, sheltered in a wardrobe as the unit was un-roofed. Soon after sunrise, Keith fired up his Land

Keith Bushnell shoots his award winning cyclone footage, the first seen in Australia. Photo, Keith's neighbour.

Cruiser and persuaded a neighbour to drive him around as he filmed the devastation.

Keith says he had been filming on the RAAF base where the base commander, Wing Commander Dave Hitchins personal transport, a RAAF Dakota, was now 'resting' in his front yard. He says he asked Hitchins about transport and was told an Air Force plane would soon leave so Keith gave his packaged 400 feet or ten minutes of film, addressed to 'The ABC anywhere', to Hitchens who in turn gave it to the RAAF pilot to deliver to any ABC outlet in Australia. The pilot duly delivered and that first film is the most famous of any shot over subsequent days, months and years. Some months later it won the inaugural Thorn Award for Television News Film. Parts of the film continue to be shown whenever illustration is needed of significant cyclone damage.

John Milbank says he had a role to play in getting the film out of Darwin but notes that the commercial TV Stations down south had somehow got wind of the ABC's film and demanded access to it, which meant they actually put it to air ahead of the ABC. This was a bizarre agreement that existed at that time. If the ABC had exclusive film, the commercial stations could demand access to it, and because their bulletins were all earlier than the ABC's effectively scoop us with our own film.

181

John says it was for that reason that much later, when the East Timor situation arose in 1975, he chose not to use the RAAF to send film south, even though the less frequent commercial flights delayed its arrival causing complaints from Sydney.

Meanwhile, at the ABC there was some discussion about how to cover events though with both radio and TV off air, there was no way to broadcast local news at that time. Then word came that there was to be a press conference by the disaster leadership.

I recall Dave going off to that conference which was on Christmas Day afternoon, he says he was wearing a bloodstained Ballarat Bertie (a beer company) t-shirt. The next day, Boxing Day, Dave started to pass blood when he urinated, so two of the ABC wives, Meri Fletcher and Maxina Andrew, took him back to hospital. There it was decided he should be evacuated and he was subsequently flown to Sydney aboard a RAAF Hercules.

Back in Darwin, Dave told us he'd been in pain throughout the 10-hour flight and it was only later that it was discovered he'd also suffered damage to his vertebrae.

All of the ABC employees and their families had gathered at the ABC studios and moves were under way to evacuate the women and children, arrangements that were made by the new arrival from PNG, sports broadcaster Don Bensted, who I think effectively took control of the ABC over the top of the manager, Don Sanders, a man who while affable and generally hands off, which made him the ideal boss as far as some were concerned, had no real feel for modern broadcasting, especially TV, and was out of his depth faced with this disaster.

John Milbank subsequently told me it was ABC management in Adelaide who had chartered a Fokker Friendship aircraft to evacuate the wives and children who, I think, went at quite short notice. I went home one night and when I came back the next day, they'd all gone.

It was also Bensted who dragged two young women, English tourists, off the street and employed them to cook meals for the ABC Staff, a situation which continued, with a change of personnel or two, for more than a month with a kitchen set up in what had been the tea-room and tool store at the end of the ground floor of the radio building. It had the advantage of a door which opened onto the car

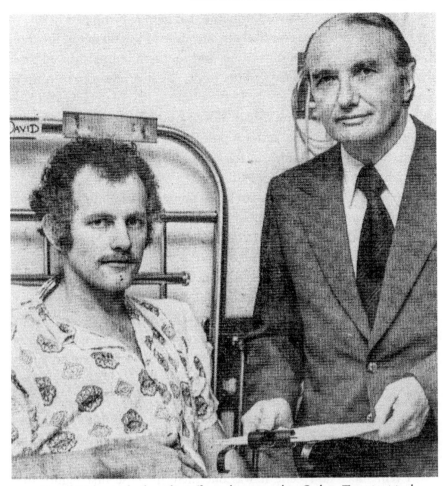

David Molesworth, the only staff member injured in Cyclone Tracy is visited
in hospital in Sydney by the ABC General Manager, Talbot Duckmanton.
Neither look impressed. From Radio Active *report,*
Graeme Halprin collection.

park between the radio and TV buildings and that was where we ate in the first days.

Later a canteen was set up on the first floor in what had, some years before, been the newsroom and this operated until about the end of January. This was run by a husband and wife team who had major arguments whenever the bloke had too much to drink, which was quite frequently. One report talks of him threatening his wife with a cleaver.

I don't think I'm alone in thinking that despite being part of one of the biggest stories I was ever likely to encounter, I was unable to function as a journalist. Southern film crews, and southern journalists took over the newsroom, leaving us very little to do. We did, however, turn up to work each day.

Most of the ABC men had moved onto the premises and were dossing down in a variety of locations: the newsroom, Keith Bushnell's hole in the wall editing suite, in Telecine or VT, Master Control, or what was then the film library.

Because of my cats, I chose to live at home and commute. I managed to salvage a single bed and dried out a mattress and sheets under the protection of the insulated main bedroom as it continued to rain on and off, it was the wet season after all.

The bed and mattress were probably from the spare room which had been my dark room and which, at the time of the cyclone, contained all of my negatives and every photograph I had taken over the previous three years.

As a result, the only pre-cyclone photos of Darwin we have are those which were in the camera, about two, and those we had sent to family and which they subsequently gave back to us.

I also found assorted pots and pans, the kitchen cupboards were untouched, so all of that equipment survived and using a salvaged table, a portable gas stove and a couple of kerosene lamps we'd used for camping, I set up home under the floorboards.

I remember how eerie it was out there in those first nights after the cyclone. The northern suburbs were virtually deserted, not only as a result of the evacuations and people's own departures by car, but also the move to community shelters, or into city offices.

Not only was there the total absence of light, there was also hardly any noise.

You get used to insect and bird sounds, a level of traffic noise, and the sound that comes from TV's, or just ordinary people noise, and this was particularly the case in Darwin where you could turn off the sound of your TV and still have a good chance of hearing the program because the neighbours' TV's would all be tuned to the same thing.

In that dystopian landscape, it was easy, especially at night, to think you were one of the last people alive on earth. Dark, quiet, the only

Author's house after Cyclone Tracy. The window visible through the triangle is the bathroom where he, Eric and the cats sheltered. Author photo.

sounds were from a distant handful of small two stroke generators which recluses like me were using for power, or the odd dog barking. The cats, meanwhile, were staying very close.

Bill Fletcher obtained a flattop truck of about three tons capacity and in the few days immediately after the cyclone a group of us went around the homes of ABC employees retrieving those household goods they hadn't salvaged themselves, or belonging to staff who were away on holidays.

Our first target, naturally, was the booze supply after which we'd concentrate on the valuables which ranged from pianos, we moved two, to camphor-wood chests, statues, paintings, favourite chairs and the like,

All of this was carted into the ABC and stored in the TV studio where the floor was marked out with masking tape delineating each family's possessions. It was a little pathetic to see a family's worldly goods confined to a six feet square patch of studio floor.

At one stage it was suggested we should break into a warehouse in Winnellie to liberate some goods which would be useful at the ABC— mostly paper towels, garbags, soap and toilet paper.

185

I liberated a large bag of dry dog food for my three cats who were all staying very close to home, obviously very spooked by what they had gone though. They were at home when I left for work and when I came back.

I have a recollection of Eric and I digging a hole in the front yard to bury the perishables from the fridge, including the turkey, which went off very quickly when we lost power. I don't know when we did this, but I do know we couldn't dig a deep hole because the ground was rock only a few inches below the surface.

The smell was fairly horrible but the prospect of flies was worse, particularly as Darwin had been unusual for its lack of the flies which were ubiquitous elsewhere in Australia, especially in summer.

Eric quickly tracked down and moved in with other friends from the Theatre Group who lived in a fairly old, but largely undamaged low level house somewhere in Winnellie.

Sometime in that first week we did the same task at the ABC with food from the fridges we collected and which were lined up in the corridor outside the TV studio.

We buried this in a trench dug in the median strip outside the ABC in Cavenagh Street. I often look at the trees growing there and think of that compost.

On Boxing Day, or maybe the day after, I was in the newsroom making yet another attempt to see if there were any telephone lines. I picked up one of the four lines we had and surprisingly got a dial tone.

It was an STD phone, that is, capable of more than just local calls, so I rang my parents in Perth. No answer, so I rang Patsy's mother, Elva, who lived in Geraldton.

She answered and I was able to give her the first message she'd received about my survival. She was very relieved. I tried my parents again without success then Bill Fletcher walked in. I told him there was a line and he should use it quickly because it might drop out. Bill rang his own parents, his wife Meri's parents and I then tried my parents again and got through to them. Not long afterwards when someone else walked in, we tried the phone but it was dead.

About the same time a telex line connection was made from what had been the Manager's office, upstairs in the radio building. We were able to keep it open more or less permanently from then on and it gave us our first direct and permanent link to the ABC Newsroom in Sydney.

It enabled us to get word stories out directly and improved our cyclone recovery coverage immensely. Bill, Dick, John Milbank and I slowly began to take responsibility for producing local news bulletins which were more often than not just a series of what would previously have been regarded as community announcements about aircraft departures, warnings to save water, and directives from Stretton or other community leaders.

Mike Hayes had driven south with his family and, we found out later, had rolled the vehicle down Mataranka way, fortunately without injuries. Keith Bushnell in his own account, notes he left a day or two after the cyclone having filmed, apart from his historic footage, what many thought was the final tribute to Darwin, a piece by Mike Hayes which included a to-camera piece of him sitting in a gutter lamenting what 'had once been a bloody good town'.

In what was a fairly magnificent effort, the radio techs had got a studio back in action and all of the other links to the transmitters, including the towers, repaired and using the emergency generator had ABC Radio back on air about midday on Boxing Day.

A group of us were sitting on the front steps of the TV building when announcer Howard Baker came on air to say that ABC Radio was broadcasting again and played the theme from the popular Australian TV series of the time, *Rush*.

It's an evocative piece of music and even now it brings tears to my eyes, as indeed it did then. I think I was crying not only for the music but also for the feeling that it meant we were back in communication with the people of Darwin, and the world.

Other communications were being restored and on Boxing Day, I think, I received a telegram from Patsy saying she would stay in Bali until she was able to come back to Darwin. I knew, though she couldn't be expected to, that it would be a long time before flights between Darwin and Bali would be restored so I sent her a telegram telling her that her travelling companion's husband, Harry Mashke and I were both alive and safe but that she should go to Perth and I would meet her or contact her there when I could.

Harry had been at the airport a day or two before the cyclone and, typical of him, had found a couple of young travellers just arrived from Asia and without accommodation so he'd taken them into his house, a privately-built elevated house in Rapid Creek. This house was virtually cleared to the floorboards and Harry told me later that he and the travellers had made a dash for the low level house next door, diving in through a smashed window.

On the way he was hit on the head by a piece of flying wood. When I saw him a few days later he told me he had come to his senses in Adelaide River with the two young travellers in his car.

When he asked what they were doing there, the young people told him they were all heading south.

Harry said there must be some mistake, he wasn't leaving, so he left them and turned around to return to Darwin. As he told it, when he got back close to Darwin there was a police road block where people were being turned back, so he went bush and drove around the road block.

When I saw him, outside the ABC, he gave me a transistor radio, one of a handful he'd scrounged, and told me I should get a tarpaulin from the council. I don't think I saw him again until we returned to Darwin at the end of January but he stayed on. I do remember thinking that he was a bit strange and I thought he'd obviously been traumatised by the cyclone and head injury. Later he told me he had the same thoughts about me.

About two days later I got another telegram from Patsy saying she would wait in Bali until I could join her. Clearly she hadn't received my telegram yet and I was getting agitated about her and about what she might be hearing.

Patsy and Lyn had just returned to Denpasar from a very peaceful few days staying at a losmen on the rim of the caldera of Mt. Batur. Their first stop had been at *Poste Restante* for mail and it was there that they first heard that Darwin had been hit by a cyclone, though they thought it was a reference to Selma several weeks before. When they learned Darwin had been devastated by Cyclone Tracy, they quickly caught a bemo to the little village of Batuan where they had been staying with the family of a Balinese teacher. They had met Agung Putra when he spent some time on exchange at Wagaman School earlier in the year.

He translated Indonesian news reports but those reports concentrated on stories like disease being rife and dogs being shot. They made contact with the owners of a yacht in Benoa Harbour who could receive shortwave radio from the BBC World Service but its coverage was mostly about cricket, a test match being played in Melbourne.

Patsy says she sent telegrams to the Red Cross, to the ABC in several states, and to the Australian Embassy in Jakarta but received no response from any of them.

Finally it was a letter and telegram from her mother which arrived ten days later on the same day as my telegram, which was marked 'National Disaster Emergency Message' and it was those messages which prompted her to fly to Jakarta and then to Perth.

She says that when they finally learned of the extent of destruction, she and Lyn began a daily routine of visiting Denpasar markets, *Poste Restante* and Merpati airline as they tried to determine their best course of action. 'Darwin kaput', the locals would tell them, throwing their hands in the air but smiling hugely.

Meanwhile I was also concerned about whether I could keep the cats alive for her although I deliberately hadn't mentioned they were alive in case I had to have them destroyed, or they died, before we were reunited.

By the end of the first week after the cyclone, probably about December 30, the ABC's Manager for South Australia, Graham Taylor, and perhaps another southern heavy or two, were able to fly in to inspect the damage.

Taylor gave us troops, the remaining local journalists, technicians, Bensted and the visiting TV crews and journalists a rah-rah speech on the forecourt at the front of the TV building saying things were now so under control that they could consider sending the southern TV crews back to their home bases, and what a magnificent job they'd done, and they could now leave things to the locals and the replacements who were being brought in on a roster basis.

Naturally, I had to stick my neck out, and probably in typical forthright manner said, 'That's all very well but what about those of us who went through it all and who are still here?'. Taylor wasn't happy with that. He fixed me with a fairly icy stare and said that was entirely a

c/- AGUNG PUTRA
BATUAN-SUKAWATI
GIANYAR BALI
31st December 1974.

Dear Mum,

Nothing else to do but check the mail each day & keep sending letters. I have had no word from Richard yet & Lyn nothing from Harry. I think it best I stay at the above address until I find out where I can join Richard. If he's staying in Darwin I might as well stay here until I can get back. If he's had to move out I can join him wherever he is or he could join me here. I'm getting impatient - it's hard just to wait - not knowing how he is or where he is. Please as soon as you know anything telegram me at above address. I can't return to Darwin by air for a month but I could get to Perth from Jakarta (on Java). We have friends at the wharf keeping eyes open for boats going to Darwin.

I have written to you already, Alex Creswick, Australian Consulate - Jakarta, ABC - Adelaide, the Darwin Relief centre - NSW & of course Richard. Have also sent him a telegram. Some of the letters must reach someone who knows where he is & how he is. We are being well looked after here but haven't been able to get much news lately. There doesn't seem to be anyone else here in our situation. I'm having some clothing made here very cheaply. My money situation is good. The cost of living is very cheap here. I'm not very good at waiting. There are many things we could do here & places to see but haven't any interest in anything except getting information about Richard.

2nd Jan. A letter today from Richard dated 21st Dec. Of course his news is completely out ddate now. Love Patsy

Letter from Patsy in Bali to her mother asking about my post cyclone situation and showing her anxiety over the lack of information.

Manager ABC South Australia, Graham Taylor addresses remaining staff
outside the TV Studios. Photographer unknown, courtesy of ABC Archives.

matter for the Chief of Staff. This was the first time any of us had been given any indication there was some course of action open to us other than just staying.

Later I asked John Milbank if I could be relieved, because I wanted to get somewhere where I could communicate with Patsy, get the cats into safety and just put some distance between me and Darwin.

While I had been staying under the house, I'd been combing through the wreckage, both in the house and in the yard, and I'd collected what I thought were the precious things I should try to save. Some of the things were mundane: kitchenware, pots, crockery, but I also found things like Patsy's engagement and wedding rings which she hadn't taken to Bali. I put her wedding ring on a leather bootlace and hung it around my neck.

I kept wearing this, at her insistence, until about six months later when I was taking part in a Cavenagh Theatre Group production in the ruins of the Theatre. I used to take it off for the performance and, on this occasion, forgot to put it on when I changed at the end of the show. That night the change room, below the stage, the only part of the theatre to remain intact, was broken into and the thieves found and took Patsy's ring.

191

Told by John Milbank I was free to leave, I decided that I would drive to Perth. By this stage Eric also wanted to get out of Darwin and his friend Howie who had done lighting for Cavenagh Theatre Group was prepared to join us. One of the ABC Announcers, Laurie Bruce, had family in Perth and that was where his wife and children would end up.

He asked me if there was any way I could take his vehicle, a Holden Ute so I said I would drive it, Eric was keen to drive my MG and Howie had a Corolla sedan about 11 years old which had lost all of its side windows, though windscreen and rear window were intact.

I loaded the ute with the goods I had salvaged, and those belongings Eric wanted to take, and we all went to Darwin High School where there was a community canteen operating, and where people like us intending to drive south, could obtain a free supply of tinned or packaged food, totally unnecessary as it turned out.

I was keen to get away but New Year's Eve was coming and both Eric and Howie wanted to stay for that.

I finally issued an ultimatum and, as a result, we left about 10 p.m., though it may have been a little later, on New Year's Eve. I suppose I have to wonder how much we had drunk. I don't think I had had an excessive amount but it was a stupid time to leave, though it did mean we would travel through the cool of the night which would benefit the cats. We each took one of them.

Banks had been offering limited services for a day or two so I was able to clean out my cheque account which had about $120 in it.

Between us we had just over $300 and I don't know how we thought that would be enough to get us to Perth but I think we were all prepared to write cheques as necessary.

We struck the first problem at what were then known as the 13-mile bends, when I had a head on collision with a car coming the other way.

Fortunately it was only wing to wing. I pulled off the road, noted that I'd lost the right hand headlight, and looked back at the vehicle I'd hit. It was also on the side of the road. Eric, who was following me, also stopped.

I am not proud of what followed but I didn't think to go back to see how the other driver had fared, or if I did, I rejected the thought. I just pulled the mudguard off the wheel, got in and drove on to a police roadblock about a quarter of a mile up the road.

While I was being processed, asked where I was going, etc, the driver of the other car pulled up having turned around and chased me. He was not only angry, he was drunk. He claimed I was on the wrong side of the road. I am not prepared to say I wasn't, though I don't think I was. However, the Holden was fairly well loaded and it certainly developed a bit of a sway at speed. The policeman on duty listened to the story. I called on Eric as an independent observer though he wasn't a very good corroborator of my claim I was on the correct side of the road.

The other chap pointed out to the cop that we were clearly in cahoots. To give him his due, the cop wanted to calm things down and insisted we exchange names and addresses. We did and I promptly lost the paper. So obviously did the other chap because I never heard from him.

Somewhere north of Pine Creek, the MG had a puncture and as the spare may have been a dud I think Howie had to go into the nearest town to buy a new tyre which took most of my money.

The first experience we had of the incredible support network which had grown up outside Darwin was at Pine Creek where we were directed to the community hall and given food, a voucher for fuel and the offer of clothing. We refuelled and drove on to Katherine arriving before daylight. By this stage it was obvious the cats were going to travel with difficulty, even at night they were feeling the heat and showing signs of distress. In those days our cars weren't air-conditioned.

We waited in Katherine until the hospital opened and I asked for some sort of a sedative I could give the cats for the next stage of the journey to Kununurra. Again we were directed to a community area where we could get food and fuel vouchers. This became the norm for the rest of the trip.

It was becoming clear that we were ill-prepared for such a journey. The Holden was starting to burn a lot of oil and Howie's tyres were not too good. The MG's spare was useless and the exhaust pipe, which Howie had attempted to fix before we left, was becoming so noisy Eric was wearing ear protectors.

We also had a variety of other minor technical problems. It soon became clear too that travelling in convoy was going to make it a slow trip. We couldn't seem to coordinate our stops so when one needed to stop, we all stopped, and each stop became longer.

Travelling west. Rest stop, Eric with Boodie Cat, and Howie. Author photo.

Late in the afternoon we were close to Kununurra but the Holden's oil level was so low that the warning light was glowing all the time, even though I was by that time using the heaviest grade of oil.

We decided I would stop and that Howie and Eric would take the three cats to Kununurra and try to get them on an MMA flight to Perth, consigned to my parents.

They would then return with more oil for me, or if necessary, tow me into Kununurra. They returned about two hours later in very high spirits.

Arriving in Kununurra they'd gone to the airport and consigned the cats to Perth.

This had taken another slab of money but then they'd been directed to the town oval or community hall where they had to register and were asked what they needed. They'd mentioned money and were immediately reimbursed the money it had cost to send the cats south. They were also given vouchers for accommodation, meals and for any necessary repairs to all of the cars.

In Kununurra again we booked into the motel using the voucher, had a shower and a meal, then I got in touch with a chap I had met

Evacuation drive. Three cars at Fitzroy Crossing. Author with ute, Howie's Corolla, Eric with MG. Photo by Howie, author's collection.

previously through relatives of both Patsy and mine who'd lived in Kununurra a few years before.

He immediately organised a party for us and we all got very drunk.

It turned out he also worked for the town's biggest car dealer and as a result our work vouchers became a complete bearing and diff job on the Holden, a full set of new tyres for Howie's Corolla and a couple of new tyres and some other work for the MG.

We left Kununurra two days later in virtually rejuvenated vehicles. At every centre down the west coast we were given the same sort of treatment: accommodation, food, fuel and any necessary repairs. It was magnificent and a terrific job on the part of the WA Department of Community Services and the people who helped us.

The trip took a total of ten days. Only isolated memories remain: of the caravan set up at the junction where the Broome road left the Northern Highway and where we turned up to be told by the emergency services officer manning it that we were late (he had radio information about all of those on the road. We explained we'd had to stop at an Aboriginal mission to again make yet more repairs to the exhaust of the MG); of being embarrassed about sleeping in a luxury hotel room in

Broome when our only clothes were starting to get a bit grubby; of driving flat-out over a black soil plain south of Halls Creek, at night, ahead of a rain storm we knew would turn the road to a quagmire (Howie had a Cibie Super Oscar spotlight on his car while I was missing one headlight so I drove to the right and just behind him with Eric behind me and we tore across the plain in a tight bunch, that one huge light illuminating the road ahead for a kilometre); of coming over the crest of a hill at 70 mph to see Howie in his windowless Corolla easing through the water over a floodway below and unable to stop, overtaking him in the creek sending a huge wave of water right through his car (I stopped and while I sympathised, thought it very funny. Howie was very pissed off, mostly because he thought I'd flooded his cassette player. I hadn't, fortunately).

We finally split up at Geraldton where I stayed with Patsy's mother, Elva, while Howie and Eric took advantage of the community facilities.

Elva told Patsy later she had been forced to wash some of my clothes, salvaged from the mud around our house, four times to get them clean. Among those salvaged items was a double sided hand stitched quilt made by Elva which Patsy has to this day.

It was probably about five o'clock the next morning when the phone rang. It was Patsy. She had just arrived at my parents' home in Perth after the flight from Jakarta and was expecting, or hoping, that I would be at her mother's place

By this stage it was about two and a half weeks after the cyclone.

As soon as I decently could I left Geraldton and arrived at my parents' home later that day. I was met by a gaunt Patsy who was recovering from dysentery and was very emaciated. We were, naturally, very glad to see each other. And all three cats were alive.

Having left Darwin, I thought I would not go back. I could have gone back to a job at ABC Perth had I wanted, or indeed one in Adelaide. The News Editor offered us all the opportunity of placements elsewhere if we wanted them, and I was prepared to look on Darwin as an interesting episode, but a closed chapter in my life.

However, Patsy was adamant that she was going back to Darwin, it was her home and she needed to see what had happened.

Because there was a permit system in force for a return to Darwin, we had to be able to demonstrate that we had necessary work, and a place to

Australian Department of Social Security

This is to certify that the bearer was a resident of Darwin on 25th December 1974.

PLEASE RENDER EVERY ASSISTANCE POSSIBLE.

NAME ..RICHARD..A..CRESWICK..

STREET ..22..SHAW..ROAD...

SUBURB WANNERROO..

NAME OF SPOUSE: PATRICIA ·   NO. OF CHILDREN ....

For further enquiries telephone 20-3386 or call at 5th Floor Mt.Newman House, 200 St.George's Tce, Perth.

DIRECTOR

Author's cyclone assistance pass issued by the Western Australian Government.

live. Communications were being restored and we were able to ring Harry Mashke and ask him if he could offer us temporary accommodation.

It amounted to a mosquito net and mattress on his Berrimah factory floor but the officials didn't need to know that. The ABC arranged my return and we began the task of trying to get a permit for Patsy.

This meant going into Perth's St George's Terrace, to an office where permits were issued. This office made contact with employers in Darwin and made judgments about issuing permits based on the response from Darwin.

We had quickly confirmed that there was work for Patsy in Darwin and she was approved for return but we couldn't translate that into a permit being issued in Perth. After a couple of days of being fobbed off, and with my departure date approaching, we were in the office again, and again being told there was no permit for us when Patsy started to cry in frustration. She then suggested with some acerbity that the official get on the phone immediately and demand to talk to someone in Darwin while we waited. He got straight through, spoke to someone who, as it happened, knew Patsy and that she had been confirmed for a permit and authorised its immediate issue. Unfortunately the first aircraft seat was only available the day after my flight but it didn't matter because we were going back.

I arrived in Darwin on 30 January 1975 and Patsy a day later, just one day short of three years after we had first arrived. Recovery and

Patsy gets her first look at her former home. Author photo.

rebuilding of Darwin was slow but took place in a spirit of camaraderie which can best be found when people share adversity.

There were many wonderful moments, particularly in the first year, and a lot of exciting things but also some which created considerable anger or frustration.

I have talked often of Cyclone Tracy as a peak experience, not one I would happily undergo again, but one which I am glad to have experienced. That seems to be a feeling shared by some who experienced it but for others it remains a deeply traumatic event. Nobody knows what long-term scars might linger as a result of going through what was undoubtedly a very stressful event.

No survivor I know doesn't get twitchy whenever winds start to strengthen and some sounds, like the rattle of loose corrugated iron or the cyclone warning signal, they make me feel very uncomfortable.

Having survived Tracy, there is a feeling of invincibility but there is also the knowledge that Darwin, and building construction, are very different from what they were 47 years ago. We are better prepared for such an event.

Bill Fletcher's recollections

'I transferred from the ABC Hobart office to Darwin in January 1971. I was a new appointment prior to the introduction of television to Darwin in August.

'I was allocated a house at 7 Blake Street, Gardens Hill. The street led to the PMG transmitter and end of the microwave link from Mt Isa to Darwin yet to be built. The original ABC radio offices were also in that street.

'The house was built in the late 1950s and had originally been the manager's house until he moved to a new residence in Larrakeyah.

'In late November 1974, our house was scheduled for minor repairs and repainting. We were required to move out but as there was nowhere to put us, a caravan was hired from one of the news typists, Mary Fraser and placed on the block. We used the facilities in the house but slept in the caravan.

'The work was being done by a Department of Works day labour gang. We were promised everything would be completed before Christmas, but they didn't quite make it. Our possessions were stored in the storeroom under the house and largely survived intact.

'On Christmas Eve there were six of us in the house: me, wife Meribeth (Meri), son Simon, aged 3, son Dhugal, 11 months, my brother Terry who had been working in the NT during his university vacation and a friend from Papua New Guinea, Martin Raurela.

'Although there was a Christmas party at the ABC, I left work after the 7 p.m. TV news as I wanted to see the latest forecast and realised that a major cyclone was going to pass near the city.

'The first sheets of corrugated iron came off the roof sometime after 10.30 p.m. and we filled the bath with water as instructed and moved in there with some food for the children. Luckily it was a large bathroom and we were all able to fit without trouble.

'The house disintegrated around us and in the morning all that was left was the structure around the bathroom/toilet. We were all okay apart from being very cold and wet. The caravan was also relatively undamaged and quite liveable. A large wooden window frame had fallen on one end and kept it from moving or blowing away. A very large mango tree on the adjoining block about 10 metres away was no longer there.

'On Christmas morning we emerged from the wreckage after the wind and rain had stopped, about 6 o'clock or 6.30 not believing what we saw: houses had vanished, powerlines were down and the poles twisted beyond belief.

'Shortly after this, Dick Muddimer called by and came to check that we were all okay. As previously mentioned, Dick had walked from his flat in Stuart Park and was on his way to the Blake Street transmitter to see if he could get a message out to Sydney that Darwin had been destroyed. He called in again later to say he had got the message out to a PMG technician in Mt Isa who had promised to relay it to Sydney, which he did. After that Dick walked into the office in Cavenagh Street to see what had survived and to start work.

'We cleared away the debris from around the caravan and Meri was also able to get something to eat for us all. My car was under the house, surrounded by debris and with a large piece of timber through the rear window.

'About half-past-nine Mike Hayes arrived in his Mini Moke and we went into the office to see what could be done. The streets were covered in debris and it was a slow journey.

'When we got there, we saw John Milbank and Dick Muddimer plus a number of other staff who had spent the night in the radio building which was intact apart from some broken windows. That building had a generator so all was relatively good.

Opposite: Bill Fletcher's house with virtually undamaged caravan. Photo, Bill Fletcher

Right: ABC Reporter, Dick Muddimer, in this photo training for the annual NT News Walkabout. Photographer unknown, possibly NT News.

'There was no emergency generator for TV but the trailer mounted OB generator was hooked up to provide lighting and later for the refrigerators that were salvaged.

'Without phones or telex machines there was some discussion about what we should do and Mike Hayes and myself were given the job of checking on ABC staff in their houses around the city and looking for stories to send out as soon as we got some communications back.

'We set off in the ABC Land Cruiser and spent several hours checking on staff and their houses though with all recognisable landmarks destroyed locating those houses was difficult.

'Rumours were already spreading like wildfire. The most prevalent being that the cyclone had done a U-turn and was heading back and that large numbers of people had been killed in buildings just around the corner.

'We were able to reassure people that the cyclone was not coming back and checked out the numerous alleged deaths stories only to find they were untrue. People had certainly been injured but we didn't come across any deaths on that trip. Many people told us they were packing up and leaving town with whatever possessions they could recover.

'Returning to the office we found there were still no communications and we learnt there was an emergency meeting of senior public servants, police and others at police headquarters in Mitchell Street.

'Mike and I went there and much to our surprise we were allowed in, maybe because we were from the ABC. During the discussions we were able to tell them we had just spent time in the northern suburbs and that many people were packing up their possessions and leaving town. This confirmed some of their own information and plans were made to assist them by providing free fuel, car repairs to keep people moving, and food and clothing through community groups and organisations such as the Salvation Army down the track.

'Returning to the office, Mike started writing up a story on what we had seen and I was pondering how we were going to get it south. About this time a good friend and assistant harbour master, Captain Colin Wood, came by to tell me his wife Jenny had been killed when out in the yard trying to retrieve a pet dog. Their two children were in the house and unscathed.

'He had spent the night at the wharf dealing with shipping problems including the Navy patrol boat HMAS *Arrow* hitting the wharf.

'He also told me the West Australian state ship *Nyanda* had berthed that morning and was in radio contact with Perth. He suggested we see Captain Roy Marsh who might be able to get a message out for us.

'We did this and while a little dubious at first, he asked the radio operator to send our news story to Perth for us on the ship's radio. A thorough gentleman, he also offered us something to drink, a meal and a shower. I think we accepted the cold beer and meal. We must have looked a sight in old clothes and looking rather scruffy after our activities throughout the day.

'We went back to the Studio and found more staff had arrived along with their families including Meri, our children, brother Terry and friend Martin.

'The TV studio and other offices were converted into dormitories with mattresses on the floor. Being Christmas everyone had big stocks of food and these were brought into the office.

'Fridges and freezers were quickly retrieved from houses and lined up along the corridor in the TV building. A few were filled with beer.

'Some of the wives had organised themselves and the rec room in the radio building into a makeshift kitchen. I particularly remember Dawn Yates and Gail Watson but there were others as well. We all got something hot to eat and slept in the TV building.

'Some of the ABC houses were destroyed while others suffered relatively minor damage.

ABC TV studios post cyclone. Note people on the roof. Photo courtesy of ABC Archives.

'Those who could, stayed in their homes but the ABC studios were a better option for most as there was some power, showers, toilets and a dry roof over our heads.

'Either that night or the next morning we were told ABC wives and children were to be evacuated by Fokker Friendship aircraft to Adelaide as soon as possible. The aircraft brought in the ABC's South Australian

203

manager Graham Taylor, a relief journalist and other essential personnel required in Darwin. We were told at the time, the ABC management wanted existing staff to get back to work until sufficient relief staff could be brought in and there was no chance of that happening while wives and children were around.

'On Boxing Day, most of the wives and children were flown out. A few of the wives who did not want to leave their husbands stayed behind to help feed the remaining staff. I said goodbye to Meri and the boys not knowing when we would see each other again. She wanted to be safe and get out of Darwin with the kids but at the same time wanted to stay.

'Some of the newsroom direct lines started working intermittently and it was a matter of picking up each one to see if there was dial tone. Sometimes they only worked for a few minutes and at other times until you hung up and then went dead.

'Manager Don Sanders had a friend who owned a trucking business and a couple of us went to Winnellie to pick up a flat top truck. We spent part of each day visiting the homes of staff who had been on leave and salvaged what we could for them. It turned out not to be a lot. What we did find was stored in the TV Studio.

'The rest of the time we went about covering the stories of the day.

'Film was still being shot and entrusted to flight crew or a passenger to hand over to an ABC staff member in whichever city the plane landed. To the best of my recollection, it was all safely delivered.

'It would be fair to say we were all in shock and there was little enthusiasm for work. Decades later someone told me we all probably had PTSD but that hadn't been invented yet.

'Barry Hamilton, the husband of one of our news typists Margaret, was a builder and he was quickly put to work to make temporary repairs to the houses that had received relatively minor damage such as broken louvres and holes in the cement sheet cladding to make them secure as much as to stop squatters moving in.

'Relief technical staff, journalists and cameramen and women, were arriving as flights permitted and Darwin staff flown out on leave as they were replaced. Many never returned.

'No such plan was in place for journalists and it came to a head when Richard Creswick asked SA manager Graham Taylor at the daily briefing séance when journalists would be relieved? A rather flippant reply of: 'that was up to the News Department', was received.

'John Milbank, the JIC, was put in a difficult position. I don't remember exactly what transpired but Mike Hayes left by car soon after and I flew to Adelaide.

'I remember standing up in a Hercules transport all the way to Adelaide where I was met by the news editor, Mark LeNevez, for a briefing on Darwin before flying on to Melbourne and then Hobart the next day. David Molesworth had been evacuated injured days earlier.

'Dick Muddimer regarded Darwin as his home and returned to his flat in Stuart Park refusing to leave. Although the entire complex of three flats was un-roofed, Dick obtained a parachute from an aviator friend, Ossie Osgood, and with help stretched it over his unit giving some waterproofing until a navy crew re-roofed the flats some weeks later.

'On New Year's Day, my brother and a friend drove out in my car to Tasmania. Once there my car was condemned as the rear roof pillars had cracked and it was unrepairable. As for my PNG friend, Martin Raurela, the ABC helped repatriate him to Port Moresby three or four days after Christmas. In those days strict conditions were imposed on PNG residents leaving the country and severe penalties applied if they did not return on time. Being an old PNG hand, Graham Taylor understood this and helped to get Martin repatriated.

'A New Year's Eve party was held in the radio building rec room and a good but subdued time was being had by all until at some point an already broken window was kicked and the sound of breaking glass brought festivities to an abrupt end.

'I was glad to be leaving Darwin but had every intention of coming back. Meri's first words to me were, 'When are we going back home to Darwin?'. It took a couple of months but we managed to get there.

'One or two things which brightened our day: after a few days a hotel manager came to the office to see if we had any communications down south and if it was possible for him to make an urgent phone call.

'There was no one around so we agreed and in return he told us that the hotel fridges were to be cleaned out and the contents dumped in the next day or so. If we wanted to grab a few cartons we were welcome to do so.

New Year's Eve, 1974. (l to r) Ian marshall, Graeme Halprin, Leigh
Halprin (not ABC), Jim Eustice, Rodger Andrews, Bruce Watson, Alf
Amrein, David Nordsvan. Photo Graeme Halprin collection.
Photographer unknown.

'A bunch of us duly arrived in the trusty truck the next day and filled some garbage bags with beers and then got them to drinking temperature in the fridges in the TV building corridor.

'As New Year's Eve approached, our supplies were dwindling and it was noted that there were pallets of the stuff outside the Information Centre building in Smith Street where the NSW police contingent was headquartered. This group was not well regarded by the populace, not least because they wore guns and that was an unusual sight on Darwin's streets. A plan was hatched to borrow some of their beer. The truck was backed up the driveway, some cartons were thrown on and we departed very quickly around the corner into the ABC. Not a sound was heard from the NSW boys in blue. Maybe they didn't see us or didn't care.'

The *NT News*

Having long since moved from the Tin Bank, the *NT News* operated from new premises in Mitchell Street, adjoining the new Police Headquarters but like so many businesses, its premises, and consequently its equipment had suffered severe cyclone damage.

In subsequent days a couple of small newsletters with limited distribution had been produced but on New Year's Eve, a four page special edition announced, '*The News* is back', apologised for missing the last few days and promised a gradual increase in size and coverage as equipment and communications were restored.

Its main front-page story, headed 'We're getting on top!', quoted Supreme Commander of the cyclone disaster relief organisation, Major-General Alan Stretton telling a press conference Darwin had made an almost miraculous recovery from the Christmas Day (sic) devastation caused by Cyclone Tracy.

At that press conference he reported about 10 per cent of Darwin had been reconnected to electricity, air evacuations had reached 23 500 with the population reduced to his target of about 10 000, 80 per cent of the city's roads had been largely cleared of debris and rubble, entry permits would be needed by anyone trying to enter the Darwin area by air or road from two days later, January the first, and on that same day normal air services would resume.

The *NT News* reported Stretton's announcement that he would postpone New Year's Eve celebrations until two days later, saying he was trying to avoid a situation in which some groups would get sufficient liquor to get them in a riotous state and we would have a situation which might bring the people of Darwin into confrontation with the police.

Stretton said such a situation would be something that would break his heart.

He said he had been:

> ... plagued by garbos in the streets and everyone and asked about this and when I've explained my position to them they all agree with me.

Clearly he hadn't consulted many Darwinites.

Stretton said the State of Emergency would end on January 1, two days later, when he would hand over the warrant that gave him supreme powers to the Governor-General, Sir John Kerr. At the same time, the administration of Darwin would revert to the Department of the Northern Territory.

Front page of NT News *first post cyclone edition, four pages, December 31, 1974. This is a later reprint. Author's collection.*

Major General Stretton's much reported raid on the law court of Chief Magistrate, David McCann with photograph, was featured on the back page with a pointer to the full story, and his apology, inside.

The rest of the back page was taken up with sport including an expectation Australia would win the third test against England in Melbourne; the sloop *Love and War*, had been declared provisional handicap winner of the Sydney to Hobart yacht race and second seeded John Newcombe had scraped into the semi final of the $70 000 Australian Open tennis championship.

Dave Molesworth, a cricket tragic, notes that the third test being played at Melbourne's MCG was abandoned due to rain on day five and replaced by a limited overs match which was later recognised as the first ever ODI (One Day International).

Other cyclone related stories included Prime Minister Whitlam's announcement of an interim Darwin Reconstruction Commission until a statutory DRC could be set up when Parliament resumed in February; Co-ordinator of Emergency Services, Ray McHenry telling those who weren't willing to work to get out of Darwin; an item noting 13 children had died in the cyclone; reports of both Army and Navy relief efforts and a report that, following his stay in Darwin the Minister for Northern Australia, Dr Rex Patterson, would be calling for all new houses in Darwin to have storm proof underground shelters.

Departures

By New Year's Day almost all of the Darwin staff had either been flown, or had driven out and apart from Dick Muddimer and a couple of radio techs, relief staff were running what radio services there were.

Keith Bushnell says he had been told on Christmas Day by the National News Editor that his services were no longer required, which would seem to have been somewhat pre-emptive and though he and his friend Toni hung around for a few days staying first in his editing room and then in his caravan, both were wet so they then drove south. Along the way Keith shot film of various refugee relief centres which he delivered to the ABC in Adelaide on arrival.

Toni has her own memories of those first few days where she and Keith first shared a tabletop covered in newspapers in the newsroom, then a night in Keith's caravan. She remembers a wonderful shower in rain from the caravan roof falling into a tinny alongside.

Of the drive down south, both recall a great roadside lunch (or was it breakfast?) of everything taken from the fridge cooked by Keith on a piece of corrugated iron found by the roadside over an open fire, accompanied by a bottle of Beaujolais (or was it sparkling burgundy?) kept chilled in an esky with ice from the ABC Christmas party.

Keith has a memory of a telephone booth beside the road at Elliott with a queue of people wanting to call south. He says the phone line was open and an operator was asking people to keep their calls to two or three minutes. He says he rang his parents, told them all was well, asked them to pass a message to Toni's parents and hung up within a minute.

Toni remembers their next, and last, stop was for lunch and a shower at a school in Port Augusta 'with all supplies, food, toiletries, clothes if needed, free for those of us on the refugee trail'. She believes they arrived in Adelaide about December 30 or 31 and had some sort of New Year's Eve of which she has absolutely no recall.

How many died?

One perennial debate surrounds the number of deaths in Cyclone Tracy. Anyone looking at the scale of the destruction caused by Tracy could be forgiven for wondering why the death toll was not much higher than the officially recorded 71 deaths. Over the intervening years there have been a number of claims of mass graves, of trucks carrying bodies leaving Darwin but such reports have always come to nothing. Those who claim to have seen such things go into smoke when asked to provide proof, as I have personally found.

Two years after the cyclone I was told of a man who claimed to have been part of such an exercise. I guaranteed him every level of anonymity but nothing came of it.

Throughout 1975, we at the ABC would receive requests from regional offices across the southern states asking us to confirm claims by Noel 'Bluey' Harvey, a former Darwin *NT News* journalist, that the Darwin cyclone death toll was 250 to 300, or five to six times the official toll at that time, that he personally had helped local firemen to load 52 bodies on a truck, and other outlandish claims. We always referred them to the official figures.

Harley was apparently offering himself as a dinner speaker to Rotary Clubs, one hesitates to suggest, for the free meal. His claims prompted a question to the then Minister for the Northern Territory, Doctor Rex Patterson in questions without notice on 6 March 1975.

Hansard reports the Member for Brisbane, Manfred Cross, asked about a published article in which (Harley) had claimed the large death toll, to have loaded bodies on a truck but went further and wrote of babies being torn from their mothers arms, that eight police officers had gone missing, and that men had tied bandages around their legs and were limping in attempts to gain priority on evacuation flights.

In repeating the official death toll, the Minister said Harley's story about loading bodies on a truck required investigation because, as Minister, he should have been told. He called the babies from mothers' arms claim a possible exaggeration and described the story of police absconding as a slur on both Territory police and firemen who had done a magnificent job.

Minister Patterson said he understood that people seeing the devastation of Darwin would not be surprised if they were told 1000 deaths had occurred but the facts were that (at that time) only 49 bodies had been found and the Minister said he could vouch for it because on Christmas night he had been in the Darwin police station. He said he would put the matter in the hands of the Attorney-General because people were entitled to know the truth.

A number of lives were lost at sea with their names not added to the victims list for some years.

To my knowledge those claims by Harley have never been substantiated and in the intervening years many people involved with managing the victims have denied all such reports, instead noting that from very soon after the cyclone, makeshift morgues were operating in several places.

These included the police headquarters building in Mitchell Street and the Post Office at Casuarina, where comprehensive photographic and other records were made of the dead, they were identified where possible, and they were given a dignified burial at Darwin Cemetery in McMillan's Road.

1975 and all that

I had planned to close off this story with the effects of Cyclone Tracy because the aftermath of that event effectively took our Darwin television output almost back to what it was in the very earliest days of 1971.

However, there was to be more to the story for the ABC and, as it turned out, 1975 was a significant year in a number of ways, not just for the ABC but for Darwin and, subsequently, Australia.

A second emergency generator for the TV building meant power could be provided to get both radio and television signals to transmitters.

Radio, which at that time operated only on the amplitude modulation (AM) band, came back on air after just 34 hours offline, an amazing tribute to technical staff given the scale of damage to the town. Rodger Andrews was just one of many to comment on the eerie effect of being able to sweep the needle across the entire radio spectrum and not hear a sound.

Even Radio Australia, which had been a mainstay of radio service delivery not only to outback Australia but to millions overseas, had been put off the air with the destruction of its transmission masts across Darwin Harbour on the Cox Peninsula.

After some time short-wave transmissions resumed using transmission masts at Shepparton in Victoria until Darwin's masts and facilities were eventually restored in 1986 with programs resuming in 1988.

Early on, the decision was made to take a television service on relay through the Broadband Microwave link from Brisbane, Queensland, though this service went via an ABC regional station in Townsville.

By early February those evacuated journalists who had decided to return were back in Darwin, including John Milbank, David Molesworth, Bill Fletcher and me. Dick Muddimer, of course, hadn't left.

Our casual staff member, Barbara James, would soon be let go, there being perceived to be no need for such a position any more. She became Executive Officer to the Environment Centre and later a noted historian and author.

Our technical staff had managed to get some television capacity restored by mid February 1975 but it was still in monochrome and some of the ABC Network by that time was already broadcasting in colour with the rest scheduled to follow.

Rodger Andrews:

> The TV Studio building withstood the onslaught very well with only superficial damage. The equipment was still intact so we could have put TV to air very quickly but with most of the Darwin region without power, a situation that was to last weeks and, in some cases, months, the decision was made to evacuate all TV staff, mothball the equipment and wait and see.
>
> To maintain a radio service, fresh people were flown in and replaced in cycles until some normality was re-established. A number of announcers who had previously served in Darwin were among those who returned for short or long relief periods including Tom Blackburn, and Bill Mudie.
>
> When power was restored, Telecom were able to provide a television service from the Southern States using the Broadband Microwave link and some months later this became a colour service from Brisbane. But the Darwin studio was still monochrome and there was resistance to mixing black and white with colour.

Taking a service from Queensland meant that Darwin only had the same opportunities for local input as Queensland regional stations, in our case Townsville, namely a seven-minute window for local news leading up to the Queensland state news now going to air at 6.30 p.m. Darwin time.

Keith Bushnell's film processing equipment having disappeared off his balcony and presumed destroyed in the cyclone, meant that any film shot locally had once again to be sent south for processing and editing with the story coming back to us a couple of days later. This limited and much resented situation was to last until 1980.

One aspect of the cyclone that exercised a few people's minds was why there had been so few Aboriginal casualties, no deaths and few reported injuries.

It was suggested in some quarters that they must have had some special knowledge which forewarned them of the potential impact, longer stalks on the mangoes perhaps, or heightened activity by the green ants.

In March 1975, I was at Bagot Reserve for a ceremony marking the completion of rehabilitation of some housing and had an opportunity to put that question to one of the community's elders. 'Nah. We just listened to that ABC radio you know,' was his reply. Vindication, if any was needed, of the value of our services.

The reconstruction of Darwin—debacle and redemption

The damage of Cyclone Tracy and particularly its destruction of an estimated half of all houses and mild to severe damage to all but a small percentage of the rest, amply demonstrated the poor standard of previous housing construction.

The issue of addressing building standards was one of the reasons for early and frustrating delays by the Darwin Reconstruction Commission.

Having seen the destruction with his own eyes, Whitlam announced early in February 1975 the appointment, by legislation, of the Darwin Reconstruction Commission which would be tasked with oversighting the rebuilding of the city in a period of five years. It ultimately accomplished it in three years though not without a lot of frustration.

The DRC, as it was known, rapidly became a focus for anger and resentment by the Darwin populace and its leaders. Goff Letts called it:

> A bizarre assemblage of consultants, advisers, designers, engineers and sociologists, few with any knowledge or understanding of the Territory (who) raided the public coffers for a year for little real gain.

He said local planners were perfectly capable of supervising the town's reconstruction.

Dawn Lawrie, like Goff Letts, also had some harsh words for the Darwin Reconstruction Commission:

> Although the citizens whose lives were to be vitally affected were compulsorily excluded from their city, a barrage of politicians, advisors and consultants descended on poor Darwin like one of the seven plagues of Egypt.
>
> There was to be a new Darwin, a new grand plan, decided by experts without having to bother about

214

the opinions of bothersome citizens. Darwin being Darwin, things didn't quite work out that way. Those who could were making what temporary repairs they could but when it came to rebuilding in earnest they received a rude shock: many found their blocks had been rezoned for some other purpose and there was to be a new building code but until that was finalised no rebuilding could start.

The need for a new building code was recognised but the declaration of surge areas where there was to be no rebuilding, or limited rebuilding proved unworkable because people refused to consider surrendering their block and anyway the government didn't have enough money to adequately compensate all those in the surge zones.

Referring to her formation of the first residents' action group in her electorate of Nightcliff, Ms Lawrie said she had initially proposed it as a getting together of local residents remaining in Darwin to provide self-help and social exchange but within a week they found it necessary to start fighting officialdom.

All we wanted to do was rebuild and we realised we needed help to do that. The Prime Minister had promised that Darwin would be rebuilt and we naively expected that would mean access to low interest finance, bulk materials and skilled labour.

What we received instead was a DRC with a preponderance of southern commissioners which insisted on concentrating on the replanning of Darwin.

The first Chairman appointed to the DRC was Sir Lesley Thiess, head of the giant construction corporation bearing his name. He lasted just eight weeks.

He was followed by Tony Powell, former chairman of the National Capital Development Commission (NCDC) who, it was believed, wanted to recreate Darwin in the image of the Canberra whose design he had a large part in.

He lasted a bit longer but it wasn't until late in 1975 with the appointment of Arch Jones as General Manager and former long-serving Labor Brisbane Lord Mayor, Clem Jones as Chairman that real progress began. Darwin's

Outgoing Mayor, Tiger Brennan hands the chain of office to his successor,
Dr Ella Stack. NT Government photographer collection, NT Lbrary

own mayor, Dr Ella Stack, who had succeeded Tiger Brennan, was also one
of the few locals appointed to the Darwin Reconstruction Commission
and is credited with contributing to some of its successes.

Apart from being very slow to develop the new housing building
codes it was believed a new city would need, there were also some
proposals which enraged the locals including a proposal to ban all
building in what was known as the Primary Surge Zone, a zone which
would be inundated if a cyclone coincided with a time of very high tides,
but which just happened to include much of the most desirable real
estate in Darwin.

There was also a proposal that housing along both sides of the town
and suburban main roads would be compulsorily acquired so that dam
like bund walls could be constructed, the theory being that these walls,
suitably treed, would deflect cyclonic winds above house height.

Again those potentially affected by this plan were outraged.

Throughout Darwin and suburbs community action groups were
formed, three prominent being in Darwin itself, led by Dr Ella Stack,
soon to be elected Mayor; at Nightcliff, formed by Dawn Lawrie and at
Parap.

In the meantime, with Major General Stretton now departed, restoration of services and rebuilding efforts were being overseen by a group of community leaders led by Ray McHenry who was now referred to as 'El Supremo' and which included Police Commissioner, Bill McLaren, Director of Health, Charles Gurd, Director of Housing and Construction, George Redmond and Majority leader Goff Letts among others.

This group managed the various projects that had been set in train by Stretton, including the restoration of power involving the rebuilding of hundreds of kilometres of distribution lines across the city and suburbs, the massive re-roofing effort mounted by the Navy, and other building works undertaken by the Army and as accommodation became available, a workforce of tradesmen from interstate.

Somewhere to live

With some tardiness in the house rebuilding program, the Government imported large numbers of caravans and demountable buildings which were either given free to residents for location on their blocks or, in the case of demountables, placed two to a block.

One aspect of the rehabilitation involved the wholesale clearing of the damaged houses across the worst hit northern suburbs. Radio announcements would advise residents which section of a suburb would be cleared a few days hence so former residents could comb their blocks for any items of sentimental or other value they could find. Sometimes Navy staff would provide assistance in such searches if requested, particularly if heavy lifting was needed.

In due course two huge front-end loaders linked by a chain would drive down parallel streets drag clearing anything in their paths: fences, vegetation, house piers, dance floors, as the bare floorboards were known, everything.

Huge mounds of the debris were piled in the streets to be transferred to trucks and taken to various dumps, but not before they had been picked over by enterprising would-be builders and scavengers.

Our house in Jingili was one to suffer that fate after our return and Patsy spent a lot of time combing the wreckage before it happened.

The unit in Eden Street the day we moved in and squatted February 2 or 3, 1975, with the little Datsun ute. Author photo.

I have already obliquely referred to our post-cyclone return to Darwin at the end of January 1975 but after two uncomfortable nights in Harry Maschke's workshop, Patsy and I decided we might be better off trying to live in the wreckage of our home so I obtained a big tarpaulin and with the help of colleagues Dave Molesworth and Dick Muddimer, proceeded to tack it under the floorboards, a fundamental mistake. Naturally it rained, the floorboards above leaked, the tarpaulin filled with water and ripped to shreds.

It was then that Dick Muddimer pointed out that the group of three flats in Stuart Park, of which he occupied the middle one, had been re-roofed by the Navy and those on either side, a one bedroom and a two bedroom had been abandoned by their renters, so we should move in and essentially become squatters.

We chose the single bedroom unit, it having fewer walls from which to remove mould, and moved our meagre salvaged possessions in. Not long afterwards Dave Molesworth, our former tenant, Eric Dowsett and his mate Howie moved into the two bedroom unit.

One of the advantages of having taken on an insurance man as a tenant and house sitter was the issue of household insurance. When he first moved

Richard putting in a corner peg on our land at Howard Springs a week before the cyclone. Patsy chose the block for its natural bush. Author photos.

into our house, Eric asked if we were insured. We pointed out it was an ABC house to which he responded: 'ah yes, but you have contents'.

So we insured the contents and three weeks after the cyclone we received a nice little cheque with which we bought the little Datsun Ute which became our workhorse.

I tracked down the owner of the units, a Mrs Moretti and offered her a modest rent for the unit which she was happy to accept and we lived there happily for nearly nine months.

Early in our time in Darwin we had visited a fellow teacher of Patsy's who lived with her husband in a breezy open shed on a five acre block in the rural community of Howard Springs. It reminded Patsy of happy childhood holidays on rural properties and she was keen to live that way too.

So a week before Cyclone Tracy we had put a deposit on a nicely treed five-acre block of land in a short street in the same community. On our first visit to the land days after our return we were distressed at how many trees had been blown over, even that far out of Darwin. An early purchase was a chainsaw to give us access to what would eventually be our house site.

Over the following months, Patsy collected many plants from gardens before they were cleared putting them in all sorts of containers and creating a moveable garden for when we finally moved to the block. At work she was one of a team cleaning up schools and collecting usable resources as well as collecting unused tins of food from schools which had been used as temporary accommodation or evacuation centres. For months we distributed tins of food from broken and therefore reject cartons to many of our friends

In the meantime, electricity was finally restored to the flats in the form of a power box with four general power outlets (GPOs) for three-pin plugs attached to an end wall. In my ignorance, I wondered how difficult it could be to get power from this box to each of the flats so I fabricated three power boards, each with a couple of double GPOs, wiring each to a long extension cord and installed one in each flat. This meant each flat would now have outlets for four electric appliances: fans, lights, electric jugs, toasters or such like.

To get the necessary extension cords for all these appliances I climbed into the exposed rafters of the unroofed and now abandoned Cavenagh Theatre and liberated a bunch of the cords which had been installed to light the stage. There were dozens of three core flex cables, each with a female plug at the end, so they only required a male end to be fitted and I had a number of extension cords of varying lengths for each flat.

My fellow evacuee, friend and now neighbour, Howie, was an electrician by trade, and he checked the electrical circuits in our flat and found that the power circuit was secure which meant that if I made an extension cord with two male ends, I could use one of my power outlets to provide power to all of the power outlets in the walls of our unit.

Even I understood the danger of such an arrangement, the potential for a handful of 240 volts, so I chose to liven the least accessible power point, the one directly behind the refrigerator, well decorated with a warning to destroy that particular cord after use, and we instantly had half a dozen extra outlets for fans and lights. It was luxury after months of kerosene lamps, candles and torches.

About September of that year, 1975, we moved into a primitive shelter we had erected on our block at Howard Springs and using lots of

The Patris *provided emergency accommodation for many people for some months. NT Government Photographer collection, NT Library.*

salvaged materials swapped for other building materials scrounged from the clean up program, we started to build a house.

Life goes on

Meanwhile, a somewhat unusual addition to the emergency accommodation had arrived in the form of the former cruise ship, the MV *Patris*, which for about six months provided accommodation for a lot of single people, men and women, and a few families.

There were, reportedly, many social problems aboard the ship but our cameraman Keith Bushnell, having returned from his evacuation drive, lived aboard for several months, and enjoyed the experience because, being a keen and competent poker player, he supplemented his regular income with winnings from the frequent games played on board.

As an aside, the departure of the *Patris* provided one of my own less successful, if more memorable, film stories.

I was doing what is known as a piece to camera (PTC) about the ship's departure, ostensibly lamenting one of the quietest cruise ship departures ever seen with no farewelling crowds, streamers, bands playing, etc. but a lone woman bystander kept adding her thoughts: 'Yes, it's a pity, isn't it? Yes, you would think more people would be here', and so it went on until I had to stop and point out I was trying to do my PTC.

In the meantime, from being just a porthole behind me, the ship was well down on the horizon before, on maybe my twentieth take, I managed to get the piece right.

It has since been preserved and used to be trotted out for training sessions as an object lesson in how NOT to do a piece to camera.

My mate, Peter Garton, told me recently he had been invited to the 1975 ABC Christmas party for the first time and his only memory was of the goof reel and, particularly, my *Patris* departure effort.

Keith says that with the film situation not improved and with an air ticket sent to allow him to attend the Thorn Media Awards at which his cyclone film would receive an award, he left the *Patris* and Darwin again, this time not to return for some years.

As mentioned above it was only with the late 1975 coming together of the Jones Boys, Arch and Clem, that significant progress on housing and other reconstruction began.

Dirt in the hand

August 1975 saw the culmination of a nine-year land rights struggle by the Gurindji people of Wattie Creek when Prime Minister, Gough Whitlam arrived to give the title to their land to the leader of the 1966 walk off, Vincent Lingiari. As previously mentioned it was Liberal Prime Minister, Billy McMahon who, in 1972, had set the Aboriginal Land Rights Act in motion by accepting the Wave Hill Station owners' offer of land for a living area for the Gurindji.

As it involved the Prime Minister, this was a story being covered by the ABC from Sydney but the ABC in Darwin was invited to join a small party flying down to Wave Hill in an RAAF Dakota.

Heading the party up was the Acting Administrator, Frank Dwyer, a small humourless man of whom more later. Also aboard were the Air Force Head, whose plane we were using, the Naval Officer Commanding Northern Australia (NOCNA), Commodore Eric Johnston, later to

Prime Minister Gough Whitlam and Gurindji leader, Vincent Lingiari
share a bottle of champagne provided by Robert Wesley-Smith. Maybe NT
Government Photographer.

become NT Administrator, some journalists, among them Rex Clark, by then working for Goff Letts, me and possibly a few more.

Essentially it was a junket because the nationals would cover the story which would come to us as part of the 6.30 news from Brisbane so all I had to do was write a brief story for our local radio news bulletins. While the officials sat up the front of the aircraft drinking whiskey on the return journey, we few plebs travelled cargo at the rear of the plane and drank beer which was nicely chilled.

I have mentioned elsewhere wharfie, Brian Manning, and the activist Rob Wesley-Smith's connections to the Gurindji and at their invitation they were also on our plane and thus among the small crowd which witnessed the iconic and symbolic moment when Gough Whitlam poured some red earth into Vincent Lingiari's hand.

Some years later Wes was to tell another ABC reporter that the famous photograph of the sand pouring was actually a re-enactment of the first pouring which, he said, he had photographed but the *SMH*'s photographer wasn't happy with so asked for a rerun.

There is a less well-known photo of Gough Whitlam drinking champagne from a bottle watched by Vincent Lingiari. Wes says he had supplied the champagne and while Vincent Lingiari had taken the first small sip, photographers kept asking Gough for one more shot causing Wes to shout: 'don't drink it all Gough'. To which, he says, Whitlam replied: 'keep your shirt on Wesley'.

Gough's miscalculations

Early in 1975, Prime Minister Whitlam, made an appointment which, together with a series of scandals, would have significant consequences before the year was out.

He appointed his Attorney-General, the brilliant but flawed Senator Lionel Murphy to the bench of the High Court.

The appointment caused outrage in some parts of the legal fraternity, including on the High Court itself. Then Murphy became embroiled in a scandal which saw him face a number of legal hearings over several years terminated only by his untimely death from cancer.

Convention had it that if a senator left mid term, a replacement from the same party and state would be nominated by the state government. However, the conservative Premier of New South Wales, Tom Lewis, decided to break convention and appointed as Senator Murphy's replacement Cleaver Bunton, who had been a long-term and popular Mayor of Albury, but who was not a Labor man. Whitlam and Labor were outraged and Labor senators gave Bunton a hard time on the floor of the Senate.

Then, in July 1975, Whitlam lost another Labor vote with the sudden death of Queensland senator Bertie Milliner. The casual vacancy convention should have seen Milliner replaced by a Labor Party nominee and the party put forward one name, that of Mal Colston.

However, the Queensland Premier, the eccentric and corrupt Johannes (Joh) Bjelke-Petersen, asked for a list of three names which Labor refused to supply. When Albert 'Pat' Field, a Labor Party member but a critic of Whitlam, allegedly offered himself for the position, Bjelke-Petersen appointed him.

The ALP promptly sacked Field from the Labor Party and then challenged his appointment on the grounds that he had still been employed as a Queensland public servant, an office of profit under the Crown, and thus illegal, when he accepted the appointment.

The challenges, which went to the High Court, kept him out of the Senate for most of his short term and when the Liberal Opposition refused to provide him with a pair, another convention broken by the Liberals, Whitlam was outnumbered in the Senate, one of the factors that enabled the Coalition to repeatedly block Whitlam's supply bills which ultimately led to The Dismissal.

Cleaver Bunton, though not a Labor nominee, was later described as a true independent, voting for legislation on what he saw as its merits, and he did not support the Coalition in its blocking of supply.

East Timor

In May 1975, ABC Staff who had gone through the cyclone were offered an R and R airfare to their home states but Patsy and I, having been in Perth so recently, chose to put our fares towards a much cheaper flight to East Timor.

We had booked into Peter Mu's Perola Oriental (Pearl of the Orient) losmen where Patsy and Lyn had stayed two years earlier. It was a simple structure—a long passageway with rooms on either side and shared bathing facilities.

We spent several days exploring the small town and on one occasion were offered the chance to take a ride into the country to visit a school for orphans and a small mountain village. We accepted even though it would mean sitting in the tray of the single cab utility for some time.

We were as surprised as he was when, the next morning, the honoured guest for whom the expedition was planned, turned out to be the ABC's Darwin Regional Manager, Don Sanders.

The trip took several uncomfortable hours and was interrupted for a stop where haggling took place over the purchase of a young goat which, legs bound, was flung onto the cabin roof to bleat piteously as we drove on.

We finally reached our destination, a small village in mature bamboo groves high in the mountains. There we waited while a fire was lit and several containers made of short lengths of bamboo were stood upright in the flames to cook. When the bamboo burnt through, the meat was deemed cooked but too short a time later we were eating the rather tough goat accompanied by rice also cooked in coconut milk in a piece of bamboo lined with banana leaf. When it was cooked the bamboo was split producing a nice cylindrical cake of rice which proved delicious.

Meanwhile we had arrived in Baucau to scenes of jubilation.

The Portuguese government, which had been wracked by a series of coups over the previous few years and ultimately a popular uprising, had announced it was offering East Timor self government. Guinea-Bissau in Africa had been granted its independence in 1971 and Mozambique and Angola were to follow.

An act of self determination was to take place in the near future and in the meantime the Portuguese soldiers were so happy to be going home they were tearing around the town in army trucks blowing horns, firing their rifles in the air and generally enjoying themselves.

In 1974, when political parties were allowed to be formed in the Portuguese colony, three groups emerged as significant contenders for any election. They were Fretilin, the Revolutionary Front for an Independent East Timor; UDT, the Timorese Democratic Union, a coalition of businessmen wanting East Timor to remain part of Portugal, and Apodeti, the Timorese Popular Democratic Association which favoured integration with Indonesia.

In August 1975, UDT staged a coup in the capital Dili which led to a short, sharp civil war in which it was claimed two to three thousand people died and from which Fretilin emerged victorious after two weeks.

Fretilin's victory surprised some observers and in September 1975, news journalist, Dave Molesworth, talks officer Jim Bonner, who had succeeded Trevor Watson, and cameraman, Peter Lipscombe, were among a group of Australian media invited to Dili by the Fretilin leadership to show that all was calm and under control. Others in that small group included two women who had reported extensively on East Timor, writer Jill Jolliffe and photographer, Penny Tweedie, along with Penny's partner, a cameraman, Clive Scollay.

On 28 November, Fretilin unilaterally declared independence. Just over a week later, on 7 December, Indonesia invaded and a 24-year war of resistance began.

Darwin media party at Dili Airport. Jim Bonner and Jill Jolliffe at left, Clive Scollay and Penny Tweedie at right. Cameraman Peter Lipscombe at rear. Photo, David Molesworth.

I think it would be fair to say that most of those in ABC News/ Current Affairs supported the independence movement in East Timor, even more so after the Indonesian invasion, the murder of the Australian journalists who became known as the Balibo Five and later, the execution by Indonesian troops of Roger East, a journalist who was familiar to many of us as one of the media advisors in the Darwin Reconstruction Commission.

Our Darwin newsroom continued to give coverage to the Falantil (Fretilin's armed wing) resistance which, despite an overwhelming and cruel invasion force, continued to fight a guerrilla war until, in 1999, a post-dictatorship Indonesia offered an opportunity for another act of self determination, in which despite harassment from Indonesian troops and pro-Indonesian armed militias supported by those troops, the populace overwhelmingly voted for independence.

Rob Wesley-Smith became an ardent and active supporter of the East Timorese resistance movement and frequently clashed with officialdom for his protest activities and, later, for helping to operate a clandestine radio connection with the resistance movement, generating yet more coverage from the ABC and a sympathetic journalist at the *NT News*, John Loizou.

Because the radio operation was illegal, the conspirators were constantly under surveillance and being pursued by Communications Department officials with orders from the Federal Government to shut them down.

The Dismissal

Remembrance Day 1975 saw the most egregious act of betrayal and the greatest act of constitutional vandalism ever experienced in Australia in the sacking of the Whitlam government by his own appointed Governor-General, Sir John Kerr, with the active connivance of the Opposition Leader, Malcolm Fraser.

On 11 November, a day of infamy for Labor supporters, Dave Molesworth and I were having a counter lunch at the Marrara Hotel when our cameraman of that time, Peter Lipscombe, phoned to tell us Whitlam had been dismissed.

Because of daylight savings, our national 12.30 news, broadcast on delay, was reporting events one and a half hours out of date while the Commercial station, 8DN, was already reporting the dismissal. We scuttled back to the office to see what local aspects could be followed up.

In return for Whitlam's dismissal, Kerr had stipulated that on his appointment as caretaker prime minister, Malcolm Fraser would call an early election.

That same day a double-dissolution election was called which meant all 127 members of the House of Representatives and all 64 senators were up for election.

Incidentally, Whitlam had announced in 1974 that the two Territories, the Northern Territory and the Australian Capital Territory would both elect two Senators at the next federal election.

So in addition to re-electing the single federal member, Sam Calder, Northern Territory voters elected two senators: former Member of the Legislative Assembly for Alice Springs, Bernie Kilgariff for the CLP and high school teacher, Ted Robertson for Labor. The CLP/Labor sharing of Senate positions continues to this day.

At that election, held on 13 December 1975, Fraser's Liberals won 68 seats, the National Country Party 23 and Labor just 36, a result Kerr would later use to justify the dismissal.

The events surrounding the dismissal would be felt for years. At every public event crowds of Labor supporters would boo and heckle the Governor-General while the Prime Minister, Malcolm Fraser, experienced the same reaction for some years.

Tired and emotional

In 1970 the independent publisher, Gordon Barton, merged two publications, his own *Sunday Review*, and Tom Fitzgerald's *Nation* into a new publication called *Nation Review*.

Aimed at Australia's new urban, educated middle classes it provided mocking political commentary, offbeat cartoons, film, book, theatre and music reviews as well as covering subjects like food, wine, chess and motoring in a satirical style.

Known as 'The Ferret', its list of contributors read like a who's who of contemporary anti-establishment writers, cartoonists and iconoclasts and it rapidly became required reading for many of us.

One of its contributions was the coining of the phrase 'tired and emotional', a euphemism for drunk, or very drunk. It was a term which was aptly used in some coverage of the Governor-General's increasingly uncomfortable public appearances.

Commercial television

In a book about the introduction of television to Darwin, and although this is about the ABC, it would be remiss of me not to at least acknowledge that in November 1971, the commercial television station NTD8, funded by a consortium of local businesses, commenced operations under its manager, the gentlemanly Fred Yeates. Being independent of the commercial networks it was able to cherry pick programs from all three existing southern networks with that variety making it a popular alternative to the ABC for those more interested in light entertainment.

NTD8 was also damaged in Cyclone Tracy but took much longer to get services restored with a limited service being offered from October 1975.

Because by then, the ABC had a monopoly on the broadband bearer, NTD8 was limited in its abilities to access national news stories or programs from interstate. However, when the ABC returned to full local programming in 1982, NTD8 was able to launch its first news service under the direction of Rex Clark. One of the original members of that news team, Andy Bruyn would go on to be the channel's general manager until his retirement. In 1990, NTD8 became part of the National Nine Network.

Post Scripts

To conclude this book, I have selected a series of what I think are interesting vignettes about aspects of Darwin's and the ABC's long, drawn-out, post-Tracy recovery.

Liberal contempt for public broadcasting

Having first joined the ABC in 1968, returned in 1982/83 and been employed again from 1996 to 2001, I have lived through and observed the results of periods of austerity imposed by conservative governments, which seem to have no love or even respect for this important national institution.

The 1975 election of the Fraser government would prove disastrous for the ABC and cause what some called a long, slow decline in its fortunes.

Blaming the Whitlam government's alleged fiscal profligacy, Fraser had his treasurer, John Howard, cut tens of millions of dollars from the ABC's budget soon after their election. The decline wasn't reversed until well into the Hawke Labor Government's term beginning in 1983.

In 1986, in an attempt to convince the Labor Government of its need for and entitlement to increased funding, the Commission and its supporters came up with the famous eight-cents-a-day campaign which claimed that maintaining the ABC cost every Australian just eight cents a day. It worked and the ABC got a funding boost.

When a later LNP government, this time led by John Howard as prime minister, imposed more cuts on the ABC, opponents were able to point out that the ABC then cost each Australian only four cents a day. No matter, funding was cut again.

Another Whitlam initiative for the ABC was the 1975 announcement of a staff-elected commissioner. This position was immediately abolished by the Fraser Government, restored by the Hawke Labor Government in 1986 and once again abolished by the Howard Liberal Government in 2006, only to be reinstated by Julia Gillard by an act of parliament in 2012.

As I write, the ABC is enduring the eighth successive year of funding cuts from the Abbott/Turnbull/Morrison governments which, against all evidence, deny any cuts.

More post-cyclone effects on the ABC

In 1976, ABC Darwin benefited briefly from a programming change emanating from Brisbane when a second small broadcasting window became available three nights a week for 12 to 15 minutes just before 6 p.m., Darwin time.

Talks and rural took two of the slots and the third was offered to the newsroom which I was asked to present. Called *Today '76* it was almost all studio based with live-to-air interviews although an occasional story recorded using the OB van could be included.

As there were only two cameras, the Nodding Neddies, we could only have two chairs for interviewer and talent. In between stories and while I was doing my intro to the next story, one interviewee would leave the guest chair and the next would quietly slide in,

It was a bit of a hard slog arranging three or more interviews on the lead stories of the day but given we only had seven minutes of local news five nights a week, we thought it worth doing.

Three stories from the time stand out. The first related to the appointment by the Fraser Government of a new Administrator, John England, another retired Liberal politician, to replace Jock Nelson.

I had been trying to get access to England for much of the day but had been thwarted, as had other local media, by the Assistant Administrator of the time, Frank Dwyer, a short, slight and pompous martinet.

Late in the afternoon in desperation, I rang Government House direct.

The phone was answered in the kitchen by a young woman who, without covering the mouthpiece said to an obviously more senior person, 'there's a bloke from the ABC wants to speak to his honour, what should I do?' 'Put him through,' was the reply I heard and almost immediately I was speaking to John England himself. 'Could we do an interview?' 'Of course.'

So I rounded up the OB van operators and twenty minutes later we were sitting beside the swimming pool, interview in progress when Dwyer came out through a side door, saw what was happening and stormed off looking very angry indeed.

The following day I heard that the editor of the *NT News*, the late and unlamented John Hogan, had been heard to demand loudly and angrily, 'How the fuck Creswick had got an interview and the *News* hadn't?'.

The second story arose from a rumour that there was a split developing between the Country Party and Liberal wings of the reigning CLP. This would have been a significant story because the CLP had only been formed a few years before and there had been debate over which party was the senior. Initially, it was the Country Party because it had all five Legislative Councillors but after the 1974 Legislative Assembly election the Liberals notionally held eleven or more seats. I took the issue to my best contact, Les MacFarlane, a Country Party member, who confirmed it was on and agreed to appear on the program.

This was the lead story and I read the intro, turned to Les and asked if the split was happening. He looked at me innocently and said no. Dumbfounded, I tried from a slightly different angle and still got the monosyllabic reply, tried again for the same result so thanked him and cut out of the interview. 'You bastard,' I said to him afterwards. And he shrugged, apologised and said, 'Things changed'. There never has been a split.

The third story related to the announcement that our cameraman of the time, Chris 'Froggy' Soulijaert, a Frenchman obviously, was to be the last, his services no longer viable in the strange circumstances of the time. With his help, I put together and scripted about a ten minute compilation of the major stories our reporters and various cameramen had covered since the 1972 arrival of Keith Bushnell. Including an interview with Froggy, it was a fairly emotional story and, I think, was also one of the last *Today '76* programs I was involved in.

Refugees

The end of the Vietnam War in 1975 with the capture of Saigon saw large numbers of Vietnamese opponents of Ho Chi Minh and the Viet Cong, flee the country. In April 1976 two boatloads of refugees arrived in Darwin Harbour having by-passed official channels by which refugees could come to Australia, namely selection by Australian officials in refugee camps established throughout South-east Asia.

I was at the wharf for their arrival, having been notified by contacts in the Department of Immigration but was advised that we should not show any faces for fear they might be identified and their relatives in Vietnam suffer retribution.

Several other boats arrived subsequently but most of the many thousands of Vietnamese refugees who sought refuge in Australia came by air.

Also within days of the civil war erupting in East Timor, refugees were heading to Darwin to escape the violence, many of them injured. In August, nearly 1200 sailed into Darwin aboard a Norwegian freighter, the *Lloyd Bakke*.

Another 272 refugees were expected to follow aboard the 500-ton coastal trader, *MacDili*, which would go on to make several more evacuation voyages then and following the Indonesian invasion in December.

Malcolm in Darwin meets protesters

In May 1976, Malcolm Fraser was in Darwin to officially launch the start of work on a new Christ Church Cathedral being built to replace the small stone building destroyed in the Cyclone.

Fraser had arrived by air the previous evening and, being on the night shift, I had gone to the Travelodge Hotel in the hope of getting an interview. However the PM was whisked in through a back door and shortly afterwards, Darwin's mayor, Ella Stack, a medical doctor, arrived to treat him for some issue. Naturally, she wouldn't answer questions so the small group of media were left to surmise that he was probably tired and emotional.

Following the Cathedral launch the following day, Fraser stood on the back of a flatbed truck next to Brown's Mart to address a noisy crowd of hecklers and announce that the Northern Territory was to get self government in 1978.

Although a significant advance on where the Territory was, the announcement was greeted with some derision because most Territorians wanted statehood. From posters being waved it was obvious there was also residual anger over his role in Whitlam's dismissal.

Newsroom changes

Our former casual journalist, Rex Clark, in 1972 had taken up the permanent job he had been promised at the *NT News*. However, by 1975, he had become disillusioned with the editorial situation there so was given a job back at the ABC.

Of course, the post-cyclone news situation at the ABC wasn't particularly rewarding or stimulating so, in early 1976, he accepted a position as media advisor to the Legislative Assembly's Majority Leader, Goff Letts, who was by then deeply involved in setting up a Northern Territory public service as well as other preparations for the forthcoming self government.

Around that time, the South Australian news editor, Mark LeNevez, wanting to downsize the newsroom, recalled John Milbank to Adelaide where he went on to become the state's local government reporter, ending his 20 years there, in 1997, as Chief of Staff.

LeNevez had come to Darwin to announce the changes and to ask which of the reporting staff should be promoted into the Chief of Staff role. The contenders, Dave, Bill and I were given the opportunity to state our cases.

I told him I believed Dave Molesworth was the best person for the job, being the most experienced of the three of us and having worked in

Melbourne, Hong Kong and New Zealand, had international experience neither Bill Fletcher nor I had.

LeNevez said he wouldn't give the position to Dave because the Darwin newsroom was his only ABC experience, which I considered stupid. In that case, I said, it should be me because I had some seniority.

In the event, he appointed Bill which, upon reflection proved to be an inspired choice. Bill was a good administrator and a tough fighter for restoration of, and improvements to, the newsroom's broadcasting capabilities.

It was largely through his efforts that full week-night news bulletins were restored in 1980 and, in 1982, the restoration of full local programming occurred, while, in 1987, a properly, and professionally staffed film and videotape archive service was begun. He went strongly into bat over other issues as well, including a dedicated TV reporter in Alice Springs.

Rural living

Late in 1976, a life-changing personal event occurred when our son Benjamin joined our family.

For most of the previous 12 months we had been living in one of the Government issue caravans alongside the steel framed house with a seven-metre veranda that we had commissioned from a local company, NAC.

We had the building roofed and using materials mostly salvaged from the cyclone debris, or swapped for items our rural area friends had salvaged, with the help of friends including Dave, we clad and lined the building, fitted doors and windows and connected water and electricity.

A medical condition meant Patsy was forced to spend the final three months of her pregnancy on her back in hospital which gave me a window of opportunity with another good friend, Derek Morgan, to complete the installation of an inside bathroom and toilet to replace the outside squat over holes dug with a post hole digger we had been using until Patsy went into hospital.

Ben's arrival, a month early, marked the start of several wonderful years on our first rural block.

We needed special permission for the caravan to be taken outside the city's boundaries. Author photo.

It is worth noting that when Ben was attending university some twenty years later, with the old hospital closed and providing temporary space for Charles Darwin University, some of his classes were held in the rooms that had been the maternity ward occupied by his mother.

The start of normalisation

1977 was characterised by the near completion of the reconstruction program of the DRC with the city's population almost back to its pre-cyclone level.

The ABC's Darwin newsroom again wishes to express its appreciation for your help and co-operation in the past year.
Those of us still in Darwin hope you can join us for our annual newsroom christmas festivities, from five o'clock onwards in the newsroom,1st. floor,TV building on Tuesday, December 21, 1976.

Invitation to the newsroom Christmas Party.

Canberra reunion (l to r) Bruce Watson, Adrian Payne, Don Sanders, Rodger Andrews, Graeme Halprin, Mike Hayes, Dave Nordsvan. Gerry Orrin front. Photo, Rodger Andrews collection.

Bill Fletcher and Rex Clark, now an event official, check out a part of the Queen's motorcade route. Photographer unknown, Bill Fletcher collection.

*Rocksitters endurance record attempt. The author, Lesley Stewart, one of the
original rocksitters, the ringpull chain on her stubby cooler indicates how
many beers she has consumed, and Rex Clark. Photo,
Ledwidge/Erismann collection.*

Some of the TV staff who hadn't returned were having a reunion of
their own in Canberra.

Among other stories of interest was a visit by Queen Elizabeth to see
the progress being made in the reconstruction.

As one of her duties, the Queen also unveiled the plaque outside the
council chambers commemorating those who died in the cyclone.

Naturally, it was all hands on deck and apart from being at the
airport for Her Majesty's arrival I was also in the new city mall when she
did a walk with the formally-gowned mayor of the time, Cecil Black.

Also in the mall were pupils from Stuart Park Primary who my wife,
Patsy, was accompanying.

Asking the children later about their impressions of the Queen, all
responded that they particularly liked the fur-trimmed robe and gold
chain 'she' was wearing. The queen was actually wearing a simple floral
patterned dress and hat.

Darwin has always been known for its characters and for its offbeat
activities but few exemplify that more than the Darwin Rocksitters Club

Dawn Lawrie, Independent MLA, launches the Rocksitters Club. She cut a ribbon and then opened each participant's first can of beer. The author with tape recorder, on left. Women were not required to drink as much as the men. Photo, Ledwidge/Erismann collection.

formed by photographer/cameraman Beat Erismann, Baz Ledwidge and others in June 1977. The venture, which involved sitting on a rock at East Point and drinking beer on a Saturday afternoon, evolved into an international phenomenon which led to challenges over beer consumption and duration of stays on the rock. It even spawned an ice hockey competition.

Although the original rock has long since been consumed by the sea, the sitting/drinking ritual continues.

1977 was also a year when the colourising of Darwin's television service occurred and the process to normalisation could begin.

Several TV staff who had left after Tracy, returned to Darwin, among them my former neighbour and presentation officer, David Nordsvan, and our old friend, Rodger Andrews, back to oversee the colourisation program.

As he explained:

> The cost of colourising the Southern Capitals had been enormous and the question became how could a colour service be justified for fewer than 50 000 people?
>
> Fortunately, around that time Sony had developed its new Umatic BVU system with portable videotape recorders (VTR's) coming into service. Another Japanese Company, Ikegami, had developed small portable colour cameras so South Australia's Engineering Division looked closely into the costs of providing the Darwin Studios with a complete colour transmission capability using this cheaper and smaller equipment. Financially it was achievable so approval was given and equipment purchased.
>
> This meant local news and programs could be revived, hopefully ending the criticism by Darwinites about the parochial news from the South.
>
> Two Ikegami 77 cameras were installed on the existing remote controlled Pan and Tilt Heads in the studio, the Nodding Neddies. These had been tamed by the genius of Gerry Orrin the Maintenance Supervisor.
>
> Four Sony BVU 200 videotape recorder/players were installed, with editors and colour monitors and a station wagon was provided with a portable videotape recorder to allow news and current affairs programs to be recorded in the field, essentially a downsized version of the OB van. The studio cameras were also used as these outside vision sources. The existing vision mixer was capable of colour and the use of other technical fixes meant Darwin was colourised at far less cost than the BAPH stations but became just as capable in terms of producing local programs.

The ENG team in action. Rodger Andrews with Camera, Bill Fletcher carries the Sony BVU recorder. It really was a two-person operation. Brunette Downs races. Photo, Bill Fletcher collection.

This new TV reporting regime was called Electronic News Gathering (ENG, pronounced enj) and being videotape meant instant replay with no more time consuming film processing.

Unusually, this turned out to be a situation where Sydney did not get first benefit from new technology because the introduction of videotape caused a major industrial dispute, the issue being who should operate the new cameras.

The film cameramen argued that only they, as accredited cinematographers, should use cameras while technical operators argued that because videotape cameras were electronic, they should be operated by technicians. It seems petty but it was a dispute that lasted five years.

The Darwin newsroom got a special dispensation to use ENG because we had not had a film cameraman for more than a year, so only had techs to operate the cameras.

It meant, however, that some techs required a considerable amount of direction from the journalist about what shots were needed for a story, something we hadn't had to think about when we worked with professional cameramen.

Early in my experience with Keith Bushnell he had attempted to give me some rudimentary instruction in camera work, against a time (heaven forbid) when I might need to actually shoot some film. He showed me that there are really only a few shots available to the film cameraman: a pan left, a pan right, a tilt up and a tilt down, a zoom in or a zoom out and a tracking shot.

However, he explained that by holding a shot for some time at both the beginning and the end of the moving shot, the film editor would have an additional suite of static shots from which to choose. It proved a valuable piece of instruction and indeed I did have very occasional requirements to wield a camera.

One lesson we very quickly learnt was how easy it was to shoot far too much videotape, knowing that it could be recorded over many times. Videotapes for the BVU recorders were three-quarters of an inch wide and came in sealed cassettes of ten, 30 and 60 minutes duration.

The shortest videotape was as long as the biggest reel of film used by film cameramen and where film incurred an additional cost in the need to process it, an incentive to keep things as short and tight as possible, the same did not apply to videotape.

Videotape did also tend to encourage sloppiness, after all what did it matter how many takes it took to get the perfect piece to camera? However, the downside of that came when it was time to edit and too much tape had been shot. Unlike film where everything remains visible, spooling speeds for videotape while retaining vision were limited. Go too fast and you lose pictures.

So at the end of 1977, ABD6 was effectively able to broadcast in colour, like Queensland, and with ENG we had almost the equivalent of our former news camera capability. But we still only had seven minutes for local news.

Legislative payback

In August 1977, the second Legislative Assembly election was held and unlike the CLP whitewash of the 1974 election, this one brought significant change, not only the emergence of the Labor Party as a political force but the fact that in winning six seats, they defeated five of the seven Executive Members, including Majority Leader Goff Letts. It was a shock result.

And for the second time, I anchored the ABC's television coverage of a parliamentary election which, on this occasion, required specific slots to be made available by Queensland in the evening's programming. I have no memory of who the party commentators were.

Although the CLP held power easily, winning 12 of the 19 seats, the popular vote was much closer with the CLP winning 40.1 per cent of the vote to Labor's 38.2 per cent.

Nightcliff Independent Dawn Lawrie retained her seat but Ron Withnall lost his seat of Port Darwin to the Star Cinema owner, by then Tom Harris Junior, which must have been galling.

The executive members who lost their seats were the Deputy Leader, Grant Tambling who lost his seat of Fannie bay to Pam O'Neill; Dave Pollock who lost MacDonnell to indigenous candidate, Neville Perkins; Roger Ryan who lost Millner to Jon Isaacs; Liz Andrew, a former colleague of Patsy's at Wagaman Primary School, who lost Sanderson to June D'Rozario and Majority Leader, Goff Letts, who lost Victoria River to Jack Doolan.

The other seat to change hands was Arnhem where the long-term incumbent, Rupert Kentish, was defeated by Bob Collins. Paul Everingham, the slow-talking but sharp-thinking and progressive member for Jingili, was elected Majority Leader and would guide the Northern Territory very successfully through the transition to self government just under a year later.

The Opposition Leader was the member for Jingili, Jon Isaacs, a union organiser who had arrived in Darwin a few years before to shake up the moribund North Australian Workers Union.

One other aspect of the 1977 election that was unusual, and even a touch cynical, was the decision by the CLP to nominate two candidates

The Second Legislative Assembly. Back row (l to r): Noel Padgham-Purich, Tom Harris, Milton Ballantyne, Rod Oliver, Roger Vale, Nick Dondas, Jack Doolan, Bob Collins, Neville Perkins, June D'Rozario.
Front row: (l to r) Dawn Lawrie, Ian Tuxworth, Marshall Perron, Paul Everingham, Les MacFarlane, Jon Isaacs, Jim Robertson, Roger Steele, Pam O'Neill. Noel Padgham-Purich collection, NT Library.

for the seat of Tiwi being vacated by Hyacinth Tungutalum, a Tiwi Islands man who had been the first Indigenous Australian elected to a state or territory parliament.

The CLP nominated an agricultural scientist, well known dingo, goat and wallaby breeder from Darwin's rural area, and mother of six Noel Padgham-Purich, as well as a candidate from the Tiwi Islands, Cyril Rioli, a former champion Australian Rules footballer. Perhaps coincidentally, Noel was the wife of the recently deposed Secretary for Mines, Phil Purich ,and had been a stalwart of the Country Women's Association.

Labor was essentially forced to follow suit and nominated my businessman friend, Harry Maschke and Tiwi Islander, Bernard Tipiloura. The Padgham-Purich/Rioli team won and Noel Padgham-Purich, having collected more votes than Rioli, was elected Member for Tiwi.

Later that year, I organised a media farewell lunch for Goff Letts at a popular back-lane restaurant operated by one of the ABC's former casual typists, Cri Pas and her partner of the time, Bob Hobman.

Self Government Day, July 1, 1978: Chief Minister, Paul Everingham addresses the crowd flanked (left) by Opposition Leader, Jon Isaacs and (right) by the Administrator, John England'. Photo, NT Government photographer collection, NT Library.

Schoolchildren are presented with miniatures of the new Northern Territory flag featuring the Robert Ingpen design of a stylised desert rose. Photo, Education Department, NT Library.

There we presented Goff with a pen and a ream of paper and urged him to write his memoirs. As I write they are finally, 44 years later, about to be published and, having read a manuscript, I am again in awe of his achievements and his connections.

Self government

On Saturday July 1 1978 Patsy, Ben in his pram, Dave Molesworth and I joined a happy crowd of about 6000 people on the Esplanade opposite the famous Darwin Hotel for the ceremony to mark the beginning of self government.

Earlier, Paul Everingham had been sworn in as the Territory's first Chief Minister by the Administrator, John England, along with his newly minted ministers.

At ten o'clock, the new Chief Minister, flanked by the Opposition Leader, Jon Isaacs and the Administrator, gave a rousing and well received speech, offshore, the HMAS *Derwent* fired a 17-gun salute, the RAAF staged a fly over, the Robert Ingpen-designed Territory flag with its black, white and ochre stylised Sturt's desert rose was raised for the first time, in the presence of its designer, and an MP who fancied himself as a country and western singer sang the grossly inappropriate scatological song, *When the gins come in from Oenpelli Mission.*

A garden Party had been held at Government House the previous night with the Governor-General, Sir Zelman Cowen, and Lady Cowen among the guests. However, they played no part in the following day's official activities, presumably because these were held on a Saturday, the Jewish Sabbath. Was this an organisational oversight?

As for me, it was the first day of my new career as the first Public Relations Officer for the Northern Territory Electricity Commission (NTEC), formed from the amalgamation of three former Commonwealth utilities covering generation, transmission and distribution, and commercial operations of Darwin's electricity supply. It was just three months short of ten years since I had joined the ABC in Perth.

A much later newsroom reunion. Back (l to r): David Molesworth,
Keith Bushnell, Margaret Hamilton, Bill Fletcher.
Seated: the author, Mary Fraser.
Front: Dick Muddimer.

ABC Darwin's first
Senior Broadcast Officer, Rodger
Andrews (left), back in Darwin
fifty years on, with the author.

Acknowledgements

I have discovered that writing the acknowledgements is one of the hardest parts of writing a book not only for who you should include, and what for, but also the concern about missing out someone important. This book might not have been written were it not for the encouragement of three people: my wife, Patsy, who is always the first and best critic of anything I write, though she says I ignore her suggestions, which is not completely true. Patsy is much more logical than me and seeks to protect me from my tendency to write and act in haste, as well as from the potential for libel suits or breaches of copyright, traits which I do not always fully appreciate; Keith Bushnell who features fairly strongly not just because his arrival in Darwin was such a pivotal moment for television coverage but because he and I went on to do so much together in subsequent years; and Dave Molesworth, fellow newsroom hack but one of the best news producers I have known and still a good mate, even if he does support St Kilda. It might not sound important but he allowed his reporters to have their own voice which some editors do not.

My son, Benjamin, who missed me for so much of his childhood because of the unsociable hours working at the ABC imposed.

My siblings, Carol and John, for keeping me grounded. We don't see each other as often as we should, living at the three points of a continental triangle but over the years John, initially a film editor, has been an important contributor to various of my ventures.

I need also to acknowledge my mother, the late June Creswick. Even in times of economic hardship she ensured our house always had books and we were encouraged to discuss issues of importance to us. It was she who bought our first typewriter, a little portable, which was how I began my first creative writing, my handwriting being execrable.

Rodger Andrews recollections made a major contribution to the content and shape of this book and the recent revival of our friendship has enhanced it. The only original member of the pre-TV newsroom still living, and still in Darwin, Bill Fletcher was one of many former colleagues who contributed recollections, words and photos as news of the project spread. He became heavily invested in the project and rounded up many of the photographs and reminiscences collected here. Others included Graeme Halprin, Joyce and David Nordsvan, John Milbank, Glenn Taylor, Judith Stevenson, Bill Mudie, Rex Clark, Trevor Watson, Tom Blackburn and scrapbook keeper, Mary Fraser.

Old mate Peter Simon was generous in allowing me access to his (as yet) unpublished book on that great crusading editor, James Frederick (Jim) Bowditch, a journalistic hero to some of us. Kim Lockwood offered some timely observations as well as corrections around his father's legacy and Gill Chalmers, peace activist who was given the opportunity to be what she called a real journalist under Jim Bowditch's tutelage, had interesting insights into life for a young woman in Darwin before television.

Liz McDonald's insights as a teenager provided a different perspective as did several other women friends who arrived in Darwin well before television, Carol Conway, Christine Silvester, Joanna Parish and Pamela Morgan or who, like Marilynne Paspaley, were here from their very earliest days. Mickey Lo, mechanic extraordinaire, who kept many of my sports cars mobile for years, isn't mentioned by name but offered insights into his growing up as a Chinese Australian child and man.

Ken Conway, long-time friend, fellow thespian, fellow Harney Beacher and fellow Friday Luncher, was always able and willing to offer advice and provide corrections or company while Peter and Pam Garton, also Harney Beachers, filled in gaps around early environmental activism, a subject with which they remain engaged.

Harry Maschke, astute businessman, philosopher, serial political contender and friend has given much more than his brief appearances in this book would indicate in a lifetime of friendship.

The loquacious and restlessly energetic Robert Wesley-Smith whose appearances in the book do not do justice to his position at, or near, the centre of numerous activist causes over more than half a century in Darwin and whose photographs illustrate some of those stories.

Richard Luxton another longtime Territorian with historical interests.

There are some unwitting helpers like Nicolas Rothwell of the *Australian*, for his insights into Colin Jack-Hinton; the unknown historians of websites like *Monuments Australia*, the *Australian Dictionary of Biography* and local academics who provided confirmation of a few important dates and places via publications such as *Northern Territory Historical Studies: a journal of History, Heritage and Archaeology* published in 2016 by the Historical Society of the NT; Dr Brian Reid, of that Historical Society, who was encouraging when I first asked him to consider the book seven years ago.

Much of my understanding about early NT times comes from reading authors whose names are mentioned in the text but one of my favourite Territorian writers, WE (Bill) Harney gave me an insight into life of and with Aboriginal people through his many books, an interest enhanced by the fact that, with a group of Territorians of similar vintage to us, Patsy and I share ownership of the land that Harney obtained by lease in 1946 and called Daramunkamani.

Members of this Harney Beach family, now into its third generation, have been important in every aspect of our lives for nearly forty years and remain so.

Over the years one absorbs, almost by osmosis, the early history of the Territory but finds it handy to consult—cough, cough—Wikipedia or Google for confirmation of a date, a place or indeed a person whose name has slipped the mind at that particular moment. Wikipedia's *Dictionary of Biography* provided handy *aides memoir* for background to some of those prominent citizens mentioned.

The National Archives of Australia (NAA) online is an excellent reference point for such arcane information as the speeches and press releases of former prime ministers and other important personages. Where I have used such information, interested readers will find more with a specific search of the internet.

Malarndirri McCarthy, another former ABC colleague, a young journalist then newsreader, and now a Senator was helpful in getting access to parliamentary records around Sam Calder's efforts to get TV for the NT. It is rewarding to be part of her informal Seniors Advisory Group.

My good friend, John Flynn, was a handy sounding board for early aspects of this story and as a very good friend of one of our better politicians, Goff Letts, first majority leader in a fully elected Northern Territory parliament, ensured that I was able to use Goff's own words where he appears in this story.

Professor Michael Bird of James Cook University, Cairns, was generous in critiquing my section on Australia's first arrivals.

He pointed me to this site for more recent information: https://theconversation.com/buried-tools-and-pigments-tell-a-new-history-of-humans-in-australia-for-65000-years-8101 His own work in the same field can also be found at *The Conversation* by searching either his name or the term Sahul.

A happy coincidence led me to Des Gellert, historian of the Beer Can Regatta and willing donor of far more information than I could possibly use.

The *Northern Territory News* is quoted extensively both through its coverage of the arrival of television, and other newsworthy events including, of course, Cyclone Tracy. I hope I have given sufficient credit where, courtesy of Territory Archives, or my own extensive collection of various commemorative editions, I have accessed relevant stories.

The late Fred Walker, long-time clerk of both the Legislative Council and the Legislative Assembly is responsible for a definitive history not only of those institutions but also the early constitutional history of the Territory. I have quoted extensively from his *A short history of the Legislative Council for the Northern Territory* available in the NT Archives and Library at Parliament House.

The South Australian psephologists, Dean Jaensch and Debra Wade-Marshall, were active chroniclers of Northern Territory electoral matters around the period this book deals with and are referred to frequently in a document I consulted for its concise record: *A Chronology of Northern Territory constitutional and statehood milestones 1825 to 2007 by Dr Nicholas Horne* and found in the Parliamentary Library online. Other papers of theirs confirmed my own recollections of various political events of the time.

Joanne Van Os, friend first, author second, played a pivotal role by giving me a knock down to Derek Pugh, the prolific local author of a number of historical works. Derek himself, a giant of a man, was encouraging on the basis of reading a couple of chapters but incredibly generous in introducing me to the intricacies of self publishing, and through them to his brother, Michael Pugh, who proved willing to take on the task of shepherding the book to production.

My former colleagues in ABC Archives, Jill Forner, Val Fong and Trish Drescher, ensured my last years at the ABC were happy ones with Trish particularly helpful with various historic aspects from the vault. National ABC Archives, through Lisa Chidlow and Clare Cremin, were helpful with some early photographs.

Elisabeth Marnie guided me through the complexities of exploring the photographic collections of the NT Archives and Library as well as advising on how to actually apply for the photos I sought while Jacqui Hatzivalsamis of the NT Archives Digital Collections Team made sure the photos I sought actually got to me.

Also helpful with photographs were the joint administrators of the Old Darwin facebook group, Graham Poeling-Orr and Herb Sinclair, and the collection of interested and interesting people who contributed some of the photographs I have used. Graham is of the opinion that copyright has been relinquished/ceded in the action of posting an image to the site. However, I want to acknowledge one photograph from the site posted by Bruce Donaldson but taken by his father Don, a prolific photographer of Darwin from 1957 to the '70s. The pictures, scanned from slides, are remarkable for their clarity and detail.

I have attempted to contact those other than Graham and Herb who put up the few images I have chosen to use. If someone is offended by the use of a picture I will happily correct it in future editions. A few of the other photos are my own, many have been offered by their snappers, former staff, free of copyright onus, and they are acknowledged in the captions. A very few are of unknown provenance.

I want to thank my long time friends: journalist, author and editor, Diana Kupke, and Dave Molesworth for their enthusiasm for the task of being first readers of this book. Kerry Sharp (Doak) and Rex Clark made valuable contributions despite their claims of fading memories and my snapper colleagues and friends, Baz Ledwidge and Beat Erismann, who contributed both photos and memories of the house in Edmunds Street they shared with other notable characters.

I would especially like to thank Dawn Lawrie for her encouragement for this project as well as her willingness to write a foreword. During the period this book covers she was a popular and active local member, unafraid to speak her mind. She was also a good friend to the ABC. She was a colourful flower in a garden of elderly maleness when she became the first woman elected to a modern Northern Territory Parliament in 1971 (though not, she tells me, the actual first woman parliamentarian, an honour which fell to the long forgotten Linda Marian Berlowitz, who represented Fannie Bay from 1960 to 1962 and is worth Googling). Undoubtedly, Dawn paved the way for the many women who were subsequently elected to the parliaments which ushered in self government.

And, again, my wife Patsy whose contributions were immense.

The internet has made the task of research considerably easier but to gain full advantage one first has to know what or who one is looking for. Memory is imperfect, especially as the years place events at a further and further remove.

Much of what is written here comes from my own memory, augmented by the memories of others who were also close to the events, but mistakes, mis-rememberings and even sometimes confabulations or exaggerations are, regrettably, almost inevitable. Where these occur, I take full responsibility.

If I have unfairly maligned anyone, I apologise. If I have omitted to thank someone who should be thanked, again I apologise.

Correctons and Additions (#1)

- What happened to the cats? A week after we returned to Darwin after Cyclone Tracy, in early February, the cats were flown back from Perth and shared our flat. They all went on to live long and happy lives.

- P 181 Photograph of Keith Bushnell. This photo was actually taken by Toni Joyce, not Keith's neighbour.

- P 225. East Timor. In addition to Portugal's four colonies seeking independence, the country had two other colonies, Goa in South-west India and Macau in southern China. Goa was annexed by India in 1961 and became a full Indian state in 1987, Macau, a colony since 1557, became a Special Administrative Region of China in 1999

Appendix: Staff of the ABC

There were three main groups of ABC staff covering the period around the introduction of television and thus deserving of recognition: those who were already based in Darwin and saw TV's arrival; those who came to install the necessary equipment for television production and presentation or who were part of the influx of additional bodies, and those who would come over the subsequent three years.

* Denotes casual or part-time.

Those already here

Don Sanders, Manager
Ian Marshall, A/Manager
Peter Knudsen, rural
Tom Wilkinson, talks
Peter Turnbull, sports*
Sandra Nicholson, secretary
Alf Jervis, announcer
Richard Peach, announcer
Ric Dowling, announcer
Glenn Taylor, announcer
Mary Wilson, sound librarian
Geoff Hughes, JIC

Mike Hayes, journalist
Bill Fletcher, journalist
Dick Muddimer, journalist *
Betty Gadd, news typist
Ron Geddes, OIC radio
Mike 'Father' Yates
Henry Anderssen,
Jim Eustice
Trevor Kelly
Frank Brogan
John Starr

Installation crew, Darwin

Peter Syme*
John Johnson*
Charlie Muscat*
Mike Davies*
Bob Gully*

Dudley Wilkinson*
John Larchin*
Allen Dent*
John Eastaff*

TV additions

Roger Andrew, SBO
Bruce Watson
Graeme Halprin,
Gerry Orrin,
Roger Burnard,
Jon Davey (from Radio),
Bruce Black,
Chris Dart
Tony Foord
John Longmire
Alf Amrein (from Radio)
Adrian Payne, presentation Off.
David Nordsvan, presentation Off.

Amanda Taylor, film assistant
Kathy Palmer, news typist
Lorelle Ayre, news typist*
Alan Humphreys, rural
Colin Martin, graphics
Arthur Harris, film library
Tom Blackburn, announcer,
Jan Storer, production assistant
Esther Lang, sound librarian
Dick Muddimer, journalist
David Molesworth, journalist
Richard Creswick, journalist
Glenn Taylor, talks officer

Newcomers, 1972 to 1974

John Milbank, JIC
Kerry Sharp, journalist*
Barbara James, journalist*
Rex Clark, journalist*
Ram Raj Gopal, journalist *
Jackie Franks, journalist*
Bob Hobman, journalist*
Don Bensted, Head of Sports
Rainer Witthaus, film librarian.
Bob Roberts,announcer
John May, announcer
Howard Baker, announcer
Lawrie Bruce, announcer

John Hall, announcer
Mary Jennings/Fraser, news typist
Christine Pas, news typist*
Toni Waddington news typist*
Sandra Hayes-Ward, news typist
Annick Pouchol, news typist*
Diane Weir, news typist*
Margaret Hamilton, news typist.
Yvonne Arkell, manager secretary
Janet Brown, manager secretary
Sandy McCubbin, manager Sec.
Peter Loxton, rural
Ross Quinn, rural

Printed in Australia
AUHW020132130921
351947AU00009B/9

9 780646 839998